THE GIRLS
COME MARCHING
HOME

**Stories of Women Warriors
Returning from the War in Iraq**

Kirsten Holmstedt

STACKPOLE
BOOKS

Published in 2009 by
STACKPOLE BOOKS
5067 Ritter Road
Mechanicsburg, PA 17055
www.stackpolebooks.com

Printed in the United States of America

10 9 8 7 6 5 4 3 2 1

FIRST EDITION

Library of Congress Cataloging-in-Publication Data

Holmstedt, Kirsten A.
   The girls come marching home : stories of women warriors returning from the war in Iraq / Kirsten Holmstedt.
      p. cm.
   Includes index.
   ISBN 978-0-8117-0516-5
   1. Iraq War, 2003—Women—United States—Biography. 2. Women soldiers—United States—Biography. 3. Women veterans—United States—Biography. I. Title.
DS79.76.H653 2009
956.7044'34092273—dc22
                                        2009009214

Table of Contents

For my parents,
Herb and Anne Holmstedt,
and in memory of my dear friend
Thora Morris

Jo,

11/12/09

For women warriors everywhere. Thank you for supporting all the troops — including these amazing women.

Kirsten A. Holmstedt

Introduction

"A timid person is frightened before a danger, a coward during the time, and a courageous person afterward."

—Jean Paul Richter

My cell phone showed I had a message. When I listened to it, I heard a slow and trembling female voice. The caller identified herself as CJ Robison, and it didn't take me long to realize who she was. During a visit to the Pentagon, I had talked to a U.S. Army colonel about this book. When I told him I was still looking for women to feature, he immediately responded with a name: First Sergeant CJ Robison. I didn't have a chance to write the name in my small black notebook, but I recalled the conversation with the colonel because he was so persistent. Certain words stood out in my mind—first sergeant, excellent soldier, female, seriously wounded, National Guard, Iowa. I returned Robison's call the next morning, and the same female voice, one that carried the weight of the war, answered.

Another time, I called Robison and got her voicemail. She had recorded her greeting before traumatic brain injury set in and started to affect her speech. The voice spoke fast and with authority. The contrast between Robison's more recent voice and the one from the greeting left me with the impression that I was dealing with two different people. When I mentioned the commanding voice on her greeting, Robison said, "I miss that."

Robison's voice is one of many you will hear in this book, voices I hope you will come to understand and appreciate—and never forget.

In 2003, a major experiment began on the battlefield in Iraq as a record number of American women headed into combat for the first time. There were rules banning women from combat, but they dissolved as the war continued and the front lines faded. There was simply no way to keep women from the front lines when the front lines were everywhere. Female military police, truck drivers, medics, explosive ordnance disposal technicians, and lawyers would face challenges that exceeded everyone's expectations, including their own.

In my first book, *Band of Sisters*, I explored the different roles that women were performing in combat, as well as their challenges and accomplishments on the battlefield. We learned through their actions that women can excel in combat. They can return fire when they are fired upon, rescue wounded soldiers, drive trucks on the most dangerous roads, provide security on convoys, and search Iraqi women and children. When they were shot down or wounded, many asked not to go home but instead to return to their troops.

Eventually, most of the women would come home—though more than 100 American women have been killed in combat—when their deployment was over. The more I talked to our returning female veterans, the more I realized that for some, the war began and ended on the battlefield. But for most, especially those who have gone to Iraq and Afghanistan multiple times, the war followed them home. Still others felt the war didn't even begin until they came back to the States.

For years, men have returned from war with physical, emotional, and mental scars. Thousands of books chronicle their homecomings and rightly so. Men have always fought our wars. However, now women are coming home with the same wounds, and their sacrifices warrant our attention. Like male soldiers before them, some women have become victims of war, and others have been empowered by their experiences. Many fall into both categories: they have been victims but have learned and grown from their experiences.

The same curiosity and commitment that drove me to write about one of the greatest experiments to come out of this war—women in combat—would also inspire me to find out what battles they faced on the home front. Having followed the progress of women on the battlefield, I now felt compelled to find out how they were doing when they came home. I had to finish what I started, what *they* started. In *Band of Sisters*, you heard their voices from the battlefield; now I want you to hear their voices when they came home.

Some women were physically wounded on the battlefield, but all were affected emotionally. In the following stories, you will read how women have or have not been able to reclaim their roles as mothers, wives, daughters, sisters, service members, and civilians while struggling with physical wounds, post-traumatic stress disorder, survivor's guilt, and military sexual trauma.

The Girls Come Marching Home goes to the heart of their stories. The voices on the following pages are filled with love and hate, anger and frustration, grief, pain, confusion, helplessness, joy, pride, and hope. You will hear their screams, their cries for help, and their reflections. An Army sergeant voices her desire to extend her deployment in Iraq; when she returns to the States and can't cope, she tries to dull her pain with alcohol and drugs. A Navy anesthesiologist's dedication to helping wounded troops is reaffirmed. An Army specialist speaks up when she is sexually harassed; her voice is ignored. A lieutenant proudly becomes the first woman in the U.S. Coast Guard to earn the Bronze Star. While providing convoy security in and around Ramadi, an Army sergeant regularly encounters either an IED, a rocket-propelled grenade, or a firefight. What a relief it is for her to return home, right? Not exactly. Back in Wisconsin, she faces daily battles to get herself and her boyfriend the medical care they need and deserve. An Army judge advocate officer brings her knowledge of the law to the battlefield; she returns with a new awareness of survivor's guilt. A Navy nurse and Army specialist are mistreated by fellow service members at home and on the battlefield, but no one seems to be listening. Their harsh language reflects their real and raw emotions.

For a year, I traveled the country and listened to women who had tried to outrun their fears, face their demons, or both. Some avoided help while others pleaded for it. Some wanted to die; others wanted to go on but didn't know how. Some came home to supportive spouses and children while others had to pick up the pieces of a shattered home life. Some became small business owners, continued their military careers and were promoted, started college or re-enrolled, got married, had children. Some used their new voices to become motivational speakers or run for political office. Some embraced their Purple Hearts; others saw the awards as a burden.

Since a relatively large number of women were entering combat for the first time, a similarly large number of women would return home after surviving combat. That reality was counterbalanced by a limited number of resources—such as counselors and doctors—who were trained to work with women traumatized by their battlefield experiences. Neither our female warriors nor their support systems were prepared for their return. Family and friends, as well as the agencies that were supposed to take care of our soldiers, were taken aback by this new and surging phenomenon. Who would be there to help them? As one female Marine told me, "The transition back home is never as joyful as the ticker tape showering down on Broadway."

During a visit to the 4th Battalion on Parris Island, where female recruits are trained to become Marines, a female drill instructor recalled an experience she had in Iraq with great satisfaction. She was on a convoy that got pinned down by Iraqi insurgents. She ordered her Marines to open fire, and they responded exactly as they had been trained to do. When she finished telling the story, she said, "Oh, and by the way, they were all women." She was full of pride discussing these events for the first time since she had returned home. That voice—and the voices of all our female service members—needs to be heard.

We know that women have made a major contribution to the war effort, yet when they come home, many don't speak up. Instead, they keep quiet and do their jobs until someone else turns the spotlight on them. This book is that spotlight.

Note: In certain instances, names were altered at the request of the soldiers to protect their identities.

Stacy Blackburn

Light in the Darkness

ARMY SERGEANT STACY BLACKBURN WAS RIDING IN A CONVOY FROM Camp Ramadi to Fallujah when soldiers spotted three male Iraqis about seventy-five meters away. One was carrying a grenade as he walked back and forth on an overpass. The other two were less visible. They were on lookout, bobbing in and out of view. In no time, the convoy would be driving under that overpass. The soldiers were about to be ambushed.

"Take him out! Take him out!" a soldier shouted.

Blackburn, a twenty-one-year-old from Detroit, was standing in the turret of the third truck and manning the M60 machine gun. She heard small-arms fire ahead. The Iraqis were shooting at the first truck. The soldiers returned fire. Blackburn had been in other firefights, but not at such close range. Usually, when she took gunfire, she couldn't see who was shooting at her. The close proximity to her target gave her an adrenaline rush. She felt powerful knowing that she could both cause and prevent harm in one trigger pull. She feared that power, but it was also soothing because it meant she could protect herself and her soldiers.

With the vehicles heading his way at about fifty miles per hour, the Iraqi carrying the grenade on the overpass didn't retreat. Instead, he held his ground and started throwing stuff at the soldiers. A sergeant in Blackburn's truck ordered her to shoot. She peered down the barrel only to discover the enemy was a boy. *That can't be. He's so young.* He looked about seven years old, the same age as Blackburn's nephew, Demarco.

"Take him out! Take him out!"

Blackburn needed the other soldiers to yell at her because her instincts were telling her not to shoot the boy—shooting a little boy is crazy. She's a good shot and could have killed him with her first round, but instead she hesitated. When she finally fired, she shot over the boy's left shoulder, intentionally missing her target. In training at Camp Atterbury, Indiana, she shot at adult targets, not kids. She had to remind herself that the goal was to kill the enemy before he destroyed her and her buddies. Never again would she hesitate. If she didn't know it before, she learned that day that danger and terrorism have no age, face, color, or gender.

Blackburn is five feet, five inches tall with brown skin, hazel eyes, and shoulder-length black hair. Accenting her desert camouflage was a light green headband with Psalm 23 on it. It made her feel as though she had extra protection from head to toe.

Like many teenage men and women who join the military, Blackburn was running both to and from something. She was looking for—craving—relationships in which she could trust others. Her biological mother gave her up for adoption a few months after her birth. Her adoptive parents, Theresa Drake and Roy Hoelscher, split up when Blackburn was five. Drake raised Blackburn. She moved Blackburn and her younger brother from Detroit to southern Indiana, where Drake worked the midnight-to-seven shift at Our Lady of Peace Hospital in Louisville. At the young age of eight, Blackburn and her brother slept at a neighbor's house. In the mornings, Blackburn was responsible for getting herself and her younger brother up for the school bus, which she did without an alarm clock. She made sure that she and her brother ate breakfast, combed their hair, and had their books ready.

She took charge. When she played school with her friends, she was the teacher or principal. If she had played Army, she would have been the drill sergeant. In high school, Blackburn excelled in the classroom and in basketball, softball, and track. She didn't go anywhere without her basketball. She wanted to play in the WNBA before it existed.

Blackburn devoted a great deal of time to her school work and sports to escape an unpleasant home life. She also didn't want to cause her mom any additional heartache. While Blackburn was in middle and high school, her mom moved in and out of two abusive relationships. After one physical battle, Drake told Blackburn and her brother to never jump in, just run out of the house. The lessons Blackburn learned from the abuse were to be tough and avoid displays of emotion—characteristics that would serve her well in the military.

Along with seeking healthier relationships, Blackburn yearned for peace on a much grander scale. After her junior year of high school, she returned to Detroit, moved in with her brother and his family, and enrolled in Martin Luther King Junior/Senior High School. On 9/11, she sat in a classroom and watched the terrorist attacks on television. The attacks gave her a whole new outlook on life. There was darkness at home, in the country, and in the world, but she wasn't going to give in to it. She could and would make a difference. She would be a light in that darkness. She would help make America secure for her future children. She had considered going to Xavier or Purdue University but decided to put her formal education on hold. She believed she could make more of an impact in the military. So as a high-school senior, she joined the Army's delayed entry program. Within a week of graduation, she left for Army basic training in Fort Leonard Wood, Missouri.

On a good day in Iraq, Blackburn dodged bullets and incoming mortars, sidestepped improvised explosive devices (IEDs), and avoided being ambushed. But there weren't many good days, not in 2005 and 2006.

She deployed to Iraq in 2004 as a combat mechanic with Bravo Company of the 983rd Engineer Battalion, a reserve unit from Southfield, Michigan. During the first several months of her deployment, she was stationed at Camp Speicher in Tikrit. Because of the high number of attacks on the camp and Blackburn's gung-ho and motivated personality, she was put on security duty in less than a month. She provided security at the front gate fourteen hours a day, searched vehicles and Iraqi women and children, stood watch at a tower just inside the camp, and reported suspicious activity.

After several months of working security, Blackburn learned that her company was moving from Tikrit to Camp Ramadi, one of the most dangerous areas in the world at that time. But before they could move, they had to get a feel for how difficult it would be to relocate. With a small convoy of four or five gun trucks and minimal congestion, the drive from Tikrit to Ramadi might take only a couple of hours. However, that short drive could easily turn into an all-day mission if it involved more vehicles, pot holes on the road from IEDs, Iraqis making crude gestures, and IEDs concealed in guard rails, overpasses, dead animals, and garbage. How risky would it be to move the soldiers, their supplies, and heavy equipment between cities? What deadly surprises could they expect from the insurgents along the way? And what additional perils were awaiting them at Camp Ramadi and in the city of Ramadi?

"Hey, you like action, right?" Blackburn's staff sergeant asked her one day. "Get your crap ready. You're about to go on missions clearing roads and setting up cordons."

For the next couple of months, Blackburn was the only female in a platoon of about forty soldiers to travel on convoy security missions between Tikrit and Ramadi. She started out as a gunner and alternated as a truck commander and driver. She didn't mind being the only woman. In fact, she kind of liked it. She chose a male-dominated profession knowing she would be told women couldn't do certain things. She enjoyed proving the guys wrong and earning their respect. She welcomed the challenge.

Since she had taught herself to be tough and not to show emotion, and because she projected a confidence that put other soldiers at ease, no one knew Blackburn was scared to death during those early days on the road. It wasn't that she was afraid of dying, although she admits that each time she went out on a mission, a part of her didn't think she was going to make it back. She wasn't consumed with her own mortality or that of her fellow soldiers. Instead, she worried about how her soldiers would respond when they were ambushed or hit by an IED. Could the ones who survived hold it together when they saw another soldier maimed or killed?

The day Blackburn moved to Camp Ramadi, ten or so mortars were fired into the base. The conditions didn't improve while she was there. Camp Ramadi was small—about four square miles—and constantly under attack. The explosions always hit too close for comfort. Blackburn's truck became her refuge. Starting with the day she arrived, if she were near her vehicle during an explosion, Blackburn would crawl inside, pull in her weapon, close the hatch, lock it up, and stay there until she had to use the bathroom. No place was safe on Camp Ramadi—not the chow hall, not the SWA huts (Southwest Asian huts, a type of prefabricated building), not the shops. Some got used to the attacks, but not Blackburn. She was always aware that a mortar could soar in at any moment. Where it would land was anyone's guess. At that time in the war, there wasn't a sound system at Camp Ramadi to warn soldiers of incoming mortars, so the attacks were always a surprise, and the boots on the ground had almost no time to react. If they were lucky, they would have enough time to throw their bodies behind a nearby stack of sandbags erected to protect them from potentially deadly shrapnel.

When Blackburn arrived at Camp Ramadi, there was talk about what the female soldiers were, and were not, allowed to do. Could they go off base? The discussion waned as a growing number of female soldiers such as Blackburn, Specialist Rachel McNeill, and Sergeant Jessica Yancy were needed to fill positions on tactical movement teams that escorted civilians, third-country nationals, and VIPs traveling in Anbar province.

If Blackburn didn't feel safe on the camp, imagine how she felt on the roads? Nearly every time she went out on a convoy, they were attacked by sniper fire, IEDs, mortars, and deadly decoys designed to distract soldiers from their real target. The attacks never let up; the stress level never abated.

While training for her deployment, Blackburn learned to look for sudden changes in the environment, for people and animals scattering, or for the streets to be empty. The Iraqis knew who the bad guys were and would make themselves scarce when trouble was brewing. One time, when Blackburn was convoying from Camp Ramadi to Camp Corregidor, she saw an old man appear out of nowhere and ride his bike past the slow-moving convoy. He rode down an alley. Blackburn thinks he was going to alert others that the convoy was coming. Moments later, the old man returned to his bike. This time, he was armed with a gun that he was trying to conceal beneath his long robe. Blackburn felt bullets whizzing past her head. Small-arms fire ensued. The soldiers, including Blackburn, opened fire on the old man.

Blackburn fought the enemy nearly every day, but the small-arms fire with the boy on the overpass and the old man on the bike stand out because they were the unexpected faces of the war.

It's one thing to be told at training back in Indiana that she'd be fighting children and old men. It's another to look down the barrel and see them, to have the ability to take their lives. Those are some of the images she'll never shake. It's hard for her to think of herself as the light in the darkness when she's the one extinguishing the candle.

She also can't forget the man walking his dog in the middle of the road with the intent of causing the trucks to swerve and hit an IED that had been planted on the side of the road. The soldiers couldn't waver. They were ordered to drive in the center of the road whenever possible, regardless of who or what was in their path.

Even animals were tools of war. Insurgents were known to cut open dead animals, load the carcasses with explosives, and stand them up in the middle of the street. If a truck hit them—*boom*— the explosives would go off, crippling a vehicle and its occupants. To swerve meant to risk hitting an IED on the side of the road and experience a similar fate. Blackburn was riding in a truck one day when she spotted a donkey in the middle of the road. It was still alive and looked as though it was having seizures. As truck commander, it was her responsibility to radio back to the rest of the convoy when she saw something suspicious in the road. They realized the donkey was alive when they saw its tail swish. The convoy rolled by the animal without incident.

The most violent time of the year was Ramadan, a holy period during the ninth Islamic lunar month. Camp Ramadi was mortared twenty to thirty times a day, all day long. The insurgents were also trying to coordinate an effort to overrun small U.S. bases in the area, such as Ramadi, Corregidor, Tiger, Combat Outpost, and Blue Diamond. Blackburn couldn't take the relentless bombing. She had practically stopped walking to the chow hall. The base was supposed to be the safe haven, but it felt anything but safe. To get to the chow hall, she had to walk across a softball field, a frequent target for mortars. A nineteen-year-old Marine walking to chow two weeks after he arrived was killed by a rocket. He bore the brunt of the blast, and his friends walking behind him were spared. On the small bases, the odds of being hit seemed so much higher than on the larger bases. Granted, they were a smaller target, but when a mortar did land at the camp, chances were good that someone would get hit by the mortar or its shrapnel. Blackburn preferred going on convoys to staying at Camp Ramadi. If she was going to be a target, she wanted to be a moving target.

Blackburn's convoys got hit by so many IEDs that most of them blend together. A few stand out, though, like the time she went out on a convoy just after the trucks had been up-armored for additional protection against IED explosions. Every other truck in the convoy had been fitted with the armor. The ones that hadn't been up-armored were strategically placed between those with extra protection. In order for all the trucks to be protected, there had to be a certain amount of space between them. As Blackburn was driving along, she could tell they were too spaced out. They needed to close the gaps. She sped up to get closer to the truck in front of her when she spotted huge mounds of sand on the side of the road that looked like a hiding place for an IED. She was right. As soon as Blackburn drove past it, the IED exploded. Shrapnel sprayed into the back of her truck. They kept rolling.

Another time, she was driving through Baghdad when a daisy chain exploded. A daisy chain is a series of linked IEDs, sometimes as far as twenty-five or thirty feet apart. Blackburn was providing security for third-country nationals when one of the lead trucks hit an IED. Two trucks later, another one hit an IED. Blackburn was in the fifth or sixth truck. She didn't get hit, but a third-country national ahead of her did. His mangled body hung limply from the window and door.

There was almost always an incident when the convoy took the most direct road, Route Michigan, from Camp Ramadi and Camp Corregidor. They were constantly attacked during the fifteen-minute drive. They couldn't let their guard down either on the road or when they reached their destination, since Corregidor was usually attacked by rockets while she was there and wounded soldiers were constantly being medevaced to the closest hospital.

Because of all the stress and suffering around her, when Blackburn woke up in the morning, she made a habit of acknowledging that she was alive and okay. She asked herself, "How am I going to get from point A to point B without getting hit?" It would have been foolish for her to ask, "Am I going to make it through the day? Am I even going to wake up?" Any feelings she had about killing and death were eventually replaced with numbness. It's not that she didn't care. She just preferred to think about protecting her soldiers.

Blackburn could handle just about any physical challenge that came her way. What she couldn't deal with—and what will stay with her forever—are the losses of fellow soldiers, whom she worked with day in and day out, because once they were gone, she couldn't bring them back. They had become part of that family she so desperately yearned for.

Twenty-one-year-old Specialist Kendall Frederick was born in Trinidad and came to the United States when he was fifteen years old. He dreamed of becoming an American citizen. He joined Junior Reserve Officers' Training Corps while he was in high school. Blackburn thought he was a funny kid because he liked to dance as if he were the sexiest person in the world, yet he was really skinny. He never ate. He was a happy kid with big eyes who bounced around and listened to Bob Marley.

Before they left for Iraq, Blackburn was Frederick's squad leader. She noticed he and a young female soldier liked one another and their relationship was moving fast. She took them under her wing and treated Frederick like a younger brother. Blackburn was also dating a fellow soldier at the time, so she and Frederick shared the bond of their secret liaisons. Then they deployed. Frederick transferred out of Blackburn's company, but they still saw each other.

Frederick was hoping to get his citizenship papers while he was in Iraq. He was on his way back to Camp Speicher after getting fingerprinted, the last step in what had been a long and drawn-out process to achieve his dream, when a makeshift bomb exploded near his vehicle right outside the gate at Camp Anaconda. He was killed October 19, 2005, about ten months into his deployment. He was granted U.S. citizenship posthumously.

As Blackburn's first tour was winding down, she asked for an extension. She had no way of knowing at the time that she was probably experiencing the beginning stages of post-traumatic stress disorder (PTSD). She wanted to stay and protect her buddies. She was a veteran now. She couldn't go home knowing American soldiers were still battling it out in Iraq. She had a purpose on that battlefield, whereas back home, her mission in life wasn't as clear. She had also become an adrenaline junkie and had a hard time imagining what she was going to do with all that excess energy.

But there was another reason why she didn't want to go home. There had been a battle going on in Detroit between her mom and stepdad. He was a crack addict and, some years ago, had tried to choke her mom. Having been on the front line in Iraq, it wasn't likely Blackburn would continue to play the role of the powerless daughter who stands by and watches a man abuse her mom. She was a child when her mom told her to "run out of the house" if a fight broke out between her mother and stepfather. She says she is a child of God and a loving person, but she also knows what happens when she gets mad. Iraq was where she needed to be because of the emotions she was feeling. She hated her stepdad for what he did to her mom. Blackburn realizes she is just one of thousands and thousands of children who come from abusive families. She also knows she had a purpose in Iraq: to protect her fellow soldiers in a way she couldn't defend her mom.

She also struggled with her relationship with her mom. When the abuse began between her mother and a man, it put a strain on the mother-daughter relationship. Being on the battlefield eased the tension between them. Blackburn wrote and called her mother, and in those letters and phone conversations, she found renewed compassion.

Blackburn's extension was granted. McNeill and another female soldier, who had become like sisters to her, departed in December. Before they left, they helped Blackburn move from her SWA hut into her new barracks and bought a Christmas tree for her room. Blackburn hadn't realized how much their departure would affect her. McNeill was the only one she trusted with her life. She looked to her for security and fun. The two of them had video cameras and loved recording everything and everyone. Between their risky missions, McNeill made Blackburn laugh and feel better. When McNeill left, the soldier who refused to show emotion cried. Darkness was coming.

As she was preparing to convoy to a smaller camp outside Ramadi, Blackburn got pulled from the manifest. A friend of hers who did missionary work before he was called to active duty went on the convoy, and his truck was hit by an IED. Blackburn was on base when the bloody bodies came in. She couldn't believe it. It was one of the first tragedies she would experience with her new unit. They lost many soldiers during the first several months Blackburn was with them. This war was taking anyone and everyone. Ramadi saw some of its heaviest casualties in the war while she was there. It seemed like every other day communication was being shut down because soldiers in the area of operation were being killed. Sometimes, Blackburn just laid awake all night and listened to the steady sound of medical choppers flying in and out of Camp Ramadi. The feeling that death was all around her was hard to avoid. Would she be next?

For the next eight months, Blackburn did a variety of jobs. She fixed gun trucks that were damaged by IEDs, drove on short convoys through Ramadi, provided security at the glass factory while the Army and Iraqi police were training their new recruits to become Iraqi policemen, and served in a field logistics and equipment (FLE) group.

FLE groups took turns providing security at various towers outside Ramadi for Marines and soldiers traveling through the area. They would stay at a tower for twenty-four to twenty-seven hours at a time and then rotate. Each group was made up of four or five soldiers. Blackburn was the noncommissioned officer in charge of her group, which consisted of two medics, one radio operator, and one mechanic. They hid about twenty yards off the main road in big rectangular boxes made of wood and partially buried in the sand. Each cave had camouflage netting and a five-by-five observation tower with a .50-caliber machine gun and thermal sights, along with their personal weapons. Blackburn carried an M249 SAW (squad automatic weapon), M9 Beretta, and M16 rifle with a scope. Two soldiers stood watch in the tower and walked around while the others were expected to sleep. It was hard to rest, though, because the insurgents constantly targeted them with RPGs. So they played card games, read the same magazines over and over again, and tried to catch field mice. Adding to the stress was the tension among the soldiers. They didn't all like each other, so Blackburn had to rotate them.

By March 2006, Blackburn had been in Iraq for about fifteen months and was having a hard time coping on the battlefield. Fear was getting the best of her. She was becoming paranoid. Her fear of walking to the chow hall intensified. Once she got there, she panicked because everyone could see her. On a convoy, one of a soldier's main objectives was not to be seen. In the chow hall, everyone could see her. She felt exposed and vulnerable. She eventually stopped going to the chow hall and lost a noticeable amount of weight. She replaced food with cigarettes, increasing the number she smoked a day from three to forty.

Blackburn loved her shop and the soldiers she worked with, but eventually, she lost her ability to joke and banter with her buddies. She didn't want to talk to anyone she worked with or anyone back in the States. She walked around dazed and numb. She could tell she wasn't feeling good but didn't want anyone to know. Symptoms of PTSD build up over a period of time, but to Blackburn, it seemed like she went from happy to destructive overnight. She never saw it coming, never expected to lose it.

By now, she had gone on more than 200 convoys. Twenty were hit by IEDs. Three different gun trucks she was driving in were destroyed.

During a bombing on base one day, Blackburn hid behind a Jersey barrier and started to cry. Two soldiers saw her off by herself.

"What's wrong, Sergeant B," they asked.

She told them she was tired. She'd had enough. She needed to go home. She couldn't deal with the war anymore. She had lost twenty-five pounds over the past month. She couldn't eat, couldn't sleep.

The soldiers got her staff sergeant, who knew if Blackburn was crying, something was wrong. She never cried in public or showed any signs of weakness. The staff sergeant took her to the combat stress clinic, where she was diagnosed with chronic PTSD and insomnia. She was prescribed twenty milligrams of Celexa, an anti-depressant, to ease her anxiety and ten milligrams of Ambien to help her sleep. Later, her intake of Celexa was increased to forty milligrams. She was also put on rest-and-relaxation, working the last months in country as a squad leader in the motor pool and going to the combat stress clinic twice a week.

Blackburn carried an M249 assault rifle for a while, along with an M9 Beretta pistol and M16 rifle. She continued to carry them even while on medication because she wasn't considered a threat, and she was in a combat zone and had to be able to pro-tect herself. If she had been stationed on a bigger base, such as Al Asad, she may have been relieved of her weapons. But she was on Camp Ramadi, which was significantly smaller and constantly under attack. Some of the unstable soldiers in her unit, such as those who had been diagnosed as bipolar, had the bolts removed from their weapons. That way they could still carry their weapons and avoid the stigma of having their weapon taken away.

In June, shortly before Blackburn left Camp Ramadi to transi-tion home, she was singing at a Sunday-morning worship service when she heard an explosion. Everyone jumped. The chaplain told the choir to keep singing, only louder. God would take care of them. Then there were more explosions, this time right out-side the chapel. *Boom! Boom!* Blackburn's M16, which had been leaning against the wall, fell to the ground. As they prepared to leave, another mortar landed nearby and shook the chapel and its occupants. They waited five minutes and then walked outside only to find that two rows of SWA huts were on fire. Blackburn ran across the street, past the store on the camp, to her barracks. She ran upstairs to her room and onto the balcony. She looked past the church and saw the SWA huts ablaze. She was ordered to stay inside until they got an all-clear, but she grabbed her weapon, Kevlar helmet, and flak vest and ran down the steps to see if any of her soldiers had been wounded. Blackburn had been living in one of those SWA huts before moving into a barracks.

The night Blackburn left Camp Ramadi, the Black Hawk helicopter carrying her and other soldiers came under fire. She had experienced combat every other day. Why should this day be any different?

Blackburn has a strong outward demeanor. She likens it to that of a drill instructor—serious and intimidating. When she walks into a room, she doesn't ask people for respect. She expects and demands it. She says she's not arrogant. She has a natural respect for everyone and expects the same in return. Some people assume women are weak. She doesn't want to perpetuate that stereotype. When other soldiers see her, they see a fighter. Now the fighter was coming home physically, emotionally, and mentally broken. How would others see her? Could she pull herself together?

She wanted to surprise her parents, so she didn't tell them she was flying in. At the Detroit airport, Blackburn rented a car and took Interstate 94 east to the Southfield Freeway. She was driving eighty-five miles per hour. It felt so good. The Humvees she had been driving could go only sixty or sixty-five. She was swerving and jumping curbs. To an observer, such as a state trooper, she would have looked drunk. She got pulled over.

"Did I do anything wrong?" she asked, then explained she had just returned from Iraq.

The state trooper urged her to be more careful and sent her on her way.

When she pulled up to her parent's house, a worn-out Blackburn got out of the car, dropped to her knees, and started to cry.

After being in the desert for two years, the mere sight of green grass brought her to tears. In Iraq, she had been stripped completely bare of all the comforts of home.

The reservists didn't receive an immediate welcome-home celebration. That would come months later. They were given three months to rest and recuperate. This period nearly killed Blackburn. It was more dangerous than any IED or firefight she experienced in Iraq. She likened the first twenty-four hours she was home to going through detox without a guide. She was restless, couldn't sleep, and wouldn't eat. She hated coffee before she went to Iraq but started drinking it when she wasn't on convoys because the caffeine helped her maintain that same jittery feeling she got on missions. Now she was drinking one cup of coffee after another.

As soon as she arrived in Detroit, Blackburn knew she couldn't stay there. She couldn't take being home. She had to get away. She described herself as a rolling stone. When something happened that made her feel uncomfortable, she packed her bags and left. Another term for this might be fight-or-flight. At that time, everything made her uneasy. In Iraq, she feared mortar, gunfire, and IEDs. At home, she was afraid of her memories. When she sat still, what happened on the battlefield started to sink in and haunt her. She slept only an hour or two each night. Nightmares and tremors kept her awake. She saw blood from American soldiers and the Iraqis she had a hand in killing. She slept only an hour or two each night.

She flew to New Orleans, where her best friend, Marine Lance Corporal Emetria Henderson, was stationed. Henderson had served in Iraq and returned home before Blackburn. She would understand her buddy's feelings. She knew the guilt of coming home when others didn't. She understood Blackburn's intense desire to go back to Iraq even though she had just been there for two years and hated it over there. She knew that Blackburn had been on the battlefield twice as long as many and that her adjustment back home could take double the time.

In New Orleans, Blackburn and Henderson partied at night to ward off the demons and spent their days recuperating. They talked about Iraq and compared feelings. Their conversations seemed to take the edge off Blackburn's anguish. But in reality, she wasn't making any progress. She was repressing her feelings with drugs and alcohol.

Blackburn's two-week vacation to New Orleans turned into a month and a half. It also contributed to her deteriorating health. She started taking the drug Ecstasy. Doing drugs went against everything Blackburn believed in before she went to war, but she was a different person when she came back from Iraq. She barely knew herself anymore. Taking drugs was the quickest way for her to get out of her head. She knows it was cowardly, but she was mentally unstable at the time. Drugs seemed like the best option. When it came time for her to return to Detroit, Blackburn was reluctant to go. Home didn't feel like home. She stayed with her mother for less than a week before packing her bags. She could move all she wanted, from Iraq to New Orleans to Detroit, but she couldn't escape the war because now it was inside her.

Drake was so grateful to have Blackburn home in one piece that at first, all she saw was a perfect daughter and soldier. Then she began to notice that her usually bubbly and laughing daughter had become quiet and withdrawn. She stayed up all night and was often gone. Eventually, Blackburn started talking to her mom and showing her videos from Iraq. It was then that Drake realized the horrors that her daughter had experienced.

Blackburn transitioned from the reserve unit in Michigan to one in Fort Sheridan, Illinois, because she didn't want to be in

Detroit anymore and still had to finish the last six months of her contract with the Army. She moved to Chicago, rented an apartment, and looked for a full-time job. She had decided that if she found a full-time job that she liked, she would leave the Army for good. But she couldn't find one. She blames it on her service in Iraq. She said employers saw her service listed on her job applications and figured she was crazy. Maybe she was right, or maybe she was just paranoid.

In Chicago, Blackburn ran into an ex-boyfriend and soldier who was also into drugs. They partied, and by the time he left for Fort Drum, she was addicted to cocaine. She found a provider in the city, but it was too far to drive. When she got a job working at a bar/movie theater/eatery, one of her coworkers hooked her up with a dealer.

While Blackburn continued on this downward slide, the Department of Veterans Affairs (VA) was trying to contact her for a mandatory post-deployment evaluation. She avoided the VA because she was afraid that if they evaluated her, they would think she was crazy and medically discharge her from the Army. She wasn't ready to leave the military. At the time, it was the only place she felt comfortable and sane. She wasn't sure how long she could survive in the outside world. She was angry with the Army because she felt they were trying to cut their losses and get rid of her instead of helping her. They would rather kick her out and give her a year or two of benefits than have her stay in and rehabilitate her. She felt alone, very alone.

After watching the events of 9/11 five years earlier, Blackburn had decided to join not the Army but the Marine Corps. In the eleventh hour, a sister-in-law who was in the Army persuaded her to become a soldier. Soon after, Blackburn felt she had made a mistake. "I was raised to be the best at whatever I did," she said.

"So if I find that there's a better branch out there, I want to be in it." She put in for a conditional release from the Army several times over the years. She wanted to complete her four-year enlistment in another branch. She finally got an honorable discharge from the Army in spring 2007.

Blackburn was happy to be out of the Army, but she was still searching for those lifelong bonds that often are found between siblings—and soldiers in combat. And she still thought the Marine Corps was the answer. Nevertheless, she got another full-time job working in the bakery at Meijer's department store and loved it. She baked and decorated cakes. She also was high all the time, doing lines of cocaine between jobs at the bakery and the theater. For the most part, she was able to function on the job. She messed up a few cakes, but if she was too high or tired to decorate cakes, she had the option to do something else.

For ten months, all she did was work, do lines of coke, work, do lines, work, lines. She slept only two hours a night and was wasting away. She made false promises to her family. She'd tell them she was coming home to see them and never show up because she knew she couldn't hide from her family the fact that she had lost twenty-seven pounds in a month and a half. She had been in a relationship that had gone sour, got more and more depressed, and didn't feel she had anyone to turn to.

One day, she woke up and realized she was self-destructing. The more drugs she did, and the more alcohol she drank, the worse she felt. She could no longer afford the high cost of drugs, so she threw away her rent money on liters of Rossi wine and packs of cigarettes. She'd start drinking around six or seven in the morning, an hour or two before work. Drinking was a welcome habit at first because it masked her feelings of inadequacy and worthlessness and blurred the image of the desperate woman reflected in the mirror. But then she started getting bloody noses while walking up and down the aisles in the movie theater, and her body ached.

I can't do this anymore. I'm going to die. I need help.

She decided to join the Marine Corps to save her life. "I would have been dead by now if I hadn't joined," Blackburn said. She knew no one would challenge her like the Marine Corps.

She left Chicago, moved in with her mom in Detroit, and started hanging out with her old friends. But Blackburn had changed, and her best friend didn't like what she saw. She was hurt and angry that Blackburn was doing drugs, so Blackburn started drinking vodka instead. She'd drop one bad habit and replace it with another.

One night, while attending a party at a friend's house, Blackburn snorted some cocaine, triggering a flashback. She ran from the bathroom to the kitchen, grabbed a knife, and climbed into the bathtub.

"They're after me," she said, curled up in the bathtub. "They're after me." She was hyperventilating and waving the knife.

"They're trying to take the knife from me," she said. "They're not going to get me. I'll do it to myself before they get me."

Then she passed out.

Her friends poured water on her to wake her up and drove her to the hospital down the street. Blackburn's breathing was shallow. She had nearly overdosed. The doctors gave her smelling salt to wake her. When she came to, she was violent and aggressive. After she was treated in the emergency room, she was transferred to the intensive-care unit for observation. She was moving in and out of consciousness, her vitals were low, and she was dehydrated. They had to strap her to the bed because she was hallucinating. The next day, Blackburn was transferred to the psychiatric ward. When her mom and dad visited her, she could see the hurt in their eyes. She was embarrassed. Now they knew her secret. She never wanted to be a failure or disappoint anyone. She never wanted to hurt anyone.

Blackburn walked out of the hospital in her gown and went home with her mom, to what was now a safe environment. She showered and stayed on the couch for a couple of days as she went through withdrawals and cravings for the drugs and alcohol. Between her mom's prayers and Blackburn's strong will, she was able to quit the drugs.

When she finally got hydrated and got rid of the shakes, she had a mere three weeks to get in shape before leaving for boot camp. She replaced her drug addiction with exercise. Every day, a buddy in charge of the recruiting station would pick her up and take her to the gym, and she would work out on and off all day long.

Twelve weeks after starting boot camp, Blackburn graduated at the top of her company and received a meritorious promotion. Lance Corporal Blackburn began working as an individual material readiness list manager/asset manager for Marine Aviation Logistics Squadron–31 in Beaufort, South Carolina. Her job was to keep inventory of support equipment. She could make a lateral move to another position after two years. It was a tough job for her to do after spending two years in Iraq.

In her new position, Blackburn felt like an adrenaline junkie stuck in a cage. She didn't feel that she had a purpose or that she was making a difference. She wanted to go back overseas. She had some unfinished business there. "I felt like if I went back over there, I could reverse what happened to me back here," she said. It didn't have to be Iraq. It just had to be somewhere outside the United States. That's because the camaraderie in the Marine

Corps is so much more meaningful and intense when the troops are away. There aren't any family members or civilian friends to lean on. The troops have to rely on one another. She wouldn't be so lonely, and the temptation to drink would feel less powerful.

Blackburn started getting on with her life and thinking about the future. Her plans included earning a bachelor's degree in criminal justice and spending twenty years in the Marine Corps. As she moved forward, however, she also had to deal with combat-related triggers and setbacks. About nine months after completing boot camp, Blackburn got into a little trouble. She had been back from Iraq for two years and was in Meridian, Mississippi, in training for her Marine Corps job. She was in a bar drinking beer and playing pool. She walked outside to have a cigarette. A scuffle broke out between several Navy and civilian police officers. Blackburn called her sergeant to let him know what was going on and to tell him she was not involved. But then she tried to help break it up. The next thing she knew, she was having words with a base security officer who she says wasn't fond of Marines. Because she was in a bar setting and became belligerent with a security officer, the Marine Corps sent her to drug and alcohol rehab in Pensacola, Florida.

At rehab, she spent time learning how to cope with her emotions. Blackburn wrote in a journal about emotions she had suppressed. She was soul searching, trying to find some peace, and perhaps even a bit of the old Stacy, the one who saw 9/11 play out on her classroom TV and wanted to make a positive difference in the world. As she was trying to regroup, tragedy struck.

On Friday night, August 15, 2008, Blackburn was on duty at the air station. She was supposed to go out with her Marine boyfriend, Corporal Tony Martinez-Ramirez, that night but had to work instead. He stopped by to see her, teasing Blackburn about having to work and not being able to party with him and their

Marine buddies. That's the last time she saw him alive. About 1:30 the next morning, Blackburn got a call from another friend. Martinez and the other Marines had been drinking alcohol when one of them pulled out his .45-caliber pistol. Not knowing it was loaded, he jokingly pointed the gun at Martinez's forehead. "You're not going to shoot me?" Martinez said. Seconds later, his friend shot him.

Less than forty-eight hours after Martinez had been shot, I was scheduled to meet Blackburn in person for the first time at Plums restaurant in Beaufort. She was coming from Charleston Memorial Hospital, where Martinez had just been taken off life support. He died soon after.

Blackburn came to the restaurant with two stocky white male Marines, Lance Corporals Jose Ghiorzo and Gabriel Goelz. Walking down the street, they looked like two body guards, one on either side of her. And at that moment, they were probably feeling intensely protective of her. Martinez was their buddy, too, and they had been at the party with him when he was shot.

Blackburn's eyes were dry for the first time since learning her boyfriend had been shot. She wore her sorrow on her tear-stained face. Nothing could hide the grief she was feeling at that moment. She took time to talk, but not to eat. She was there to talk to me about her combat experiences in Iraq, but it was this most recent battle in the States that she wanted to talk about.

The male Marines ordered three Coronas, one for each of them and one for Martinez. Corona was the deceased Marine's favorite beer. The full bottle with a lime wedged in its throat stood in the center of the table for the duration of the meal. Condensation, or maybe tears, trickled down the side of the bottle.

It was difficult for Blackburn to get involved with someone after spending two straight years in Iraq. She lost battle buddies over there, people she loved. She didn't want to risk getting close to someone else and losing him. She and Martinez talked about her struggles. He understood. When she did finally get close to someone, God knows she didn't expect to lose him to a gunshot wound. "I thought I didn't have any more tears left, and then I walked in the hospital room and saw him," she said. Now she doesn't want to make friends again. She's confused but finds clarity when she's talking to other Marines, who are like family to her.

On November 3, 2008, Blackburn and her best friend, Emitria Henderson, were both promoted to corporal. Blackburn was promoted in Beaufort, South Carolina, and Henderson in Djibouti. Blackburn was going to counseling for her PTSD at Parris Island. She loved going where Marine recruits are trained, because she sees and hears the drill instructors, who motivate her. But she still struggles every day. She has panic attacks that make her feel like she can't breathe. One time she started screaming something about Iraq and tried to jump off a deck. A corporal grabbed her and settled her down. She's not sure what triggers these incidents.

She has nightmares, which increased at the end of 2008 when several Marines committed suicide during a two-month period at Beaufort Marine Corps Air Station, where she worked. She wonders what makes her a survivor. Why does she choose to live when others take their lives? She said she didn't want to disappoint her family and friends. She still drinks to drown her demons and loneliness and takes Ambien to help her sleep.

Blackburn struggles to keep the light inside of her shining, much like the flame of a candle that flickers in the breeze but keeps burning. It takes a great deal of effort to keep the light burning. Being a leader inspires Blackburn. At twenty-five, this corporal has figured out that maybe, for now, she is meant to guide younger Marines who are starting down the tumultuous path that she has already traveled. As she finds her own way out of the darkness, she can light the way for others.

In spring 2009, Blackburn was deployed to Afghanistan.

CJ Robison

Still in the Fight

On February 27, 2004, Army Master Sergeant CJ Robison went on a convoy from Camp Taji to Camp Ridgeway to drop off third-country nationals and vehicles. On the four-hour drive back to Camp Taji, Robison was kneeling on the front seat of a soft-top Humvee, with her back to the windshield. She had her laptop in front of her as she tried to e-mail the convoy's coordinates back to the operations center at Camp Taji. When she sat the normal way, the sun shone down on her computer, and the glare made it impossible to read the writing on the screen.

About an hour into the drive, an IED exploded next to the driver's side of Robison's truck. The explosion rocked the Humvee and shot shrapnel into the vehicle. Luckily, none of the soldiers was hit by the flying debris. However, the explosion happened just eight feet from Robison, and the sound was deafening. It felt like someone had popped the inner tube of a tire next to her ear. She asked the soldiers in her truck if they were all right, but she couldn't hear their responses. Her ears were ringing. She couldn't even hear the voices on the radio. The explosion pissed her off.

Kiss my ass. It's unbelievable when someone attacks you and you can't see them. It's such a chicken-shit thing to do. You want to come out and fight? Come out and fight. The enemy can see us but we can't see him. And I can't see the soldiers behind me to know if they're okay.

Between the plume of black smoke from the explosion and the dust kicked up from the gravel road, Robison couldn't see to get her bearings. She could barely see inside her own vehicle, never mind the gun truck in front of her and the fuel and gun trucks behind her. She turned around in her seat to check on the driver and the passenger. Having been in-country and traveling these roads for a year, they gave the impression of being unfazed. Then she kept looking in her side-view mirror until the smoke and dust cleared, and she could see the two trucks. They never got out of their trucks. They drove on. This was the first time in Robison's twenty-year Army career that she felt she didn't have control over the safety of her soldiers. It made her sick to her stomach.

After being hit by the IED, the convoy still had to drive through Baghdad to get to Camp Taji. They were doing fine until they reached a series of traffic circles in the city. At the second circle, they were forced to stop because of traffic. They were surrounded by tall buildings and a market with baskets and other items hanging everywhere. As soon as they came to a stop, the Iraqi people in the market started moving toward the trucks. It was a dangerous situation for a small, four-vehicle convoy.

When forced to come to a stop, one soldier in each truck was supposed to stay with the radio while the others got out and posted security along the perimeter of their vehicles. Robison began to dismount when someone yelled that they were taking fire. She couldn't hear the shots because her ears were still ringing from the IED explosion, but she could feel the breeze of a bullet as it shot past her head.

"Get the soldiers back in their trucks," Robison shouted. "And tell the front truck to make a hole."

The soldiers remounted their trucks and sped off.

Most people would consider it a bad day when an IED exploded near their vehicle and they took fire. Not Robison. She considered it one of her best days in Iraq. This mission occurred early in her deployment, opening her eyes to the dangers that soldiers faced on the roads, and to what she and her soldiers could do to increase their safety. Of course, there were no guarantees.

A couple of months earlier, on December 13, 2003, when American soldiers caught Saddam Hussein in Iraq, Robison and her fellow soldiers in the 185th Support Battalion (National Guard) from Camp Dodge, Iowa, made preparations to deploy. They left for the Sunni Triangle on December 26, 2003, and arrived in January 2004. For the next year, they would be stationed at a forward operating base (FOB) in Taji, thirty minutes south of Baghdad. Their job was to make sure the Marines and First Cavalry had the heavy equipment, food, water, ammunition, and anything else they needed.

Robison, thirty-seven, was the noncommissioned officer in charge of support operations and also a medic, having gone through basic medical training in the Army and completed three years of nursing school at Grand View College in Des Moines, Iowa. Having already spent half of her life in the Army, she hoped to add another ten years to her career before she retired.

Her blood ran green. She had known since she was six that she wanted to join the military. That was the first time she saw her dad, a former Army sergeant and Vietnam vet, take his uniform out of the closet. "It was the greatest thing I'd ever seen." She was in awe not only of his medals but also the light blue infantry cord that went over the shoulder and hung from the lapel. She comes from a long line of men who served in the Army and the Marine Corps and was determined to become the first woman in her family to serve her country. College didn't interest her, so she joined the Army when she was eighteen.

Over the years, Robison developed into a tough, no-nonsense, hands-on leader with high expectations of herself and of the soldiers she led. She never expected her soldiers to do anything she wouldn't do. But since she was willing to do almost anything and everything, her expectations of the others were quite high.

For example, Robison's shop of seventeen soldiers provided the supplies for other troops, but someone had to transport those provisions to the soldiers and Marines on the other end. The soldiers who did the transporting were from different companies attached to the 185th Battalion, such as a truck company from Ohio; a laundry, shower, and clothing renovation unit from Puerto Rico; and heavy equipment transporters from North Carolina. Robison felt responsible for the soldiers not only in her shop but also in the other companies.

Robison didn't have to go on convoys with those companies. She could have stayed in the comfort and security of her support shop with her soldiers. But she insisted on going because she wanted to make sure the transporters had what they needed to make their missions successful, and the only way to know for sure was by going with them. She was also adamant about the soldiers from her shop going on convoys. During the first week of operations at Camp Taji, she let them know that they would be traveling with the companies to find out what it felt like to be on the road in a war zone. They had been working independently of the companies during peace time, and she felt that they hadn't been challenged and had developed large egos. She had watched her soldiers bark orders at the transporters, who spent their days out on the dangerous roads, and didn't like what she saw. Her soldiers had no sense of what it was like for the company soldiers to be away from the security of the forward operating base. She wanted them to understand—emotionally, mentally, and physically—what the transporters were doing.

Robison got to know the transporters by sight and name because when a company was going on a mission and was short a medic, she would volunteer to go. If a company had been hit the past couple of nights, Robison would choose another soldier from the battalion, and the two of them would ride on convoys that night. She wanted to send a message to the companies: the battalion wasn't going to ask them to do anything they wouldn't do themselves. She believed the soldiers would respect her and the battalion more if they saw that she was willing to go on missions, too.

Because of her "I'm not going to ask you to do anything I wouldn't do myself" philosophy, Robison was on the road about 60 percent of the time. The IED explosion in February was the first of about a half dozen that she would encounter. It was the only direct hit. The others exploded behind or in front of her. There were also vehicle-borne IEDs and mortar attacks.

As her deployment progressed, Robison started to experience a number of medical problems. She had lost all of the hearing in her right ear from explosions. When other soldiers spoke to her, she turned her left ear to them. She admits that she probably irritated the other soldiers by asking "What?" all the time. Even though she compensated for her lack of hearing by reading lips, the hearing loss was definitely affecting her job. She stopped answering the phone in the shop because she couldn't hear the person on the other end of the line. She couldn't hear the voices on the radio. When a call came in over the phone or radio, it had to be relayed to her. It was taking twice as long to get a message to her. She realized this wasn't an ideal situation but felt like she was managing okay.

Captain Rich Fowler thought otherwise and ordered Robison to get her hearing checked out right away. Robison was mad. She couldn't be bothered. She had more important things to do. She could take care of her ear when she returned home, but it wasn't her decision. Captain Saralee Sickles made the flight arrangements for Robison to fly from Camp Taji to Camp Anaconda to Baghdad.

There was a wounded soldier in really bad shape on the flight from Anaconda to Baghdad. He was sitting slumped over between Robison and the flight nurse. When the helicopter landed, Robison helped out by handing the defibrillator to someone on the ground while the patient was being handed off to the ground crew. As this was going on, Robison, who was on the edge of the aircraft, turned, lost her balance, and fell to the ground. The fall resulted in a three-inch gash that exposed her shin bone. She went to medical and saw a line of people who she believed were worse off than she was, so she super-glued the gash closed. She later learned that the fall had caused a hairline fracture.

Robison spent the next two nights at the hospital in Baghdad, where she was seen by an audiologist. He wasn't able to do anything for her. If she wanted her ear treated in the near future, she would have to fly to Landstuhl Regional Medical Center in Germany. She didn't want to leave her troops, so she returned to Camp Taji. She had gone to Baghdad to get her hearing checked, and she returned with the same hearing problem and a broken leg.

When she deployed, Robison already had two herniated disks. The pain from the disks intensified as she rode in trucks on unpaved roads and she fell several times. In addition to the fall from the helicopter, she also fell out of a heavy equipment truck. It was early morning, before dawn, still dark. A Marine unit ahead had come under heavy attack. When her vehicle stopped, Robison grabbed her medic bag and ammunition can and began to climb down the ladder on the side of the truck when her foot got caught in the webbing. She fell about six feet to the ground, landing on her back. She couldn't get up so she just lay there. No one knew she had fallen. She didn't move until a soldier kicked her boot to tell her they were mounting and rolling. She doesn't remember anything after that until the sun started to rise and the light shone into the truck. She refused to be medevaced. Again, she didn't want to leave her soldiers.

Sometime after those falls, Robison was riding in a fuel convoy from Muleskinner to Fallujah to Baghdad with emergency fuel and rations. They drove in a two-lane highway to a bridge. They ascended the bridge and were heading down the other side. They hadn't gotten the word that the bridge was no longer in use. Someone had hidden an IED in the guardrail toward the bottom of the bridge, and it had gone off. The whole bottom of the bridge had been destroyed. Robison watched sparks fly as one fuel truck after another dropped four feet onto asphalt. Then it was Robison's turn with her fuel tank. They were going too fast to stop. She feared that she and her truck would explode upon impact. They didn't. But the landing was jarring, especially with the armor plates that she was wearing in her vest.

After months of explosions, falls, and bumpy roads, Robison also started to tire easily, get headaches with increasing frequency and severity, and have difficulty seeing out of her right eye.

When she returned to Iowa in January 2005, Robison felt like she had entered some kind of fantasy land. Iraq had become her reality. Right away, the Army did something that has become symbolic of her post-Iraq experience. When Robison and the other soldiers got off the buses to greet their families for the first time in a year, they were wearing coats over their uniforms. They got about six steps inside the armory in Camp Dodge when they were told to hand over their coats. It was a frigid January day in Iowa, and the Army was more concerned with getting their coats back than they were with the well-being of their battle-weary soldiers. It was the first time Robison realized she had an unrealistic view of the Army, an institution for which she was willing to die.

Robison's family met her at the armory. A single mom, Robison has a daughter, Amber, who was in the third grade, and a son, Ben, then a sophomore in high school. Her mother and stepfather, Mary and Chuck Long, were also there. Mary watched the soldiers march in. When she found her daughter among the masses, she saw something that troubled her. Robison had a blank expression on her face, like nobody was home.

Trauma changes you.

The National Guard soldiers were given three months of leave to get reacquainted with family, friends, and former coworkers. For some, this would be easy. For others, reconnecting with loved ones would never happen. Robison fell somewhere in the middle.

Robison's home is an hour's drive from Camp Dodge. She lives in a 1,800-square-foot house on forty-five acres in New Virginia. Once she turns off the main road, she takes a dirt road for four miles to the driveway leading to her house, which sits on a hill. Bailey, their golden retriever, sleeps in a small house out back. Mary and Chuck live on a farm next door.

Originally, Ben and Amber were going to stay with their grandparents while Robison was deployed, but their grandfather was diagnosed with lymphoma just before Robison left. To make it easier for her grandmother, Amber stayed with her aunt, Sandra Saluri, in West Des Moines, about an hour away.

When a parent deploys, changes in family dynamics and leadership, along with the grief of an absent parent, can throw children into an emotional tailspin. Some founder academically and get into mischief. Robison's departure seemed to have no negative effects on Ben's academic and athletic interests. An above-average student, Ben was inducted into the National Honor Society. He also had one of the best years of his athletic career. He was the first athlete at Interstate 35 High School to qualify in the state cross-country competition two years in a row. Ben attributes his ability to adjust to the Busby family. His best friend was Cal Busby, whose father, Tim, was a high-school history teacher and mother, Jane, taught science. They treated Ben as if he were one of the family, and he spent more time there than anywhere else.

Ben did struggle a bit with the lack of interest and sensitivity of his teachers and administrators toward his situation. He was the only student at Interstate 35 High School with a parent in either Iraq or Afghanistan, and for some reason, few adults knew or cared about what Ben and his family were going through. They never asked, "Have you heard from your mom?" "How is she doing?" "Is there anything you need?" This seems so simple, considering there were only about sixty students in his tenth-grade class. It's not like he was just a number at a huge school. Everyone knew everyone. Or did they?

When the Army announced that there would be a video conference at Camp Dodge where Ben could see and talk to his mom, he was told that if he went, he would have to take zeros on all his assignments. Because Ben attended his mom's deployment ceremony on a school day, he was charged with an unexcused absence. The day his mom returned, Ben went to the principal's office and made a special effort to let the school's top administrator know he was leaving at noon to meet his mom at the armory. His principal said, "Okay, no problem." But when Ben returned to school, he was given in-school detention. Ben's mom was proud he put family first.

Ben has always been able to talk to his mom about anything at any time. She is his go-to person. When she was deployed, Robison tried to call home every Sunday, but there was a series of Sundays when she didn't call. That was a worrisome time for Ben. During that period, he heard a report that soldiers from Iowa had been attacked and some were missing. He prayed it wasn't his mother.

In his mom's absence, Ben was forced to become more self-reliant than his peers. He developed from an awkward freshman into a very mature sophomore.

Where Ben rose to the challenge while his mom was away, young Amber struggled. She moved in with her aunt an hour away and had to start a new but temporary life. The administration at Interstate 35 Community School District had the opportunity to help eight-year-old Amber make a smooth transition from Interstate 35 Middle School to Johnston Middle School in West Des Moines but didn't.

Over the next year Amber saw little of her brother or her friends back home. She made new friends at Johnston Middle School and played on the softball, basketball, and volleyball teams. She survived, but not without crying every day her mom was gone. She sent hate mail to Robison in Iraq. She'd draw a big circle with the word "Army" in the middle and a line through it. On another occasion, she bore down on a crayon as she drew a picture of herself, Robison, and Ben in a circle with a line through it and the word "retired" in a bubble over Robison's head. When there was a bombing in Iraq, friends would ask Amber if her mom was dead. She had no idea.

Visits to the park with her aunt and uncle only made Amber miss her mom more. Watching other moms playing with their daughters intensified her grief. Her aunt and uncle were good to her and tried to cheer her up, but it was no use. "I felt like I was all alone," she said. Amber couldn't really write to her mom because she was only in the third grade, but she would talk to Robison on the phone. And she could tell her aunt what to write for her in e-mails and letters.

Family members didn't know what to expect from Robison or from themselves when she returned home. They figured she would be tired from the flight. They weren't aware of the firefights, explosions, mortars, and falls. They didn't know Robison would be bringing the war home with her. They were about to embark on a chaotic and confusing journey.

Robison opened the door to a home that had been uninhabited for a year. The house felt as cold and empty as the inside of her refrigerator and freezer. The heat hadn't been turned up. The cupboards were bare. She wasn't feeling good about being home. She decided to shed her uniform and shower, thinking that would make her feel better.

Neither Robison nor her home felt important anymore. As a master sergeant on the battlefield, Robison was responsible for hundreds of soldiers. There was always a sense of urgency, and the lives of other soldiers depended on her decision-making. Now that she was home, she felt less consequential. It's not that motherhood didn't seem important. It's just that Amber and Ben had gone a year without her. She knew they were safe. She had been in Iraq for a year and had taken good care of her soldiers. Another master sergeant had been trained to replace her. Would her replacement keep the soldiers safe? Would other soldiers be wounded or die during the learning curve? Many dedicated soldiers grieved when they left Iraq. They felt they were leaving before they finished the job. Robison was one of them.

The first night home, Amber asked if she could sleep with her mom. Robison didn't think it was a good idea. She hadn't been sleeping well in Iraq, especially toward the end of her deployment, because it was taking too long for her replacement to get there. She was afraid her job wouldn't get done. She needed to train someone. She also had a sixth sense that was keeping her up at nights. It told her when something bad was going to happen. In the evening, when her sixth sense kicked in, she'd get dressed and go to the shop, only to find out that a convoy had been hit. She was right 99 percent of the time, so her soldiers called her

Sergeant 99. On those rare occasions when she did sleep, Robison was restless. One time, she had to sleep in a large room with other soldiers. When someone reached over her to get something, Robison grabbed the soldier and told him not to touch her while she was sleeping. After that, if anyone needed something from her, they would poke her with a broom.

Amber persisted. She wanted to be beside her mom that first evening. Later that night, Robison had a bad dream. She screamed, "You're a disgrace. I hate you." Amber thought she was talking to her. She got out of bed and ran to the staircase between the main floor and downstairs. Robison found her on one of the steps, sobbing uncontrollably. Amber told her what she had shouted in her dream. It turns out Robison was dressing down one of her soldiers, not her daughter. They went into Amber's room and lay down. As Amber fell back asleep, Robison lay awake. Going from soldier on the battlefield to mom in New Virginia, Iowa, would be much tougher than she thought.

Being a soldier in wartime is a sick profession. How is it that when I hear the word "deployment," I am able to effortlessly flick a switch and shut off my family? Yet when I returned from deployment, there was no such switch to reconnect me to my children and parents? It doesn't equate. I don't get to pick up where I left off. I will have to rebuild.

It was hard for Robison to grasp that life had gone on without her. Amber and Ben were another year older. Ben got his driver's license while she was gone and no longer had to be driven to the bus stop or picked up from his cross-country meets. Amber received First Communion, a Roman Catholic ceremony for a person's first reception of the sacrament of the Eucharist. The family sent Robison a tape of the ceremony.

The day after returning home, Robison called Colonel Mike Schlorholtz to find out if she could go back to work right away. She worked full-time for the Guard. He told her she had to wait at least one week. That month, Robison was promoted to first sergeant. If that raised her spirits at all, it was brief because going back to work turned out to be a disappointment. It wasn't the same. Many of the soldiers with whom she served in Iraq didn't work for the Guard full-time, so she wasn't seeing her buddies. Initially, she was put in charge of retrieving equipment belonging to the state of Iowa that was coming back from Iraq and Afghanistan. Her new job seemed trivial compared with her autonomy and responsibility in Iraq, where she took care of soldiers and soldiers relied on her.

It took only a few days for Robison's mom, Mary, to realize that her daughter didn't want to be home. It crushed her. Mary was tired. She worked full-time, her husband had lymphoma, and he hadn't fully recovered from a stroke. She desperately wanted her daughter to pick up the load she was carrying before she left. She needed Robison to be there for Amber, who was now nine and in fourth grade. Even though her granddaughter wasn't staying with her when Robison was gone, Amber was more of a challenge than Ben because whenever Mary saw Amber, they cried. Amber wanted her grandmother to fix things for her, and Mary couldn't. She felt helpless to Amber's pleas of "Grandma, I just want my mom."

Also weighing on Mary were her memories of Vietnam and the first Gulf War. Her first husband was a Vietnam vet. "This is so different from Vietnam," she said. "When those soldiers came home, they just wanted to be here and be accepted. The soldiers from this war all want to go back to Iraq. Neither situation worked." While Desert Storm was playing out in Iraq, Mary cried for those who had served in Vietnam. When the "shock and awe" bombings began in Iraq in 2003, Mary cried for a week. She shed tears every day her daughter was gone. She cried for Robison and all the troops there and prayed for a speedy resolution. "I don't have another twenty years to hold it in."

It took Robison six months to turn on the TV satellite, land-line phone, and Internet. She didn't want anything to do with the outside world. This drove Amber and Ben crazy.

"How much longer will it be before we have TV?" they asked.

"You have two channels," Robison said.

"They're fuzzy."

"I don't want TV in my house," Robison said. If she couldn't be in Iraq, she didn't want to know anything about it.

At first, she borrowed her mom's phone to make calls. Then they got cell phones.

Robison had been pursuing a bachelor's degree in nursing before she left for Iraq. Her plan was to retire from the Army and become a nurse. She would never be able to fulfill her dream of becoming a nurse. She earned her degree April 2006 but couldn't take her state boards because she couldn't remember much of the material she had learned. She was having problems with her short-term memory and continued to have difficulty hearing. She had a special stethoscope, but it was still a challenge to hear. She went to vocational rehab to see if they could help her find a job in nursing but was told that she was too much of a liability to work in the profession because of her back pain and hearing loss. This left her discouraged. She was good enough to provide medical treatment to the troops on the battlefield but not back home.

The welcome home ceremony for the 185th Battalion was held in May. During the ceremony, Robison received a Purple Heart for her hearing loss and other combat-related medical conditions. When she first learned she was receiving a Purple Heart, Robison was angry and embarrassed. She didn't feel worthy. "I lost soldiers," she said. "I had 104 come home with life-altering wounds." Eventually, as her health declined, Robison was grateful she had it because it was the only piece of paper the Department of Veterans Affairs took seriously.

It really wasn't until the Purple Heart ceremony that Robison's family realized what she had been through. She hadn't told them anything, and she played down and didn't address her problems at first. Mary realized how poor Robison's hearing was when she was sitting across the room from her daughter. Mary would talk to Robison and not use any volume, and Robison would know exactly what she was saying. She had perfected the art of reading lips. "That's when I realized she had lost her hearing," Mary said. "Then, bit by bit, it sunk in."

In Iraq, Robison made a deal with Colonel Schlorholtz. He had wanted her to take care of her medical problems as soon as she returned home, but that would have meant staying at a mobilization station at Fort McCoy in Wisconsin until they figured out what was wrong with Robison and what to do with her. She didn't want to spend any more time away from her family. So she promised that as soon as she was eligible—that is, off active federal orders and back on state orders—she would register with the VA and get her health looked after. Her most pressing medical concerns were the ringing in her ear, headaches, and the pain that shot down her back and into her right leg.

Her first visit to the VA Medical Center in Des Moines, Iowa, was on February 11, 2005, just two weeks after she had returned from Iraq. Robison thought that the experience would be straightforward and that she would be in and out in no time. Nothing could have been farther from the truth. She had to fill out numerous forms and make an appointment for a physical.

"I just want someone to look at my ear. Can you just look at my ear?"

"You need to go to the federal building first and come back to the VA on another day."

Robison set up future appointments and was directed to the federal building to register—for what she did not know.

"Are you filing a claim?" an employee in the federal building asked her.

"No, I just want someone to look at my ear."

"Here's a stack of papers. Take these next door and have the man help you fill them out."

"I just want someone to look at my ear," Robison said, as she carried the papers next door to the Department of Disabled Veterans.

Robison told the male employee that she wasn't a disabled veteran.

"I know that, but you need help filling out the forms."

"This is bullshit," she said. "I just want someone to look at my ear."

"This is the way it works. You need someone to go through all this stuff with you."

Robison was losing her patience. He asked her to tell him everything that happened while she was gone. She told him only about her hearing loss. She didn't tell him about the half-dozen IEDs, mortars, firefights, and falls. She didn't think it was any of his damn business. She doesn't like to be prodded, especially by people she doesn't know and trust. In hindsight, she wishes she had told the man everything. Then the VA would have realized from the start that she had extensive wounds and they could have caught her traumatic brain injury (TBI) earlier rather than later.

A month and a half later, she returned for her physical. She was told she couldn't have her physical until she filled out the means test.

"What's the means test?"

"It will only take you a couple minutes, but you can't get a physical until you fill out the form. They want to know how much money you make."

The means test is what the VA uses to determine how much of her care the service member will be responsible for paying.

Unfortunately, it was the man's first day on the job, and he didn't have all the answers. Robison suggested he get his supervisor because she was getting ready to lose it. A female supervisor informed her that everyone who wanted health services from the VA had to fill out the means test.

"So let me get this right," Robison said. "I'm willing to serve my country and get my ass blown up in the process. All I want is for you to fix my ear. You put me through all this shit at the federal building with a stack of papers like this, send me to the DAV, humiliate me, and now you want to know how much money I make? You have my 214s [certificate of release or discharge from active duty] that show I served in Iraq. Give me the piece of paper that shows me that you need to know how much money I make."

"I don't have anything. I have a poster I can give you."

"Lady, I'm out of patience and am ready to snap you in two like a twig. I'm not going to tell you how much I make. If you want to know, look up how much E8s earn in a combat zone. Then stick that and the means test up your ass."

The lady asked Robison to wait out in the hallway.

The next thing Robison knew, she was being escorted to the elevator. When she arrived on the second floor and the doors opened, she saw a sign: Mental Health. She thought she was going to throw up. They let Robison know that anger was a symptom of post-traumatic stress disorder (PTSD). They requested she make an appointment with mental health. She didn't. It would take six months for her to get hearing aids.

Headaches that started on the battlefield continued to plague her when she returned home and got progressively worse during the summer of 2005. As the headaches intensified, she began having problems with her balance. She'd get out of bed and fall, hitting her head against the wall and bruising the side of her face.

Over the next two years, the VA prescribed Robison sixteen different medications. She took amitriptyline to stop the ringing in her ears. Her ears rang all the time and still do. The medicine didn't help. Now she runs a fan all night long to cancel out the ringing and keep her from going crazy. She was given pills to help her sleep, calm her anxiety, and manage her depression.

She balked at the depression diagnosis. "People like me don't get depressed," Robison said. "We're super troopers."

She took Vicodin for pain, oxycodone as an advanced pain killer, methadone combined with a seizure medicine, and more. "I was so uncomfortable," she said.

Seeing her daughter on so much medication and walking around like a zombie made Robison's mom mad. She watched her daughter go off to Iraq to make things better. Then she watched her daughter get left behind by the VA system. "They're drugging them and not fixing them," Mary said. "And that still makes me angry."

Robison faced a catch-22 with the drugs. If she went off the medicine, she would be in pain. When she was on the medicine, her brain couldn't function. Either way, her quality of life was terrible. She allowed them to medicate her at first, but it got to the point where she was almost comatose. The only thing she takes now is a nerve drug and blood pressure and ulcer medicine. She has had fourteen back procedures, from epidermals to a nucleoplasti to the doctors burning the nerves in her back. And the pain continued.

As her physical health declined, Robison got more and more depressed, and her energy level plunged. She had no idea she was depressed. She just thought that she had left the best of herself in Iraq. She left her energy there. Nothing was as important as the battlefield. She couldn't sleep and would be up for days at a time. But she didn't want to talk to anyone during those waking hours. Not her mom. Not her children. She wanted to be by herself or with her soldiers. In the dead of winter, she'd sit outside on her snow-covered porch, alone, and smoke.

While all this was going on, Robison was still trying to be a soldier, one under consideration for the rank of sergeant major. In 2006, she requested a medical board to make sure she could physically do what the sergeant major academy would require of her. If she couldn't, she wanted someone else to have the slot. As soon as she requested the medical review board, Robison felt the Army was done with her.

The review process was supposed to take ninety days; it took fifteen months. They put her through hell. The medical board process at Fort Leonard Wood in Missouri was extremely difficult. She had to make three seven-hour trips from Iowa to Missouri because Fort Leonard Wood couldn't get everything done in one trip. She couldn't drive that distance alone, so her mother went with her on one trip and officers accompanied her on the two other trips. They assisted Robison with the paperwork.

As the last step of the medical evaluation board, Robison was told she would have to fly to Fort Lewis in Washington state to testify. She repeatedly asked the Judge Advocate General's officer if she had to be there. She didn't want to go because traveling is hard on her. She was informed she had to be there, so she paid $1,000 for a last-minute, nonrefundable ticket for her mom. Then she got a call saying they didn't need her.

She continued as first sergeant and trained her soldiers, but she felt like she had been put out to pasture. Her retirement was put off four times because her orders hadn't come in.

In April 2007, Robison was admitted into the Comprehensive Inpatient Brain Injury Program at the Minneapolis VA Medical Center. She still didn't think there was much wrong with her, even though she had been having balance issues for more than a year and her back and leg hurt so badly she could barely walk. She was supposed to stay at the center for seven days but ended up being there for nearly three weeks.

It wasn't until she went to the Minneapolis VA and was surrounded by other wounded vets exhibiting the same behaviors that she finally accepted she was really sick. She realized she couldn't do everything and discovered that what she had come to accept in her personal world as standard operating procedure was anything but normal.

When it came to pain, Robison felt she could suck it up. But when other things were pointed out, she realized she might be in trouble. She couldn't multitask anymore. She couldn't even perform simple tasks. She got so frustrated trying to do a child's puzzle that she threw it at the psychologist. She slept only a few hours a day, and those hours were spent slung over a chair. When she woke, the surface beneath her would be soaked from sweat.

The staff challenged Robison. They wanted her to talk to a psychologist, but she refused. Why, if she didn't think she had any problems, did she feel so threatened about talking with someone? "It was the first time I felt really scared," Robison said.

The Minneapolis VA wanted Robison to enter a seventeen-week inpatient program to treat her severe post-traumatic stress disorder. She refused. She wanted to get back to her job and her children, so she agreed to do counseling at the VA in Des Moines instead. She thought that would take care of the requirement. Unbeknownst to Robison, the Minneapolis center took that to mean that she was intentionally going against their medical advice.

Robison knew she had been affected by her experiences in Iraq, but she didn't want people labeling her. If it wasn't already obvious, she isn't keen on filling out surveys, checking off boxes, and then being categorized one way or another. "It's demeaning," she said. She didn't go over to Iraq for a year to come back and be minimized. So what if she doesn't deal with things the way everyone else docs?

She described herself as a "monster," although those who know her well would say she is anything but. It's a label she gave herself after attending the memorial service for the first soldier killed from her battalion. Robison had talked to the soldier the day before he went out on his final convoy. She told him that he was going to be okay. She felt she had lied to him. He burned alive in the truck. At the funeral, Robison was surrounded by grown men crying. Few women can remain unmoved when they see men cry. "Taps" started to play, and the dead soldier's name was called three times. Robison never cried. She never got a lump in her throat. Nothing.

A year after Robison returned home, her brother died. She didn't cry. She said she isn't normal because she doesn't express herself in the world like everyone else does. Maybe what the doctors are calling post-traumatic stress disorder is just her personality. Give her a checklist that she can fill out, one that fits her personality, and then she'll talk.

When she testified at a VA hearing for her disability claim in June 2007, Robison was asked to explain how she felt when she was in a crowd. She said she gets agitated, can't breathe, and breaks out in a sweat. She feels like she's back at that circle in Baghdad, and the Iraqis are converging on her. When she was done describing how she felt in a crowd, she was told, "That's a sign of severe PTSD."

Still, Robison didn't want to admit that she had PTSD because she sees it as career ending and as a sign of weakness. If her soldiers had PTSD, however, she would expect them, without question, to get help.

In March 2008, Robison's health took a dramatic turn for the worse. Her speech had slowed, she was sweating more profusely, it was getting harder for her to maintain her balance, and no one in the medical community seemed to be listening. One day, she called her mom at home.

"I can't breathe. It feels like my throat is closing. I can't feel my right arm and can't feel anything on the right side of my face."

"Do you need an ambulance?"

"No, you can take me to the hospital."

They got as far as Indianola, about thirteen miles out, when Robison told her mom to call for an ambulance because it was getting harder for her to breathe. She had no feeling on her right side. She could barely speak. Robison's mom thought she was having a stroke, but the CAT scan and MRI were inconclusive. She never received an official diagnosis. Her civilian doctor believed her condition resulted from complications from a brain injury she suffered in Iraq.

She wanted to go back to Minneapolis to figure out what was going on with her brain injury, but they wouldn't take her. Before they would treat her physical ailments, she had to go through the PTSD program, which she had turned down. She was in a bind. She didn't want to be treated by the VA in Des Moines but had no choice. So she saw a social worker, went to the pain clinic at the VA, and started seeing civilian doctors.

Her speech had already been affected by her hearing loss, but it slowed even more. When she's tired, her voice trembles, and she slurs her words. She worked with a speech pathologist and speech therapist, doing exercises that included blowing bubbles and blowing into a spirometer. Her arm was numb but is better. It tires easily if she holds something for too long. She uses a cane for balance when she is tired or has a long way to walk.

In the final months of her Army career, Robison told her soldiers she could no longer do what she asked them to do. It was time for her to retire. Those last months were worse than being in Iraq. She felt everything slipping away. Two months later, in May

2008, Robison was medically retired. With her retirement went her identity as a soldier. It was a loss for which she hadn't prepared.

"I love the Army, but it doesn't miss me as much as I miss it," Robison said. "And I just couldn't believe that could happen. I just couldn't believe they could go on without me. I couldn't believe it."

Robison set a few goals for herself when she retired, including writing a book about her soldiers and speaking in front of a congressional hearing about the battles she fought with the Army and the VA when she came home from Iraq. She also wants to work with traumatic brain injury patients. But after her retirement came and went, she wasn't up to doing much of anything. She never expected to get out of the Army early or to be sick. Now she was both, and she didn't know what to do. She was lost. She laid around feeling sorry for herself. She couldn't get motivated.

The kids would say, "Let's watch TV."

"I don't feel like doing nothing," she'd say.

The kids started watching the women's college softball world series. Robison didn't feel like watching, but she didn't have much of a choice. It was on the TV in front of her. Early on in the series, she became enamored by one of the players. She watched Megan Gibson pitch for Texas A&M, and by the second game, Robison was off the couch, yelling and cheering her on. Gibson's team lost in the finals, but her skill and poise under pressure left a lasting impression on Robison and many others. Gibson was named the Big 12's player and pitcher of the year. It is the only time in Big 12 history that the same student-athlete has won both awards.

Robison was especially impressed that Gibson didn't get emotional while leading her team of warriors. Robison needed to get her drive back so that she could help and lead others. She needed to know there was still a place for her with the Army, that she still belonged. To make things right with herself, she believed she had to work to help ease the transition for returning soldiers.

The old Robison wasn't one to dole out compliments and tell people they were important, but she was changing daily. The new Robison cut off one of the flags from the uniform she was wearing when she got her Purple Heart and sent it, along with a letter, to Gibson.

Gibson went on to play professional ball for the Philadelphia Force. Viewers can listen to the games live on their computers, and Robison was listening one day and heard the owner, Tom Kleinman, say they couldn't get anyone to attend the games. The stands were empty. Robison e-mailed Kleinman and said they needed to advertise in Iowa. As they corresponded, they discovered they are both vets. He served in Vietnam. Robison told him about her experiences in Iraq and coming home, her brain injury, and her interest in Gibson. Next thing she knew, she was on her way to Chicago to see a game and meet Gibson and her teammates. Robison had the time of her life.

It was a Saturday night over Labor Day weekend in 2008 when the phone rang around nine or ten. The soldier on the other end of the line was calling to alert Robison that the Army wanted her to deploy. She threw up. She knew the call was a mistake. She had been medically retired and wouldn't be going, but her buddies would be going. "It's hard to think they'll go without me."

A couple of weeks later, she traveled to the Tampa Pain Clinic in Florida to get some help with her back and leg pain. "That was a bust," she said. She came home with two blood clots in her arm. In the eighteen days she was there, the staff never got to treat her back and leg pain. She had such severe headaches that they had to run Dihydroergotamine, a drug used to prevent and treat vascular headaches such as migraines and cluster headaches, through her veins every eight hours. The headaches didn't get any better. She continues to get two to three severe headaches a week that knock her off her feet.

What the Tampa Pain Clinic did do for Robison was open her eyes to what was going on with her VA treatment and medical records. The folks in Tampa said they would send Robison recommendations for follow-up care because they saw neurological damage from her brain injury that could be treated with physical therapy. Robison asked for a copy of *all* of her medical records, including her mental health file.

When they arrived, she spent six hours reading through the paperwork. She found 120 errors in the charts. Her age varied from eighteen to forty-nine. Sometimes she was a male, sometimes a female. Other people's files, including their names and Social Security numbers, were in her charts. Her files implied multiple times that she wasn't reliable.

It's no wonder she had to fight with the VA to be awarded disability. They had gotten her basic story wrong. They were under the impression she had fallen out of a Humvee and hit her head when she actually fell out of a heavy equipment transporter and onto asphalt. And that was only one of many incidents that affected her. There was no record of her blood clots. She was furious.

She fired the nurse practitioner who was trying to overmedicate her. She wrote a letter to the House of Representatives and the Senate. She terminated her healthcare services with the VA after reading in her records that her health had declined and not improved while she was being treated by the VA. The high number of errors and inconsistencies in her medical records also concerned her. She stayed with the VA as long as she did because she felt it had a responsibility to take care of her. She was entitled to quality healthcare. She has Tricare, which is health insurance for members of the military and their families. That's good enough for her. It beats the daily battles with the VA. She rated 50 percent temporary disability from the Army and 80 percent with the VA. The patient collects whichever is the higher of the two.

In October 2008, soldiers from Robison's former unit left for Texas and later for Iraq. This was an extraordinarily difficult time for Robison. She felt she belonged with them. Even though she loves her parents as a daughter should and loves her daughter and son as a mother should, she wanted to be with the soldiers. The Army was her life—her identity—for twenty-two years. "It's one thing when you have a choice to give that up," she said. "It's another when it's taken from you. I felt like I was being cheated because I really wanted to go."

Leading up to their departure, the soldiers called Robison to run things by her. She'd pace the floor in her home, answering their questions and longing to be with them. The Army had raised the requirement for the number of combat lifesaver bags for truck companies. The soldiers were authorized to take additional bags with them to Iraq but hadn't received more. What were they to do? They also wanted to know what nonrequired training would be most beneficial to them. Robison suggested teaching them how to change a tire in five minutes because if you sit on the side of the road for too long in Iraq, you'll get mortared.

She did her best to stay away from Camp Dodge and not interfere with the leadership, but it wasn't easy. She craved time with her friend, Captain Sickles, with whom she had served in Iraq and who was redeploying. But Sickles has children, and Robison understands the importance of spending time with family before deploying.

Sickles called Robison the morning she was leaving and asked her friend to come over to her house. They spent time together while Sickles packed. Robison tried to keep the conversation light. She felt she had let a lot of people down because she wasn't healthy enough to deploy with them. She had kept her distance from her unit because she didn't think she could handle being around them, yet staying away made her feel selfish. She felt someone was ripping out her heart and guts.

When they said good-bye, Robison told Sickles, "Anything, anytime."

Robison stayed at Sickles's house with her mom until it was time to attend the send-off ceremony. Robison could have gone but chose not to. Once the soldiers left, Robison started to watch more news on TV. She e-mails Sickles and her kids. She talks to soldiers at Camp Dodge to find out what's going on. "I want to be where they are," Robison said.

Robison feels like she's getting her mojo back, but it's different. She's figured out that what worked in the Army doesn't necessarily work in the civilian world. Civilians don't respond to orders and demands. In fact, orders might deliver the opposite response she was looking for. She's learning new ways to communicate.

She's also discovering that being a mom and being a first sergeant are not synonymous. Instead of leading her children, Robison has chosen to walk beside them in this journey called life. She feels fortunate that her physical decline has been gradual. When someone becomes ill, it doesn't just affect the individual. It affects everyone, especially family.

Trauma changes people.

Robison was becoming increasingly dependent on her children. They were doing more for her. That's not the way it's supposed to be. But they've adapted, become a team, like the Philadelphia Force. She lets them know what's going on with her health and tells them when she is sick.

Almost everything about her mom's return was hard on Amber. Some days Robison was in so much pain she couldn't get out of bed. There were weeks when Amber did all the cooking and cleaning. People would tell her to just be a kid, that she didn't need to be a parent. She wouldn't go so far as to say she was raising herself, but she has had many more responsibilities than other kids her age. It should be noted here that as the daughter of a master sergeant, Amber would have more tasks than the average child, anyway. She was Robison's youngest soldier.

Robison couldn't be as actively involved in Amber's life as she used to be. Before she deployed, she helped coach one of Amber's teams and was able to play catch with Amber. Now she can't do either, and Amber doesn't think that's fair. She wishes her mom could get her strength back. Amber doesn't have much patience for other kids her age who complain and get mad at their moms for petty reasons. She thinks they should be more grateful for having moms who are healthy and can be actively involved in their lives. She wants to tell them to suck it up.

Ben and Amber try to find the positive in what has happened to their mom and their family. They used to have to wait until their mom took off her uniform to approach her. Mary said she couldn't even deal with her daughter until she had changed into civilian clothes. Robison is softer now. Before she went to Iraq, she had a set of rules, and if the kids broke a rule, there were specific consequences. And she'd get on them about small things: "Don't put your black socks in the same drawer as the white socks." She was the enforcer, the one who made sure they completed all the chores on their list. These days, Robison is much more willing to negotiate. Rules are important, but she's happier spending time with her children at Ben's races and Amber's volleyball games and dance recitals.

They also look for humor in situations. When Amber gets into trouble, she can outrun her mom. And when Robison grounds her, she often forgets how long Amber was supposed to be on restriction.

"Is my grounding up today?"

"I think so."

Amber is grateful beyond her years for her family and friends. She sees in her mom a woman who is in pain every day yet somehow manages to smile. "She's the person who walks in the room and makes it light up if you ask me. She wouldn't say that, but I think that.

"She's still mom. She still motivates her soldiers even though technically they're not her soldiers anymore. Her personality hasn't changed at all. When I'm really sick or sad, she'll come out here [to the TV room] and hug me until I'm laughing. The one thing I love most about her is I know she's always going to be there to catch me when I fall."

Ben has a couple of heroes in his life. Most of them are athletes—U.S. Olympians Kara Goucher and Steve Prefontaine and the Chicago Cubs' Ryan Theriot, to name a few—who looked adversity in the eye and didn't back down. But it wasn't until his mom returned from Iraq that he met his first real-life hero. He has watched her look so much adversity in the eye and say, "Bring it on!"

"I don't think my mom has ever backed down from any situation," he said. "She is the single most resilient person I have ever met. Granted, she has some quirks, but if I could model myself after any human being, I would like to be at least half the person she is."

Robison has struggled with putting her children before her soldiers. She knew she was good at leading her troops on the battlefield. As a mother, she felt inadequate. "I didn't think I was capable of being a mom again," she said. "My kids loved me back into being a mom."

Navy Lieutenant Commander Mary Sutton, RN

DURING THE FIRST GULF WAR, SPECIALIST MARY SUTTON WAS AN MP for the Florida Army National Guard and responsible for guarding enemy prisoners of war in Saudi Arabia. In 1995, she became what the military refers to as a mustang, a commissioned officer who started her career as an enlisted person. She had earned a bachelor's of science in nursing from the University of Central Florida and was commissioned in the U.S. Navy.

In 2003, Sutton was sent to Kuwait, where, as an operating room nurse, she treated many casualties. From August 2007 to August 2008, she was deployed to Mazar-e-Sharif, Afghanistan, again as an operating room nurse. On her third deployment, she mentored nurses in the 209th Corps of the Afghan National Army. She got them up to speed on infection control, the proper disposal of medical materials, the tracking of cases, and the use of supplies. She mentored three nurses on how to train their colleagues. Each presented lectures on hand washing, sharps containers, and the use of the incinerator for biological waste. In return, they adopted her as their older sister, and everyone developed a mutual respect for each other's culture.

During her "down time," Sutton helped coordinate medical care for seven Afghan children to travel to Pakistan for lifesaving heart surgery. She took over this volunteer job from former Navy Lieutenant Jobe Galli, who had the program set up before she arrived through the International Children's Heart Foundation (www.babyheart.org). The surgeries were funded by generous American donations.

After seeing all of Sutton's medals on her uniform, a friend commented that they must have been expensive. "In more ways than you know," she said. "In more ways than you know."

The cost of serving is unique to each individual. While the friend was referring to the dollar cost of the medals, Sutton's thoughts immediately went to the sacrifice of being away from family and friends and the stress of combat. Some have lost limbs. Some have emotional and mental scars permanently imprinted in their minds. Others have paid the ultimate price, and their families are left to bear the heaviest burdens.

Michelle Barefield and her husband, Jeff

Who Ya Gonna Call?
The Bomb Squad

SERGEANT MICHELLE BAREFIELD ARRIVED IN IRAQ IN MARCH 2006 as a seasoned Explosive Ordnance Disposal (EOD) technician. At forty-one, she had already served in the Air Force's bomb squad for eighteen years, nearly half her life. She had gone to Qatar to support F-15 fighter jets and to Kosovo to clean up unexploded ordnance left over from NATO. But those missions paled in comparison to the danger she would face in and around Baghdad, where she and her team of three airmen were charged with defusing explosives, sometimes while under fire.

When a team leader like Barefield arrived at a new assignment in Iraq, it was customary for her to ride along on responses with the team she was replacing to see how they had been operating and familiarize herself with the area for which she would be responsible. Her first ride-along was March 29.

A native of Fremont, Michigan, the five-foot, five-inch Barefield was a scholar-athlete in high school. She earned straight A's, ran the 440 and mile relay in track, and played the violin. Despite her academic success, Barefield never considered going to college. She started working at a car dealership in her junior year and stayed there for the next six years. When she finally went into the Air Force, it was a rash decision. She was twenty-three, and things weren't working out for her in Michigan. A relationship had gone sour, so she decided to run away to the Air Force. Barefield was interested in the medical field, but the Air Force had all the medics it needed. If she was set on a medical career in the Air Force, she would have to go into the delayed-entry program. That wasn't an option; she knew that if she didn't enlist right away, she would change her mind. At that time, she was okay with any career the Air Force threw her way, including EOD tech. She didn't know anything about the "bomb squad" and didn't care. In hindsight, she says she "got lucky." She met and married her husband, Jeff, also an EOD technician, during Desert Storm while they were both stationed in Korea. Since returning to the states in 1991, Seymour Johnson in Goldsboro, North Carolina, has been their home base. They have two daughters, Amanda and Rachel.

Barefield's team was replacing Technical Sergeant Walter W. Moss Jr., a staff sergeant, and another soldier. Barefield rode with those three airmen on a routine response to an IED that a security patrol had found. IEDs were the number one killer in Iraq, and insurgents were constantly hiding them along the roads. These routes were routinely patrolled to make sure they were safe for the convoys to travel. Ideally, there would always be soldiers clearing explosives along heavily traveled routes, but it was impossible to post security on all the roads all the time. EOD technicians were frequently responding to calls to clear an area where an IED had been spotted. Sometimes, those IEDs were duds, but more often, they were live and had to be carefully assessed and defused.

They drove in a Humvee to a location about five miles outside Baghdad. There were about four trucks and a dozen or so soldiers already at the site. Barefield knew right away this was going to be a difficult response because the IED was far enough away that they couldn't get a good read on it. They were going to have to drive a robot downrange to see what kind of an explosive they were dealing with. TALON military robots are tracked vehicles designed for explosive ordnance disposal. The most widely used robot is about three feet wide, with eight-inch-wide tracks that allow it to move across the desert sand. It stretches several feet up with a camera that enables the operator to see what he's doing and has grippers to handle explosive charges. The operators refer to driving the robot, but one of the EOD technicians actually steers it by operating a remote control from a safe area. Once it reaches an IED, the robot scans the area to get a visual of its surroundings. The technician looks at a screen and sees what the robot sees.

Moss was driving the robot when he discovered two pressure plates intended to trigger an IED. The plates were made up of two three-foot-long metal strips buried on the side of the road. The Iraqis position the pressure plates in such a way that if someone driving down the road spotted the first one and swerved to dodge it, he would probably drive over the second one and trigger an explosion. It's a complicated and lethal device. It looked to the technicians as if the insurgents had spent a good deal of time setting it up. The strips were held just far enough apart by Styrofoam so they didn't touch. But the slightest pressure and *boom!*

If an IED were visible, the technicians would put explosives on it and blow it up. No need to mess with the pressure plates. No need to take anything apart and study it. They just wanted to blow it up and get the hell out of there. But in this case, the IED was buried, and the explosive charge had to be in contact with the IED to detonate. It made more sense to disconnect the plates and remove the power to render the IED impotent.

Examining an IED can require incredibly long stretches of time. Barefield and her team had been there several hours, and it was getting dark. Each time they put an explosive on one of the pressure plates and detonated it, they would send the robot down to see if it worked. By looking at the picture provided by the robot's camera, Moss saw that the explosive charges had disconnected the plates. He told the team to start packing their equipment. They were heading back to base.

While the team did as instructed, Moss walked down to the defused bomb to do a final clearance before letting the convoy through. The staff sergeant and a security soldier accompanied him. Barefield was standing about 100 feet away, watching Moss and the staff sergeant through her night-vision goggles. The staff sergeant was standing off to the side with a metal detector, and Moss was bending over to do something.

A secondary IED exploded.

Barefield heard a loud explosion, like a clap of thunder. Then she saw a huge flash of green and a cloud of smoke through her goggles.

Someone called for a medevac to get the wounded out of there fast. They formed a search party to find Moss and look for a trigger man. Barefield jumped into the EOD vehicle and drove to the site of the explosion. The third team member, a young airman, was sitting in the backseat. When she got to the site, Barefield saw a big hole. The staff sergeant was sitting off to the side with his legs crossed. His helmet had been blown off by the explosion. He looked dazed. Barefield ran up and touched him.

"Clok, can you hear me?" Sometimes, depending on how close you are to an explosion, you could have your ear drums blown out. She looked at him and made eye contact. "Can you hear me?"

"Yeah."

He was alive, had all his arms and legs.

At that point, Barefield's concern shifted to Moss. She saw the staff sergeant and the security soldier but couldn't see Moss.

"Where was Walt when it detonated?"

"He was right on top of it."

Moss, who was on his last clearance in Iraq, had led his team on 119 missions, and had cleared forty IEDs, had been killed instantly. The staff sergeant was badly burned and bruised. The soldier providing security had burns and wounds from debris kicked up by the explosion. The medics arrived and started taking care of the soldier and the staff sergeant.

Running parallel to the road was a canal on one side and a field on the other side. The airmen and soldiers began searching along the sides of the road, hoping the explosion had just blown Moss off to the side and they would find him whole. As they widened their search, they began to find small pieces of Moss's uniform, parts of his vest and boots. Barefield knew that when you didn't find a whole boot, just a piece, you probably weren't going to find a whole body.

They began collecting remains. It was horrible, but they didn't want to leave any part behind. The soldiers hadn't known Moss. He was Air Force; they were Army. But that didn't matter. If they found a scrap of a uniform, they were going to pick it up and bring it back with them. They didn't know him, but it was still personal.

When they returned to base, they had to account for Moss's sensitive items—weapons, night-vision goggles, radio. If they were lost, they had to be reported. Barefield went through the motions. She was working on autopilot. She didn't stop to think about what had happened. She couldn't. She had a job to do. If she thought about the death of a fellow airman or the near-death of another airman and soldier, she wouldn't be able to function. To think that a mother and father had just lost a son—that the Air Force had just lost its first EOD tech of the war—would be too much to bear.

She didn't sleep that first night. She had been out at the response call for twelve hours. They didn't get back to base until three in the morning. On the following day, her second day without sleep, she had to give witness statements, brief her commander, give a statement to the Office of Special Investigations, and write reports. Like a trained EOD tech, Barefield would carefully and deliberately describe what happened on the battlefield.

EOD techs are expected to recount the facts of a crime scene as if they were detectives. When speaking, Barefield might seem more like a stunned victim than a slightly affected tech. However horrific the events on the battlefield that she was describing, her vague facial expressions and monotone voice concealed her feelings. She compared herself to first responders, like policemen and firemen back home, who can't get emotional every time someone is killed or wounded. If they did, they'd never be able to do their jobs. So they detach from the humanity of the explosion, fire, or murder, and concentrate on what they are trained to do.

When she was finished giving statements, Barefield flew with her commander to a hospital in the Green Zone in Baghdad to see the staff sergeant and the soldier who had been wounded. The soldier was going home. He had numerous secondary wounds from gravel hitting him in the face as well as burns on his face and hands from the heat of the blast. His eyes were bandaged. The staff sergeant had been wounded on his back and shoulder from the force of the blast that knocked him down.

When everyone who hadn't been wounded returned to base, the chaplain talked to them. Other airmen urged Barefield to get some sleep, but all she wanted to do was talk to her husband, Jeff, who had been an Air Force EOD tech for twenty years before retiring. She hadn't been able to talk to him because when someone is wounded or killed, the military goes into a communications blackout until the next of kin are notified. When the blackout was lifted, Barefield called Jeff.

Jeff knew something was up because he hadn't heard from his wife in a while. She called before she left Kuwait for Baghdad and again when she arrived in Baghdad, but their last conversation was brief. He had been expecting another phone call, a longer one. Having served in the Air Force for so long, he knew the significance of a communications blackout. He was working as a civilian in the EOD shop at Seymour Johnson when he learned that the first Air Force EOD tech had been killed. He knew it wasn't his wife because he would have already been notified. He was easy to reach.

On the phone with her husband for the first time since the explosion, Barefield started the conversation. She was unemotional at first, but then the words came gushing out. Up to that point, she hadn't cried. Now, exhausted from lack of sleep, she began to cry.

Because they had only talked briefly since Barefield arrived in Baghdad, Jeff had no idea whom she was replacing. Jeff knew Moss, with whom he had served after Desert Storm. Jeff remembers sitting in the EOD unit with Moss in Kuwait. There wasn't much going on. Just 120 airmen and soldiers hanging out in the desert in case something happened. They started each day with a meeting, then they'd go outside to sit on the deck. Before the day got rolling, they'd drink a couple of cups of Italian coffee that Moss's wife had sent over. Jeff was saddened by the news of Moss and concerned about Barefield. He wondered how she was going to deal with the death of a fellow airman.

Barefield was tired, but she knew that if she went to bed, she would just lie there and think about what had happened. Following her conversation with Jeff, she went for a run on one of the treadmills. She ran herself to exhaustion and then took a shower. She slept for the next twelve hours. The young airman who had been sitting in the Humvee also fell asleep. Barefield felt sorry for him. He was nineteen years old, just out of EOD school, and on his first deployment. He was upset. Everyone was.

The Air Force EODs throughout Baghdad went into a mandatory safety stand-down for two weeks. The Navy filled in while the airmen used the time to mourn the loss of a fellow airman, plan and hold his memorial service, and prepare to return to work. After a week, everyone was eager to get back to work. In Iraq,

Barefield was miserable when she wasn't doing something. When the two weeks were over, she went to work as a team leader.

Since September 11, 2001, fifty-six EOD techs have been killed in Afghanistan and Iraq. The loss of so many EODs is unprecedented. They have never faced the kind of working environment they're now encountering. There are some parallels to the guerrilla warfare of Vietnam, but the techs didn't work as independently back then as they do now. In Iraq and Afghanistan, when techs are on a mission, the commands rely on them for guidance. It's hard to train to be an EOD tech. Most end up learning the job as the number-two man in a two-man team. Every situation is different, so it's the details that make the difference between a successful and unsuccessful mission.

For example, technicians have to use different distances for their safe areas each time they respond to a call because every time they go out, they have to assume someone is watching them, perhaps even videotaping them. Insurgents would put out hoax devices just to see how the technicians would respond. Then they would anticipate where the team was going to park and hide devices there.

As a team leader, situational awareness was critical. Barefield had to remember which locations she had used as her safe areas. She never wanted to park on a bridge or get her team into a potential ambush situation where there was only one way in or out. She had to remember where they had been, what it looked like the last time they were there, and what they had used as a safe area. Sometimes, insurgents would put IEDs in the same hole as before, so they couldn't assume an area was safe because it had been used before. Soon there weren't any safe areas.

If something didn't look right when she got there, Barefield had to adjust the safe area. Every EOD team had an area, or grid, for which they were responsible, and they would learn what was normal for their area of operation. If Barefield responded to the same place more than once, she really had to remember what was there before, what looked different. Was that pile of trash on the side of the road last week? Was it really a pile of trash or an IED? Wasn't that tree trunk in another location? Was that gas can or tire an IED or a marker for an IED? Iraqis didn't leave tires, gas cans, and water bottles on the side of the road without taking them. Other markers included spray paint on a rock or the ground, a pile of rocks, and upright sticks. Barefield had to have all of the necessary information about her surroundings and the IED with which she was dealing in order to make an informed decision.

During all of this, she also had to be conscious of her stress level because that would keep her aware of her fear. Once a tech dismisses her fear, she will become complacent. A certain amount of apprehension is good because it makes her more aware. Some techs think you should just do your job and ignore the fear factor—if you're going to be killed, you're going to be killed. Barefield believes in keeping the fear and stress level in the back of her mind. "It keeps me more aware of what I'm doing," she said. "I don't agree with the people who say what will be, will be."

She also believes she can have a hand in fate or destiny by erring on the side of caution. "You don't want to let your fear control you, but you want to respect it," she said. "Know that it's there. That way you can be more cautious. Being a team leader, it's not just me that I'm responsible for. God forbid if something happened to my team. I didn't want anything to happen to them."

Everything about being an EOD is stressful, from getting the call and responding, to the long hours. In a given day, they might respond to five different locations. The lack of predictability wears on them. The techs need to decompress after they have been through a stressful situation and return to a place where they feel safe. In the area of operation, EOD techs tend to be segregated from the rest of the population and left to their own because they work such odd hours, handle classified material, and are responsible for their own assortment of weapons.

Barefield was involved in five blasts in Iraq. She doesn't consider being near IED blasts a big deal because she knows Marines and soldiers who go on patrols every day and have been involved in countless blasts. She didn't get a single scratch on her. She was always just far enough away from a blast that she didn't get external injuries.

Still, she had some close calls. Once, the security vehicle in front of her ran over an IED. The convoy was small, with only one Humvee in front of her, one behind, and ten people total. When the lead vehicle hit the IED, the gunner and the driver were ejected. Barefield and her team members got out and carefully searched their surroundings. They were looking for insurgents, IEDs, and the soldiers who had been thrown from their Humvees.

The truck started to burn from the explosion. They spotted the gunner. He had landed on the road. One of Barefield's team members checked on him. He was okay—alive and no broken bones. They helped him to a safe location.

Barefield was walking around the burning vehicle when she heard someone yell, "Get me outta here!" She couldn't find anyone.

"Where are you?" she yelled back.

"In the canal."

She reached down and pulled him up. He wasn't injured. She asked him how many people were in his vehicle.

"Three."

So far they had found only two.

She hurried back to the vehicle and found a soldier in the back seat. He couldn't get out. The Humvee doors were heavy since they had installed additional armor plates. When the IED exploded, the vehicle's tires went flat and the Humvee sank into the sand. The soldier in the truck couldn't get any of the doors open because they were wedged into the ground. The more they tried to open the doors, the deeper they sank into the ground. All the guys from Barefield's team were pulling on the door, trying to get the soldier out of the burning vehicle. The tires were melting, small-arms ammunition inside the vehicle was starting to cook off from the heat. As the other EODs and soldiers tried to get the door open, Barefield reached her hand inside. She told the soldier to take his helmet off because he had a better chance of getting through without the bulkiness of his helmet. He was starting to panic. Pretty soon, his head was outside the door, but his body was still inside. Those outside the truck were pulling him as if he were a rag doll. Barefield grabbed what she thought was the soldier's vest and yanked it as hard as she could. Something snapped, causing her to fall backwards onto the hillside. It was his CamelBak hydration pack.

Eventually, they got the door open and carried the soldier back to Barefield's vehicle, where the medic started an IV. The soldier wasn't too bad off. He had some second-degree burns from the heat of the fire, but neither he nor anyone else had severe wounds. Regardless, all of the soldiers from the first vehicle were medevaced. Sometimes, the extent of a wound is masked by adrenaline or other distractions, so they are medevaced as a precaution. A severe head injury could present itself later, and if it's not treated, it could be deadly.

About the same time Barefield heard the rotors of a medevac chopper coming in, she also heard gun shots. Insurgents on the other side of the canal were shooting at them. This was all taking place in a rural section of Baghdad. There weren't many IEDs in the city of Baghdad because of the strong military presence and curfews, but the same couldn't be said for the farmlands and rural areas. The insurgents had been pushed out of the city and into areas like the one Barefield and her convoy were in.

A chopper won't land if there's enemy fire. It will keep circling until the coast is clear. The troops felt like sitting ducks. They had one security vehicle with three people, three wounded, and Barefield's team with the Navy captain. The insurgents saw an opportunity to ambush a crippled convoy that was focused more on treating the wounded than on security. When the shooting started, Barefield and the others laid down on the ground near one of the vehicles and returned fire.

The firefight lasted about five minutes. The helicopter landed and medevaced the wounded. Now they were down to two vehicles. They couldn't go anywhere because it was too dangerous to travel in a two-vehicle convoy, so they called an Army unit in the area to send an additional vehicle to escort them. When they were hit, they were responding to an IED. By the time the soldiers were medevaced, they were two hours into their response and had to continue on even though they were all so tired they just wanted to turn around and go back. Soldiers were counting on them.

Another time, Barefield's team responded to an abandoned house that the Army was using as a lookout point to find terrorists. Soldiers had climbed up on the roof and found detonating cord. The Iraqis had seen soldiers using the house, rigged the perimeter of the roof with eight or ten IEDs, and were waiting for the most opportune time to blow up the entire house. The EOD sent the robot in to do reconnaissance and discovered a wire extending from the roof down through the house, across a field, and into a canal. The wire was attached to a battery. The EOD team disconnected the wire and blew up the empty house. But the situation was still dangerous.

Many of the houses have walls around them as well as driveways. The EOD teams parked their vehicles close enough to security so they could protect them but also in an area that was easy to get in and out of. Before the EOD team arrives, soldiers have already declared a "safe area" for them to park and operate. Soldiers declared an area safe by doing a five-meter visual search before they got out of their vehicles, and once they got out of their vehicles, they would search up to twenty-five meters for secondary devices. When the EOD team arrived, the soldiers did another search. While Barefield was in the house, more than a few soldiers were walking around the "safe area." Nonetheless, an IED was found in that safe area, and if an insurgent had still been around and not scattered at the sight of the soldiers and airmen, he could have detonated the IED and killed several Americans.

On another day, the EOD techs had already driven the robot down to an IED and defused it. They were getting ready to leave. All the team members except for Barefield were in the truck. She was spotting the vehicle as it turned around. As soon as they pulled away, an IED that was hidden next to Barefield's vehicle all along exploded. Luckily, it wasn't a high-explosive round.

One of the most horrific incidents to occur during Barefield's deployment was when one soldier was killed and two were kidnapped. These soldiers had been sitting on post on one of the roads to ensure the Iraqis didn't plant any IEDs. They usually sat post on a particular road if they knew it was going to be traveled within the next twelve hours. A search team sent out to find the missing soldiers received intelligence that the soldiers had probably been killed and to assume their bodies had been booby-trapped in some way.

EOD teams accompanied the Army search patrols. Time was of the essence. The sooner they could find the hostages, the quicker they could help them. If the EOD techs were not with the soldiers, the soldiers would have to call and wait for them, which would take even more time. EOD teams worked twelve-hour shifts twenty-four hours a day until the soldiers were found. When the bodies of the two kidnapped soldiers were found, they had been booby-trapped. It wasn't enough for the insurgents to kill the soldiers they had kidnapped; they wanted to kill those who came to their rescue, too.

Their bodies were found lying on the ground, dead. The EOD team sent the robot to investigate before they went in. They manipulated the bodies with the robot to ensure the bodies were safe before they recovered them. Barefield was not on the EOD team that discovered the bodies but imagines it was one of the hardest and most rewarding responses for a team—hard because they were dead, but rewarding because they were in one piece.

Barefield was deployed from March to September 2006. When she returned home, the family took a trip to Atlantic Beach in eastern North Carolina. While there, her oldest daughter gave her a "survivor necklace," a sterling-silver circle with the word "survivor" on it. Barefield had never thought of herself as a survivor before. When she thinks of survivors, she thinks of people who live through cancer.

"No," Amanda explained, "you survived Iraq."

Soon after she returned Barefield received the Bronze Star for responding to the busiest area of operations in Iraq. That area covered 500 square miles and included Baghdad International Airport. Her leadership contributed to the safe resolution of 828 EOD emergency-response missions, including 583 IEDs, 119 unexploded ordnance responses, 81 post-blast analyses, 72 weapons caches, and 9 vehicle-borne IED missions. The destruction of 11,883 ordnance items, 78,750 rounds of small-arms ammunition, 448 IED components, and 1,100 pounds of homemade explosives significantly hindered insurgent groups in conducting attacks against coalition forces. Barefield personally led eighty missions.

She was chosen to be featured in a book called *Portraits of Courage* and as a result was nominated to attend the State of the Union address in January 2007 and sit in First Lady Laura Bush's gallery. One person from each branch of the armed services was invited, and she represented the Air Force. Barefield sat with Mrs. Bush; Mrs. Cheney, the vice president's wife; four other service members; and various other guests. At the time, she felt excited and honored to be there. She took her oldest daughter Amanda, then thirteen. Barefield was feeling pretty good. She hadn't yet felt any negative effects from her deployment.

Following the State of the Union Address, a retired Marine asked Barefield to be the guest speaker at the 2007 Goldsboro Memorial Day Service. By the time Memorial Day rolled around, fourteen EOD technicians had been killed in Iraq and Afghanistan. Barefield would include each and every one of them in her speech. It was personal. War is personal.

In the speech, she described her own EOD response team, which was made up of her, Sergeant Mike Williams, and Sergeant Schuyler Morse. She talked about how well they knew each others' strengths and weaknesses. "We knew each others' personalities. Most importantly, we knew each others' blood type, allergies, and what to say to each others' next of kin in the event that things went terribly wrong."

Barefield went on to say that she has been asked many times if she felt she accomplished anything while she was in Iraq. IEDs are still being found every day, but her team safely disposed of more than 100 IEDs, each with the potential to kill or wound coalition forces. The weapons caches they destroyed took thousands of pounds of explosives and IED-making materials out of enemy hands. So, yes, she and her team made a difference.

Memorial Day will always be significant to Barefield. She hasn't lost any immediate family members in the war, but her EOD family has been hit hard.

Possibly because she was thinking about the speech she would be giving, Barefield started dreaming about Iraq. She was also opening e-mails every week or two containing information about EOD technicians who had been wounded or killed.

Barefield doesn't think of her dreams as nightmares because if they were nightmares, she would wake up screaming and sweating. Nonetheless, they're frightening. In one dream, she was kidnapped and taken hostage. She managed to escape and get in a vehicle but was afraid to drive away because she knew there were IEDs on the side of the road. If she stayed, she would be tortured and mutilated like the other soldiers. Would it be easier for her husband to find out that she had stayed—and been tortured and mutilated—or that she had died from an IED while trying to escape? Obviously, death would be more proud and easier to accept if she had tried to escape. In another dream, Barefield was working on an IED when the vehicle blew up. She was the only one who was ever killed in her dreams. By now, she had started seeing a counselor, who suggested that the EOD in her dreams chooses to be blown up because she doesn't want anyone else to die.

More than two years have passed since Moss's death. Barefield thinks some people believe she could have prevented his death. "He was a tech sergeant," she said. "I was a tech sergeant. We both had the same level of knowledge. They think that because I was on scene, I could have prevented him from going down range unnecessarily."

It was her first response in Iraq.

"People always second-guess these situations once they are over and the report comes in," she said. "I do the same thing. We look at reports of people's injuries. Why and how were they wounded? Why did they react a certain way? I don't know if this is true. No one has said anything to me. It may just be me. Survivor's guilt."

She's the only one who gets wounded or killed in her dreams.

In addition to the dreams, Barefield began suffering from migraines and memory loss. If she was working when the migraine started, she would lie down on a bunk and take a nap. A one- or two-hour nap usually took the edge off. She felt bad because airmen would come looking for her—the boss—and she'd be taking a nap. But she'd rather take a nap than leave work for the day. She had about twenty-four airmen working for her, and they seemed to understand.

The memory loss has been exasperating for Barefield. On more than one occasion, she'd be driving in the town where she had lived for the past sixteen years and not recognize where she was. One day, she was driving her daughter Amanda to the fairgrounds two miles from their house. Barefield took a wrong turn. She pulled into a gas station to turn around and then couldn't remember which way she had just come from. She turned in the wrong direction again. Another time, Barefield was driving to her hairdresser when she had to pull off to the side of the road because she didn't know where she was. She waited to see if she could spot something familiar. Finally, after not recognizing anything, she told herself that she wasn't going to sit there all day and wait for something familiar to present itself. She was going to drive until she recognized something.

Sometimes, Barefield would come to a complete stop at a green light. Then she would either sit there until the cars started blowing their horns or until Amanda told her the light was green. "It wasn't as if I wasn't paying attention," Barefield said. "I knew the light was green but my brain was telling me to stop instead of to go."

Service members returning from Iraq and Afghanistan to Seymour Johnson Air Force Base are required to see a Global War on Terrorism deployment specialist at the base before they integrate back into society. Then airmen are required to follow up three, six, and nine months after coming home.

Barefield saw Jody Suda, a counselor and Global War on Terrorism deployment specialist, and later returned after self-identifying, which means she identified herself as someone who needed help and sought out that help. People who self-identify typically want to address symptoms they are experiencing before someone else calls on them to see a counselor. Maybe the symptoms were affecting their job performance or their home life. Suda treated Barefield for post-traumatic stress disorder.

It was a big deal for Barefield to get in touch with Suda because the airman is not necessarily an openly emotional person. She's more private. But talking to Suda and others has helped Barefield. She struggled because she wanted to honor Moss and all the other EODs who have died because they are all important to her, but thinking about them too much was affecting her personal health. Suda believes one of the most important things she was able to do for Barefield was to give her the courage to see that sharing her vulnerability is a strength and an instance of leading by example, rather than leading by invulnerability.

Barefield made a conscious decision when she came back from Iraq *not* to hide the fact that she was seeing a counselor from her airmen. She wasn't ashamed. She thinks it's good for the young airmen in her shop to see her asking for help. She's in a career where the line between being confident and being a superhero can get blurred. It's especially hard to show weakness when you're a leader in a career where lives are on the line every day. Barefield's airmen depend on her. She doesn't want them to think she is weak. On the other hand, she believes that knowing your own limitations and capabilities is a sign of strength, not weakness.

Being in Iraq taught Barefield how important it is that the younger techs get the training and knowledge they need before arriving on the battlefield. Some young airmen wonder why they have to do certain things; they think some of the training is silly and unnecessary. Barefield remembers going through six weeks of predeployment training to learn everything from low crawls and weapons qualification to land navigation and combat lifesaving. She didn't want to be there; she just wanted to go home. Yet when Barefield was in Iraq and put in situations where she had to react quickly, she used the training she had learned throughout her career to keep her and her airmen alive, including the small things that seemed so insignificant when she was learning them. When she needed to recall them, they were there.

Soon after Barefield returned, she talked to the EOD technicians in her shop at Seymour Johnson about what her team had gone through in Iraq. She wasn't afraid to let them see her emotions. She wanted to prepare them not only for what they might go through physically on the battlefield, but also what they might endure emotionally when they returned. Now the young techs can look at Barefield and say, "She went through all this, and she's still in charge."

The physical repercussions of the explosions in Iraq hit Barefield all at once, about six months after she returned. When a brain has suffered a concussion wound, it can take months for the damage to present itself. She told Suda about the dizziness, headaches, and confusion. The confusion was bothersome to Barefield because she prided herself on being a highly organized person who managed her time well. Now she was finding it difficult to perform simple tasks. It wasn't that she was unorganized; she couldn't remember things. Suda, recognizing that some of Barefield's problems were more physical than psychological, referred her to a medical doctor. Barefield's doctor told her that she had classic signs of traumatic brain injury, or TBI, and referred her to WOMAC Army Medical Center at Fort Bragg, North Carolina. She had her first TBI appointment in January of 2008.

She had blood work done, an MRI, and cognitive evaluations to test different areas of her brain. All the tests were timed. Barefield did them correctly, but more slowly than normal. She'd have to come up with as many words as she could that started with "k" or "d" and was using way too much time. She learned that there are areas of her brain that are not functioning at optimal levels. A neuropsychologist determined what areas needed help, and a cognitive rehabilitation therapist provided her with techniques to exercise her memory. She also worked with a speech therapist because she found herself pausing frequently during conversations so that her brain could search for a word. For someone with an extensive vocabulary, Barefield found it troubling that she was having such a difficult time coming up with words to express herself.

In early 2008, Barefield was promoted to master sergeant. She didn't have to test for her new rank. Every year, the wing commander gets a certain number of stripes that he can give out. Barefield's supervisor thought she deserved to be promoted, so he submitted a package on her behalf. She plans to retire in early 2010. She is not scheduled to go back to Iraq, but it's possible. She has a medical evaluation board pending because it has been determined that she is non-deployable. She still has migraines and has been diagnosed more recently with vertigo. She is also seeing a physical therapist for vestibular rehab because the vestibular area in her brain has been damaged, and it's affecting her balance.

Barefield's adjustment back into family life may have been slightly easier for her than other female military spouses. The odds are not in favor of military marriages and marriages between EOD technicians working out, yet Michelle and Jeff have been together for nearly two decades and worked together for fifteen years. Having spent twenty years in the Air Force, Jeff understood the physical and emotional challenges of war. As far as Jeff is concerned, Barefield isn't any different than the day she left for Iraq. What he means is this: whether she has a migraine or is going to the State of the Union Address, she's still his wife. He still loves her. Even though he's retired, Jeff works with EOD techs in his job as a civilian unexploded ordnance (UXO) technician for USA Environmental, cleaning up military munitions from former U.S. defense sites. When Barefield started talking about her symptoms, she wasn't telling Jeff anything he hadn't heard before. All the techs who have deployed to Afghanistan and Iraq have shown one or more symptoms of post-traumatic stress disorder. Ninety-five percent of the guys he works with are retired EOD techs, and just about all of them have been to Iraq. They've all been near explosions.

As a mother who has served on the battlefield, Barefield is concerned for her children's future. When she was cleaning up the explosives in Kosovo, the children greeted her enthusiastically. They shouted, "NATO! NATO!" as the EOD technicians approached. The children hugged the techs because they knew they were there to clean up the unexploded bombs and mines that were maiming and killing their friends and relatives.

Barefield thought that when she saw the Iraqi children, she would be able to relate them to her own children, but that wasn't the case. "I don't look at those children and see my own at all," she said. "Most people think that [American] women would feel sorry for the women and children in Iraq. But all I felt was anger and almost hatred. I was surprised. There were twelve-year-old children threatening us with IEDs and RPGs."

Lenora Langlais

PHOTO BY DRUSILLA ELLIOTT

Still I Rise

THERE ARE DAYS A PERSON NEVER FORGETS: HER HIGH SCHOOL graduation, her wedding, the birth of her child. Navy Commander Lenora Langlais's list of memorable days includes the day she was nearly killed at Al Taqaddum (TQ) Airbase in Iraq, the day a young Marine died from a massive head wound, and just about every day that has followed.

It all started around three o'clock on the morning of April 7, 2006, when the surgical shock trauma platoon (SSTP) at TQ Airbase in Iraq got a call: *IED blast. Mass casualty. Eleven Marines wounded or killed.*

Over the next twenty hours, the medical staff operated on the wounded Marines. Langlais, a forty-four-year-old senior nurse in the operating room, didn't finish until mid-morning the next day. She was exhausted. It had been a rough night for everyone, the wounded Marines and those trying to save them.

At about noon, Langlais, a five-foot-four-inch black woman with short hair, walked to the recreational tent to unwind. Even when she was tired, her smile and posture exuded confidence. She was walking on the shoulders of her parents, both of whom came from Trinidad and settled in Philadelphia. Her father graduated from the Wharton School at the University of Pennsylvania and has a PhD; her mother served on the board of education. Langlais graduated from Villanova's College of Nursing and went to work at Thomas Jefferson Hospital in Philadelphia. She joined the Air Force nurse corps for four years before leaving to care for her dying mother and then to take care of her father. She spent five years as a nurse in the Army while finishing graduate school. After Desert Storm, the Army reduced its nurse force, so she applied to the Navy and joined in 1997.

She's had three-and-a-half years of civilian training in the emergency room, oncology, and medical-surgical. She's also trained in advanced trauma life support, advanced cardiac life support, and trauma nurse critical care. When it comes to patient care, she thrives on helping the sick and wounded recover from traumatic injuries. When it comes to the business side of nursing, she follows her conscience. She doesn't toe the line or circle the wagons. She was raised to give her best and stand for something lest she fall for anything.

Soon after she arrived in the recreational center, Chaplain Terrell Byrd walked in. Byrd, black and five feet, seven inches tall, was the chaplain for Marine Wing Support Squadron 374 out of Twentynine Palms, California. He and Langlais were good friends. She liked the way he was able to pull feelings and concerns out of people, including her, while also making them feel comfortable. He urged her to go to the galley with him to get something to eat. Langlais is diabetic, takes Metaformin twice a day, and has to eat something with her medication. She didn't want to walk to the galley. It was only about a quarter mile away, but on this day, it seemed like miles.

"Commander, you have to eat," Byrd said.

"Okay," she said, reluctantly getting out of her seat.

Byrd comes from a family of nurses and knows a good nurse when he sees one. He believes Langlais is a perfectionist, a nurse to her core. He had many occasions to observe her in action in the operating room at TQ and could tell she was devoted to her profession. He saw her train young corpsmen and nurses to be better clinicians and providers. Her job never stopped. She never stopped. Her life was in the operating room. She became what battle care is all about: comforting the wounded and one another until greater care arrived.

The level of dedication that Langlais and others showed when they heard the high-pitched sound of sirens warning of incoming mortars or the rumbling of a CH-53 helicopter landing, or when they received a call on the radio, was first-rate. Langlais worked between two operating rooms, ensuring that everything was in place so the maximum amount of care could be given to each patient. Some would say doctors and nurses become immune to the wounds and deaths of their patients, but Byrd disagrees. Everyone on the medical staff, including Langlais, was affected when they lost a patient.

On their way to the galley, they ran into Dr. Darren Cherry, the flight surgeon for the Marines of Squadron 374. He is short, white, and funny. He was always telling jokes that incorporated real-life experiences. So when he got to the end of the joke and everyone was laughing, he'd say, "But I'm serious," and they would all stop laughing as quickly as they started. Langlais should have known she was going to survive that day. She was in good company with a chaplain and doc.

After eating and talking in the galley, Langlais, Cherry, and Byrd headed back to the SSTP. While they were walking down Docs Lane, the main road to the SSTP, Langlais stopped to take pictures of the doc and chaplain in front of a HESCO barrier. HESCOs had become a modern gabion for military fortifications. They are made of collapsible wire-mesh containers and heavy-duty fabric liners and are used as a temporary blast or small-arms barrier. It had become a tradition among the troops to take photos in front of the HESCOs. Langlais was also interested in capturing the different uniforms. It seems the chaplain was wearing one uniform, the doc another, and Langlais yet another.

Langlais was taking pictures when she heard an explosion in the sky. Iraqis were firing air-bursting bombs into TQ. Langlais was used to hearing incoming missiles, but these were different. They were silent until they exploded, giving no warning. She, Cherry, and Byrd took off running to the HESCOs. Then another mortar exploded right over Langlais. It sounded like packing bubbles that you pop, only in rapid succession and amplified.

Suddenly, Langlais couldn't see Byrd. The mortar had kicked up enough dust to cause a miniature sandstorm. They could hear, but not see, each other.

When he reached the wall of HESCOs and the dust cleared, Byrd saw that Langlais was bleeding. Two pieces of shrapnel had hit her, one in the neck and one in the face. Blood immediately started gushing from her neck. The impact of the blast knocked Langlais off balance, and the pain of the shrapnel forced her to the ground.

"Lenora," he shouted. Most officers don't address each other by their first names, but their relationship was unique. Byrd was often standing beside Langlais at the operating table when a soldier died or when a wounded Marine learned for the first time that a buddy had been killed. They had been through a lot together.

"Lenora, you've been hit," Byrd said. "You've been hit. Stay still. My hand is on your neck. Don't move."

She was fighting him, trying to get up. *Dude, you need to get off me!* He wanted her to stay down. She had lost a good bit of blood and was becoming oxygen-deprived.

Byrd and Cherry debated who should stay with Langlais and who should run to get help. Langlais didn't want the chaplain to leave her. Byrd stayed and applied pressure while Cherry ran to the SSTP. There was so much blood that Byrd wasn't sure where exactly his friend had been hit or where to apply pressure.

As people do when they are dying and a chaplain is nearby, Langlais gave Byrd some directives. She asked him to tell her father, husband, and children that she loved them.

"No, you can tell them yourself," Byrd said.

"You're not listening," she said.

Nothing Byrd used to stop the bleeding, including his hat, was working. He couldn't help thinking that these were Langlais's last moments. He kept talking to her, telling her to hold on, trying to get her mad—anything to keep her alive. She closed her eyes and went limp.

One of the chaplain's jobs on the battlefield was to attend to the wounded. Byrd knew his job and could do it on autopilot. When he saw another human hurting, he offered compassion and tried to make him or her comfortable. But it was different when the person was a friend, someone whom he knew and admired, someone with a husband and children back home.

As Byrd continued to apply pressure and wait for a medical team, he worried that he was losing Langlais and there wasn't anything else he could do. How long would it take for help to arrive? Should he continue to do what he was doing or try something else? When the medical team showed up, they immediately recognized Langlais as one of their own. They transported her back to the SSTP, where she had spent the previous night and that morning mending other soldiers. Now it was her turn to be stitched up and put back together.

Byrd followed protocol by retrieving his flak and Kevlar before running back to the SSTP to catch up with Langlais. When he reached the doors of the operating room, Langlais was already on the table. Byrd didn't go in. Cherry was the doctor, and he was already back there.

As he stood outside the operating room covered in Langlais's blood, Byrd kept his distance from the others. He didn't want anyone to touch him. He felt that if they touched him, he would cry. He didn't want to crack or break down. This was when the troops needed him the most. He had to be strong. A mental health provider stepped in and suggested he change his clothes.

Some members of the medical staff weren't doing much better than Byrd. They were trying to deal with their commander, their infallible leader, being their patient. The senior doctor told his staff, "Listen, we need her well, but if we don't get her under [sedation], she is going to die right here in front of us, and we're not going to feel good about ourselves." It would take two operating-room teams to get enough staff together because the members of Team A, Langlais's team, were too upset. They were crying. The scrub tech was trying to prep Langlais, and her tears were getting in the way. In the meantime, blood continued to gush out of Langlais's neck. With so much blood masking the wound, no one would know how critical the situation was until they went into her neck.

Dr. Don Bowman, the godfather of the SSTPs, which he created, was her surgeon. His first assistant was Dr. Erin Felger. Langlais is claustrophobic and got combative when they tried to cover her mouth and nose with an oxygen mask. They would have to sedate her first and then put the mask on.

In the meantime, a helicopter was put on standby to medevac Langlais to Balad, where she could get a higher level of care if necessary. Fortunately, the medevac wasn't needed; Langlais did well on the operating table. When she woke up, Bowman told her that she had given them a scare.

"We're getting you the hell out of here," he said.

Langlais refused to go. "I can't go," she said. "Look at the level of experience you have here," referring to her young nurses.

"Lenora, you need to go."

"Dr. Bowman, I don't want to go."

Bowman consulted with Captain Richard Schroff Jr., the officer in charge of Taqaddum surgical detachment. They had to make a quick decision. Could Langlais recover safely at TQ? Obviously, it wasn't safe there. But letting her level of experience go would significantly weaken the trauma care in the operating room. They wouldn't be able to get anyone with her experience on such short notice. They decided to let her recover there.

Langlais had been hit by shrapnel shortly after 2 P.M. She got off the operating table at four. At ten o'clock that night, she was lying in bed in an extra-large T-shirt and sweatpants. She had a big dressing on her neck and another one on her face, which was swollen from the fluids that had been pumped into her.

"Miss Ma'am, are you asleep?" someone whispered.

It was her corpsman.

"I'm so sorry," he said. "I hate to bother you, but there's a Marine in the next tent, and he's not doing well."

"What do you mean, he's not doing well?"

"He's as red as red can get."

"What do you mean red?"

A Marine standing by said, "Ma'am, I know you're not going to get up."

"A Marine is sick."

As she stood, she felt stiff, like she had been in a car crash.

A doc was on the way, but Langlais was closer.

"Your job tonight," Langlais told the corpsman, "is to watch my IV so the blood doesn't flow back up and cause the fluids to stop." She asked the corpsman to tell her more about the Marine.

"Why is he red?"

"I don't know. He just got really red over the last thirty minutes."

"Is he taking any medication?"

"He's just taking some antibiotics."

"What kind of antibiotics?"

"Vancomycin."

"Oh shit. Red man syndrome." That's when the antibiotics are being pushed into someone's system too fast. This was a medical emergency.

When Langlais got to the Marine, he was red from the trunk up. He had a gunshot wound to the abdomen and was packed with dressing. She turned off the antibiotic. "I need eppy [epinephrine]. I need Benadryl." She started pushing the meds. The Marine recovered, but it took a while.

When the surgeon arrived, he took one look at Langlais and said, "What the hell are you doing up?"

"We had to take care of the Marine," she said.

"You can go to bed now." The doc wasn't happy that she had gotten out of bed but was pleased that she was alert and knew what she was doing.

The day after Langlais's near-death experience, the SSTP received a tragic call. Langlais was having the dressing changed on her neck wound when the call came in. The medical staff couldn't understand what the Marines were saying on the other end of the line. There was too much screaming going on in the background. Experience had taught the medical staff that the reaction of the Marines meant it was going to be bad.

Two Humvees turned the corner toward the SSTP. Marines jumped out and carried one of their own to the tent. The wounded Marine's head was wrapped, and the wrapping was saturated with blood. A corpsman had done his best. There was commotion in the clearing area where everyone, including distraught Marines, was supposed to relinquish their guns and grenades before they entered the surgical tents. The medical staff was trying to control them as well as treat the Marine.

The wounded Marine was very close to death, but the staff still worked feverishly. It wasn't until they cut off the Marine's clothes that they realized what all the fuss was about. The Marine had breasts. Lance Corporal Juana Navarro Arellano, twenty-four, of Ceres, California, died on April 8. The severity of the head wound made it one of the worst deaths Langlais had seen. The fact that this death came just a day after she was wounded or that the dead Marine was a female didn't make it any easier to deal with. No one needed to remind Langlais how close her own fate had come to that of Navarro Arellano.

Within a week of being wounded, Langlais and Chaplain Byrd were standing in line for dinner at a cafe on base. Byrd and a Marine gunnery sergeant overheard a young Marine who was making disrespectful comments about the likelihood of Langlais receiving a Purple Heart for her wounds. The Marine was upset because she was alive and walking around while his buddies had been critically wounded or killed. In his mind, his buddies were the ones who deserved a Purple Heart, not her.

When the chaplain and gunny heard the comments, they brought the Marine to Langlais to tell her what he had said. She told them to leave him alone; his comments were his to have. She didn't feel it was necessary to verbally reprimand a Marine who may have seen more death than most individuals in a lifetime. She requested that he be allowed to eat his meal in peace. Byrd and the gunny were mad at the young Marine, but they were even angrier with Langlais for not reprimanding him. They respected her wishes and placed the Marine far from Langlais. She never saw the Marine again, but his comments served as a precursor of what was to come.

That same week, Langlais got a call from the director of the Navy Nurse Corps in Washington, DC, who is also an admiral.

"Am I to understand that you have five children?" she asked Langlais.

"Yes."

"Is that why you are there?"

"Yes," Langlais said, laughing.

Langlais's husband, Daniel, was a lieutenant commander in the Navy before retiring in January 2007. As a chief engineer, he traveled a great deal and was rarely home. That made Langlais, in effect, single mom of five children. At first, she handled this role, but eventually, she grew rebellious. She wanted Daniel to experience what it was like to stay behind, to be in charge of the discipline, school and extracurricular activities, the bills, the household. She wanted him to know what it felt like not just for two weeks but for a full six months.

While they were on the phone, the admiral told the commander that she could come home any time.

"No, ma'am," Langlais said. "I can't."

"Is there anything I can do for you?" the admiral asked.

One of the primary reasons why Langlais felt she needed to stay on the battlefield was because she knew the level of experience there. She had six nurses—two lieutenants and four ensigns—who were lacking in trauma experience.

"Ma'am, there is plenty that can be done not only for me but for the experience level out here," Langlais said. She told the admiral that she had wonderful nurses with great intentions, but when you're dealing with traumas, you need experience. "If you have lieutenant commanders and commanders standing beside you, I need them out here. I need nurses who can think on their feet." Lieutenant Commander Randy Moore was the other senior nurse working at the SSTP. The admiral said they were looking into it.

As a trauma nurse, time is life. You have to know what you're doing when you have Marines in front of you who have lost limbs from IEDs and small-arms fire, or when you have Iraqis who have self-inflicted wounds or are suffering from domestic violence, or when you have children who got caught in the crossfire. They deserve the best. It's not that the nurses weren't trained; it's that they didn't have the level of training and experience necessary on the front lines.

After seeing Navarro Arellano die, Langlais started to have nightmares. She couldn't sleep at all and stayed awake for days at a time. Sometimes, she and Byrd would be having a conversation, and Langlais would nod off. She wouldn't go anywhere without her flak and Kevlar. She was noticeably agitated at the sounds of a siren, a mortar exploding, or a helicopter landing. "She tried to stick it out as long as she could," Byrd said. "That's the Lenora I know."

One of Langlais's best friends during the deployment was Marine Captain Lisa Christenson Doring, a white female and medical service corps officer. Doring made it clear from the beginning that they were going to stick together on the deployment. She wasn't with Langlais when she was wounded and took it hard. She stayed in the background while Langlais was treated and then helped the patient in more ways than one. They didn't look alike, yet they were so similar. Langlais believes God sent Doring to her to change her way of thinking.

Their battlefield friendship was groundbreaking for Langlais, who was dealing with some racial issues, mostly with white females who lived in the same berthing during her deployment. As the only black female officer for the Navy in TQ and the most senior female officer on the base (all services included), she was shocked by overt displays of racism. With the racism, her senior status, and her "no-nonsense leadership," Langlais was often seen as mean-spirited and intimidating. She doesn't smile if something isn't funny, nor does she scratch when it doesn't itch.

For Langlais, the most insulting racial experience occurred when her medical chain of command gave her roommates time off and the use of material and equipment to build a wall in Langlais's berthing space separating her section from the other tenants, who were white females. Her chain of command authorized this after Langlais refused to move in with the junior officers, as was abruptly suggested by the white females in her berthing, all of whom were lieutenants and lieutenant commanders. Langlais didn't always get along with other women and wasn't quick to embrace anyone on this deployment.

She and Doring did get along, however. Doring was the one who got Langlais food from the galley and brought it back to her when she was unable or afraid to walk down Docs Lane. Langlais would have had many hungry nights if Doring and Byrd hadn't helped her. No one else was knocking on the door of her hooch to see if she needed anything to eat.

The first time Langlais walked down Docs Lane to the galley after being wounded, Doring was by her side. Langlais was wearing her flak and Kevlar. "Come on," Doring said. "You can do this. I know you're scared. It's okay." To Langlais, the sky seemed so vast and vulnerable. She never knew when the next mortar would be incoming.

As Langlais continued to heal, another tragedy hit close to home. Doring was married to Marine Captain Nathanael Doring, a pilot who was also a mechanic. When an aircraft was having mechanical problems, he would repair it and then take it for a test drive. That's what he was doing on May 27, 2006, when the Cobra helicopter he was piloting crashed. Doring and Corporal Richard Bennett were killed.

Langlais wasn't supposed to leave the battlefield until July, but in late May, nearly two months after she was wounded, she told her boss that she wanted to go home. She was struggling in Iraq. Service members, male and female, would have gone home with much less serious wounds. But it wasn't just the physical wounds that were weighing on her. Seeing the young female Marine die reminded her of her oldest daughter, who had been missing since September 12, 2003. Langlais has visited city morgues to view bodies, but none were her daughter. To this day, she and Daniel haven't had any contact with their missing daughter. Langlais had to go home. She had to see and touch her four other children. She was afraid that if she didn't leave soon, she wasn't going to make it home. She felt a sense of impending doom. She told her boss, "I need to go home. I'm ready to go home now." She left June 5, 2006.

When service members leave the battlefield early, they are assessed. The doc said she had been wounded and had insomnia and approved her departure. The psychiatrist said, "Not so fast." She diagnosed Langlais with post-traumatic stress disorder (PTSD). This made her livid. She knew what PTSD was because she had it before she ever stepped foot in Iraq. Hers was not a charmed life. Her brother, a Vietnam vet, committed suicide when she was twenty-two years old. Her previous husband fathered a baby outside their marriage; Langlais was six months pregnant when the other woman was nine months along. Her mother had stage-four lung cancer when she died in her arms. And most painful of the all was her missing daughter.

Langlais doesn't believe she suffered from PTSD on the battlefield. Instead, she says she had combat stress, i.e., shell shock or battle fatigue. Combat stress is a military term used to categorize a range of behaviors resulting from the stress of battle, all of which decrease the combatant's fighting efficiency. The most common symptoms are fatigue, slower reaction times, indecision, disconnection from one's surroundings, and the inability to prioritize. Combat stress reaction is generally short-term and should not be confused with PTSD. Nevertheless, the psychiatrist was convinced Langlais had PTSD and wanted to prescribe medication. Langlais refused to take any psychotropic drugs, which are used for mental illness.

Langlais was medevaced to Landstuhl Regional Medical Center in Germany. All service members who are wounded on the battlefield and medevaced have to go through a post-deployment mental and physical assessment. When she arrived, a Navy-Marine liaison escorted her to the wounded warrior section for her assessment. She was made to wait nearly three hours at the mental health clinic. Such a long wait would irritate even the sanest and calmest of people. By the time she saw the psychiatrist, Langlais was annoyed. This psychiatrist also wanted to prescribe psychotropics. Langlais argued that she was restless because of the long wait and not from PTSD. She asked for a second opinion and another provider. She didn't get either.

Langlais and the psychiatrist exchanged curt words. The psychiatrist called in an enlisted airman to stand in on the rest of the conversation. Then she asked the airman if 9C had a room available. The airman returned and said there was space available. 9C was the mental-health ward, where Langlais would spend the next twenty-four hours.

The psychiatrist told her assistant to call Dr. Strong, cold security. Within minutes, a barrage of people descended on Langlais and took her to a padded room. She was instructed to remove her ranks, which are pinned on. She did so willingly because she knew other patients who were not stable could use them as weapons. An Army medic was posted outside her door.

She had arrived at Landstuhl at 11:10 A.M. By four that afternoon, she had been locked up. The blood from the last Marine she had taken care of was still fresh on her boots. None of the documentation from that evening stated she was belligerent or threatening to herself or anyone else, only that she was in an agitated state from having to wait three hours.

When they locked her up, Langlais was furious. She didn't think they had any reason to detain her on the mental-health ward. She was like a caged lion with a sharp thorn stuck deep in her paw. She wanted out of the padded room but remained calm and read a book by her favorite author, Zane.

The staff took Langlais's large travel bags and put them in storage. She was able to keep her flight bag, which was about the size of a tote bag and carried her toiletries and anything she would need immediately. After her surgeries at TQ, Langlais's corpsman gave her the shrapnel from her neck, and she kept it in her flight bag. Every time she asked to go to the bathroom, the staff would throw her belongings out on the floor to make sure she didn't have anything sharp. The third time, about two in the morning, the vial that contained her shrapnel broke. The shrapnel was taken from her, and she hasn't seen it since.

Having the shrapnel that wounded you is a big deal. Ask anyone who has been injured, and they'll tell you the same thing. Marine Gunnery Sergeant Rosie Noel, who was wounded in the cheek by a piece of shrapnel in Iraq, said it's a tangible reminder of the day she was wounded. It's validation that something significant happened.

Langlais was admitted on an evening shift. The next day she saw a different psychiatrist who disagreed with the assessment from the previous night and discharged her. The commander of the ward agreed. Langlais asked for her ranks back and was told they had been lost. So for the remainder of her time—three days—at Landstuhl, she was called private, the lowest enlisted rank. She could live with that; she couldn't live with the fact that they had lost her shrapnel.

She went to the office of the commanding officer of Landstuhl, but he was away. The hospital knew it had made a mistake, so they gave her the nicest room at the Fisher House, which is where wounded soldiers on the mend and their family members stay so that they can be close to one another during these stressful times. They also sent her on an all-expense paid trip to Trier, the oldest city in Germany.

She contacted her parent command at Camp Pendleton to see if she could take a commercial flight home to attend her daughter's high-school graduation. They wouldn't approve it because of the incident at Landstuhl. For all they knew, Langlais did have psychiatric problems. It was her word against theirs.

Langlais came home quietly, but a storm was raging inside her. She didn't want any hoopla; she just wanted to be left alone. "I didn't want a parade," she said, sobbing, as she recalled this period in her life. "I didn't even want my husband to know I was coming home."

She reported to her command at Naval Hospital Camp Pendleton and was immediately whisked off to psychiatry. Dr. Lana Clark didn't agree with what the psychiatrist had written in Landstuhl.

While at the hospital, Langlais ran into her commanding officer in a hallway. He advised her against being dramatic about what happened in Landstuhl. He told her not to play the system. A day later, the awards office called Langlais to find out when her commanding officer could pin the Purple Heart on her. There was no way she was going to give him the honor of pinning an award on her. Service members can choose who awards them the Purple

Heart. Her commanding officer from Iraq had just returned. She asked him to do it.

Langlais is the first nurse in the Navy nurse corps to be awarded a Purple Heart. Some have received it posthumously. It's meant to be a symbol of her sacrifice but instead has been a prickly thorn in her side. She learned that people whom she'd never met and who had never been to Iraq were judging her and her performance.

"I hate wearing the Purple Heart," Langlais said. "It means two things: People are going to either label you as someone who was wounded and damaged goods, or there's tremendous animosity."

It was also brought to Langlais's attention that as soon as other nurses in the Navy heard that she had been wounded, they began calculating her retirement and disability. The most egregious thing they did, in her opinion, was to categorize and label her limitations before she had a chance to heal physically or mentally. The same nurses were also aware that this award came with great honor and prestige, and that's what Langlais suspects led to the personal campaign that the nurse corps launched against her.

In the years since she returned from Iraq, Langlais has felt as though a war has been waged against her by fellow shipmates in Navy Medicine West leadership and its senior nurse corps. It was more than a professional campaign against her. It was also a personal crusade by her nurse corps shipmates to destroy, discredit, and discourage Langlais from feeling the honor that she deserved. She was an officer with a special place in the history of the Navy nurse corps and in the Navy in general. "How dare she not know her place?" She knows her place. They just messed with the wrong naval officer—or perhaps they messed with the right naval officer. Still she rises.

While still in Iraq, Langlais felt the nurse corps had turned its back on her by not sending more experienced nurses and by not holding people accountable for their actions. They didn't help her at Landstuhl, after which she felt like the Hester Prynne of the Navy nurse corps, and they made her feel ashamed for receiving the Purple Heart.

Langlais came home eager to share with the nurse corps what she had learned as a senior nurse on the battlefield. Her experience on the battlefield had been physically, emotionally, and mentally traumatic. She nearly died. She saw others die. She had ideas for improving care for the troops. She would never be asked to give a briefing. Instead, the nurse corps went on the attack.

The nurse corps couldn't black ball Langlais's reputation as a professional trauma nurse or naval officer, so they made everything personal, from Lundstuhl to her arrival home and job assignments. Langlais was told she would be the department head of the Staff Education and Training Department, a position fitting of a commander. She went on leave for two weeks, and when she returned, she was demoted to a division officer's position while the department head position was assigned to a junior officer. Langlais was told that she would get a better leadership position at a later time. She filed an equal-opportunity complaint. Then she was pulled from that position to direct the new Deployment Health Clinic—the first of its kind—on Camp Pendleton, but she wasn't given any guidance.

She asked for help at every level to set the record straight. She went to the Pentagon and visited Chief of Naval Operation Admiral Michael Mullen's senior diversity staff. During this meeting and after she briefed his diversity staff, Mullen ordered his senior legal staff to assign the commanding officer of the Naval Legal Service Office in San Diego to represent her. Next, she called NAACP San Diego and Oceanside, the Urban League San Diego,

Republican (now Democratic) Senator Arlen Specter of Pennsylvania, Democratic Congressman Bob Filner of California, and Democratic Congresswoman Maxine Waters of California.

Langlais received some help and validation when an equal employment opportunity (EEO) command team from Millington, Tennessee, went to the hospital at Camp Pendleton to survey the climate and determined that it had a systemic problem. Because of the tangible evidence that Langlais was in a hostile work environment, the EEO team removed Langlais from the hospital and placed her in Navy Recruiting District San Diego command, where she recruited twelve people for medical in six months; none of them knew what she had been through. Finally, she was transferred to the Naval Medical Center San Diego, where her senior nurse didn't want her in her directorate. So Langlais received an assignment six buildings away from the in-patients' ward and was tasked with ordering durable medical equipment, such as breast pumps and wheelchairs, alongside hospital men and young enlisted sailors.

"All I want to do is nursing," she said. "All I want is to touch people. All I want to do is be with patients."

As Langlais was moved from one job to another and placed in positions beneath her level of expertise, her anger escalated. "If I had done what I wanted to do when I got home, my kids would have lost a mother and my husband would have lost a wife," she said. Langlais could handle injury trauma on the battlefield; no one taught her how to patch up the injuries caused by her colleagues. "The insult from my own corps is a different war," she said. "I didn't know how to fight that on my own."

These job changes happened over a two-year period. While she was being moved from job to job, Langlais's chain of command at Camp Pendleton allegedly made twenty-eight unauthorized inquiries into her medical records. "I've been treated like shit since

I've been back," she said. "But despite what they've done, 'still I rise.' I haven't given up."

Langlais called her admiral for help. The admiral refused to speak to her not once but twice because of legal reasons.

"Legal reasons?"

"We're protecting the admiral," said the deputy commander of the Nurse Corps.

"But I'm one of your sailors."

"I am sorry, Commander Langlais. I don't know what else there is to tell you," the deputy commander said.

She was a nurse with a Purple Heart calling her admiral about two injustices, at Landstuhl and at Camp Pendleton. She still hasn't heard from the admiral. The irony is that Langlais is a senior clinician who is also an administrative officer. She has deployed, she was wounded, she became the face of the Navy Nurse Corps in journals, and she was being treated like she had no rank, no clout, no experience.

On her own nickel and dime and on her own time, at the twenty-four-month mark after her return, Langlais flew from San Diego to Washington, D.C., to have a one-on-one conversation with the Surgeon General of the U.S. Navy, Vice Admiral Adam Robinson. He told her that as the U.S. Navy Surgeon General, he wanted to apologize for how she was treated in Landstuhl. No sailor or service member—especially no shipmate—should be treated the way she was. It was an injustice and an embarrassment. They should be ashamed of themselves. He was sorry it ever happened to her. He respected her request to be removed from harm's way at Navy Medicine West and placed her in a recruiting leadership position as the Lead Medical Recruiter for Medical Officer Programs at Navy Recruiting District San Diego until her retirement or until she receives a new set of orders.

For more than two years Langlais has been trying to get the incident at Landstuhl erased from her record, but to no avail. It's the only blemish on an otherwise exemplary naval career. She has never received an adverse fitness report; her professional performance has been outstanding. She has never been counseled. She has never harmed a patient. She has completed master's degrees in health-care administration and at the Naval War College–Command and Staff, and is working on a PhD in health-care administration. She's always been a leader. She loves the Navy and her profession but has been around long enough to know that there are bad apples everywhere, including in the Navy nurse corps.

While Langlais was attempting to salvage her professional career, she was also trying to cope with her physical wounds. The mortar explosion affected her right ear. At first, she thought that she had swimmer's ear and that it would pop once the swelling went down. That never happened. She has lost 75 percent of her hearing in her right ear. She wears a hearing aid. Three major nerves on the right side of her face have been severed; they may or may not regenerate. She has neurological firing—nerves are trying to regenerate—and experiences phantom pain. She's taking Neurontin to reduce the pain. She has a hard time sleeping. She sleeps about four hours a day, between eleven at night and two or three in the morning. Sometimes, she takes sedatives to help her sleep. She has a three-inch scar on the right side of her neck and a scar on the lower right side of her jaw.

Langlais is adamant about many things, including how the war affected her emotionally and mentally. "I do not have PTSD from Iraq," she wrote in an e-mail. "I have internal anger towards the nurse corps for their lack of support and how they gave the green light to treat me like shit—at least in Iraq. I knew the enemy! My hurt and anger did not surface until I came home to my parent service. 'They' are my Iraq. So now I am in a war zone without any personal protection equipment or support!"

In addition to everything that was going on in her professional life and the demands of her medical appointments, Langlais was also a wife and mother. Like everyone else coming home, she had to learn how to reconnect with her spouse and children. She was happy to see her husband and pleased he was able to run the household while she was gone.

Her kids were excited to see her scars. Once they saw that she was okay physically, they were okay. At least one of her children feared she would have to deploy again. If she went on an errand and her nine-year-old son didn't see her for a while, he'd ask if she was coming home or going back to Iraq.

In Iraq, Langlais learned the hard way that even though she is here today, there is no guarantee she will be here tomorrow. She's grateful for that lesson because it has made her focus on the important things in life. Before she went to Iraq, she thought everything was important, everything was a priority. "Iraq has shown me what I can live without, do without, think without," she said. "It has truly helped me understand what's important in life." What's important are her children and husband. She's happy to have her health, a husband who loves her, healthy children who are Christians and love one another, and a nice home in San Diego. Most importantly, she's thankful to be alive.

Life could have been much different for her and her family. They could have gotten back someone who was critically wounded and couldn't take care of herself. Her kids could have lost a mother. Her husband could have lost a wife, and her father could have lost a daughter.

"I realize how blessed I am," she said. "I took life for granted. I was a daredevil when I went over there. Life is precious to me now."

Her oldest daughter is still missing. She has handed that problem over to God, but God is still working on her feelings with the Navy nurse corps. She was wounded and survived for a reason—to wake up the nurse corps? "I opened a Pandora's box," she said.

Army Master Sergeant Ronda Warrick

RONDA WARRICK WAS A MEDIC ON THE FRONT LINES DURING HER first two tours in Iraq, "in the sand fighting for our lives so we could save other lives." As a medic, she went on recovery missions that involved taking photos of the scene, picking up remains, and doing inventory. When she returned to base, she'd look at the photos and wonder if she got everything. It became an obsession. She tried to detach herself from her work so that it wouldn't get personal, so that she wouldn't fall apart every time she went on a recovery mission. But it was tough to detach. As she took photos of the dead and put names to their faces, it became personal, very personal.

"Those are the reasons why I walk the floor," she said, pacing while talking to me on the phone from her home in Colorado. She has about 125 different files on her computer with pictures of everything from recovered vehicles and items on the road to scenes of bodies completely torn to pieces in vehicles. "They're not pictures I would share with everyone or I would send to family members," she said. "I wouldn't want those pictures sent to me."

As a convoy commander on her third and last tour, Warrick went on 488 missions outside the wire. On one of those missions, she was hit by an IED. She has pins in her left knee, and she'll get a right knee replacement in the next five years. She was diagnosed with traumatic brain injury and other wounds that have forever changed her life.

She said being wounded was probably one of the best things that happened to her in Iraq because she no longer had to sift through the debris and pick up the pieces of someone else's injuries or death to send back to family members. "I would rather be hit than have to pick up the pieces of another soldier to be sent home."

When she came home, she had digital cameras installed outside her home. She walks the perimeter of her property every day before the sun goes down. In the morning, she walks around the house. She knows she's not going to find bombs or the enemy out there; it just makes her feel safe so she can relax. She suffers from post-traumatic stress disorder and obsessive-compulsive disorder. She can't be in large crowds around others for long periods of time or shop in busy places like malls. She retired as a master sergeant after twenty-one years of service to her country and has started a self-healing business called Joining of Herbs (www.joiningofherbs.com).

Holly Harrison

Been There, Done That

Lt. Holly Harrison and the 110-foot Coast Guard cutter *Aquidneck* were preparing to escort a cruise ship out of the Philadelphia harbor. This was one of the first large cruise ships to embark with passengers from the city since 9/11, and there was a good bit of excitement in the media about cruise lines possibly being a new industry for the city. Given the media coverage, Harrison was concerned this high profile transit could make it a target for terrorists. But before she and her crew could complete this important mission, they received new orders: Stop what you're doing. Get underway. Report back to your home port. You have to be in Portsmouth, Virginia, in three days.

They were being called off a mission? That never happens. If anything, they are called onto missions. The caller was vague about the upcoming assignment but *had* hinted that "you can't sail there." Say no more. Harrison, thirty years old and captain of the *Aquidneck*, was up on her current events and knew what this meant: she was headed to the Middle East for the start of the war in Iraq.

The 110-foot ships couldn't sail to the Middle East for a couple of reasons. They were too small to carry the necessary amount of fuel to get them from here to there; another boat would have had to accompany them and carry the fuel. More importantly, going through the Suez Canal or sailing around Africa would have taken months, and they didn't have that much time. Four cutters, including the *Aquidneck*, would meet in Portsmouth and be taken to Manama, Bahrain, on large container ships. The *Aquidneck*'s crew of twenty-two would fly over and meet the ship in Manama in February 2003.

From an early age, it seemed that Harrison was destined to wear a military uniform of some sort. Both of her parents served in the armed forces. Her father, Robert, was a Marine who served in Vietnam and later went to work for the FBI. Her mother, Margaret Monthan, was in the Navy's marine mammal program until she married and became pregnant. The Navy offered fewer opportunities to pregnant women back then. In addition, when her unit deployed to Vietnam, she was the only member who didn't go because of the "lack of billeting" for females.

Harrison grew up in Vienna, Virginia, and attended Thomas Jefferson High School for Science and Technology in Alexandria, where she joined the U.S. Naval Sea Cadet Corps, which is sponsored by the U.S. Navy League. To advance in rank in the Sea Cadet Corps, cadets have to spend two weeks each year with either the Navy or Coast Guard. Between her sophomore and junior years, Harrison spent time at a small Coast Guard boat station in Yorktown. The following year, she went to Coast Guard Station Miami Beach for two weeks, where she participated in the rescue of a boat drifting out to sea and helped retrieve a fatality from a scuba diving accident. Rather than traumatize her, as her parents feared, the opportunity to help others energized her. She likes the Coast Guard because there is always something to do, from security at waterside festivals to search-and-rescues, and at the end of the day, she feels she has accomplished something.

After graduating from the U.S. Coast Guard Academy in 1995, Harrison traveled to Kodiak, Alaska, where she was an ensign on the medium-endurance cutter *Storis* and spent just about every patrol in the Bering Sea enforcing fisheries laws and doing search-and-rescues. From Alaska, she went to work as the executive officer of a 110-foot patrol boat, the *Kiska*, in Hawaii, where she did a little of everything—search-and-rescue, law enforcement, fisheries, and public service projects. Then she served as the protocol officer for the Commandant of the Coast Guard in Washington, D.C., from 1999 to 2001.

In 2001, Harrison was selected as captain of the *Aquidneck* and started doing law enforcement, fisheries, and Caribbean counter-drug work. Then came 9/11 and a new focus on homeland security, including escorting submarines and commercial ships with liquid natural gas in and out of ports and guarding ships with heavy ordnance along the Cape Fear River before they embarked to the Middle East. The goal was to prevent another USS *Cole* incident. The *Cole* had been attacked by suicide bombers in the Yemeni port of Aden in 2000.

The crew gives a ship its personality. The *Aquidneck*'s home port was Fort Macon, North Carolina, and the majority of the crew hailed from the Tar Heel state. They had a good attitude about going to the Middle East and understood how their jobs contributed to the big picture. They preferred to be a part of history rather than to sit on the sidelines, which was what they had done during the first Gulf War more than a decade earlier. Since the Coast Guard hadn't deployed for war since Vietnam, it's easy to see why family members weren't expecting the crew to go to Iraq, but they nonetheless supported their loved ones. No one wanted to leave home, but they knew what they were doing, that they were going to be a part of something, and that they were the right people to do it. No one tried to get out of the deployment.

To start her crew off on a positive note, Harrison wrote a command philosophy entitled "Aquidneck Attitude," which stated that the individual crew member's attitude would determine his experience. If he thought it was going to be a bad deployment, it probably would be. If he maintained a positive, can-do attitude, he would likely succeed.

Harrison was the only woman on her ship but doesn't think her gender was ever an issue. She said her male crew treated her like a captain. What they cared about was that she was competent and could do her job. Since women are allowed in every role in the Coast Guard, they are treated the same as the men. Everyone is viewed as capable of performing any job as long as they can meet the performance criteria. Individuals are judged based on how they perform their duties and what type of team player and shipmate they are. Everyone has a chance to succeed and is evaluated according to his or her skills and abilities, not a demographic category they have no control over, such as race, gender, background, or religion.

Before they left for the Middle East, Harrison had to take one of her firemen to captain's mast (a form of punishment) for messing up, again. He was young, right out of high school, and having a hard time growing up and being a man. She had a long talk with him and the crew. There they were, making plans for the possibility of Saddam Hussein releasing chemicals on them like he had on his own people, and Harrison had to worry about a crewmember. It was distracting all of them from their mission. She enlisted the crew to help this sailor fix himself. Eventually, he would become sailor of the quarter.

The *Aquidneck* and three sister ships—the *Adak, Baranof,* and *Wrangell*—waited to deploy while in Portsmouth, Virginia. During the four months it took to receive their final deployment orders, the crews went through extensive training. Meanwhile, the cutters were given a top-to-bottom overhaul to ensure that everything was in top condition. Harrison focused on seeking solutions to various "what if" scenarios: What if they were fired upon? What if they encountered a mine? What if the Iraqis used chemical weapons on them? She then developed plans to counter each of these threats and ran the crew through drills to test the effectiveness of each plan in order to work out any potential problems and make improvements. She knew that whatever they encountered, they would have to handle it themselves. Help would be available from other coalition forces, but it would take time to reach them. She was very aware that they had to be prepared to face the unexpected.

One area of particular concern for her was chemical weapons. The 110s were not designed to operate in conditions with chemical weapons, and Saddam Hussein had used the weapons in the past. Would he use them against coalition forces? Harrison discussed her options with a chemical-weapons expert and was told they had suits that would last a little while, but after that, they would be "out of luck." Not satisfied with that answer, Harrison researched defensive measures, wrote a detailed chemical-weapons defensive plan, and ran the crew through drills with makeshift equipment, some as simple as plastic sheeting and duct tape, to test the plan. While it may not have been perfect, Harrison was not about to let her crew's safety depend on luck.

On February 22, 2003, Harrison and her crew headed to the Middle East. Within a week of being pulled off a cargo ship in Bahrain, the *Aquidneck* set sail and was doing patrols. Harrison felt good about the boat's condition. The *Aquidneck* had been maintained in excellent condition over the years. When the crew needed its engines to run, they ran. When they needed the boat to head in a certain direction, the steering responded. The *Aquidneck* had problems periodically but nothing serious. It was reliable, and so was the crew.

Coast Guard, U.S. Navy, and British and Australian vessels were stationed at the mouth of the Khawr Abd Allah River, which separates Iraq and Kuwait. Harrison and the *Aquidneck* were the eyes and ears of the river. In addition to providing protection and assistance to other American vessels, the *Aquidneck* was charged with boarding and searching everything on the river to ensure that embargoed oil, terrorists, and weapons were not being smuggled out—all while navigating waters that were poorly charted, often treacherously shallow, and frequently mined.

When they arrived at the river, there were lots of dhows, small coastal freighters and fishing vessels with five to seven people onboard. The fishermen would cast huge nets to catch what looked like schools of sardines that had gathered at the mouth of the river. The majority of these fishermen were just out there trying to earn a day's wage; they didn't care who was fighting whom. But the Coast Guard and coalition forces had no idea who were the good guys and who were the bad guys. There was concern that some of the fishermen were aligned with Al Qaeda and might be laying mines in the waterway, spying on coalition forces, or smuggling Al Qaeda leadership, Iranian soldiers, money, and artifacts in and out of the area. The Coast Guard didn't want any ships operating in that area until they were searched. However, they were also sensitive to getting the river open to commerce as soon as possible. They wanted to get the fishermen back fishing again and the cargo moving.

So the *Aquidneck*'s first assignment after the invasion of Iraq was to sail up the river and herd all the boats out. It was a monstrous undertaking. Some of the dhows were more than 200 feet long. It could take up to half of Harrison's crew to inspect one vessel; the other half, including Harrison, had to stay on watch on the Coast Guard ship.

Since no one on the *Aquidneck* spoke Arabic, the crew was forced to use hand signals when they neared the vessels. They'd point in the direction that they wanted the dhows to go, and if that didn't work, they'd find another way to communicate through hand gestures, body language, and tone of voice. The guns they wore and those mounted aboard the cutter provided a not-so-subtle show of force, but the Coast Guard has history of working with the public, and threats of force were not necessary to get the dhow crews to cooperate.

Divers from other ships made sure nothing was attached to the bottoms of the boats. This was no easy task. The river was clean, but they couldn't see through it because of all the silt and sediment. It looked like a cup of coffee with a lot of cream. When they finished searching the dhows, sailors would spray paint the hull to indicate it had been checked. The message: if you're not needed here, leave.

The *Aquidneck* stayed at sea for twenty-six straight days before and after the start of the war. Harrison compared it with being locked in a high-school classroom and having to live and work with each other in that small space under stressful conditions for a month. You might work well together and get along with some of your classmates; other classmates you might not like so much. Either way, you would have no choice but to find a way to get along. Harrison was fortunate because, as the captain, she had a stateroom to herself. The executive officer, Lt(jg). Matthew Michaelis, also had his own room. The chief engineer and operations petty officer shared a two-person stateroom. The rest of the crew had to live in cramped berthing areas. The aft berthing area had eight racks, but they squished three more cots into it along with all the extra equipment and gear issued to everyone.

There was no place on the ship to be alone. Living with that many people for that length of time in those cramped quarters will test anyone. Harrison was lucky because most of the crew had served together for almost a year prior to deploying and had built a solid working-living relationship. Four new crewmembers from Tactical Law Enforcement Team North joined the *Aquidneck* to help strengthen its defensive posture. They incorporated themselves fairly well, but they had to get acquainted with not only the crew but also life aboard a 110-foot cutter, so it was more challenging for them. The crew was outstanding. They focused on improving things they had control over (such as figuring out a way to do laundry on a ship without any laundry machines), not things that they could not change (like the length of the patrols). There were no discipline problems or fights. Everyone figured out how to get along and give each other space as best they could.

As the ship worked its way up the river, the crew found a large freighter partially sunk in the middle of the channel. The river was shallow, so the ship's bow and superstructure stuck out. It was rusty and looked like it had been there for some time, perhaps since the first Gulf War. Harrison had been ordered to search anything and everything, whether it was moving or not, so she sent part of her crew to check out the vessel. It appeared someone had been there not too long ago. They found food supplies, gas masks, AK-47s, prayer rugs, and most importantly, crude drawings of coalition vessels that had been on the river. Whoever had been staying on the boat had been providing intelligence about the movement of coalition forces in the river. If she didn't realize it before they arrived, Harrison now knew the importance of checking everything.

Once the dhows were searched and began re-entering the river, they were everywhere. When Harrison looked out on the horizon, she could easily see about fifty boats in the mouth of the river, which was wide enough that you couldn't see from one side to the other. And searching the dhows once didn't mean that job was finished. Dhows constantly crept back into the river. The *Aquidneck* had to regularly change its routine. They would board a boat and then go back on it six hours later.

There was no rulebook out there. Harrison and her crew had to use common sense. They observed the people on the river and watched how they reacted to her crew and how those responses changed over time.

As the ship's captain, Harrison was in charge of everything from navigating the ship to executing missions. When she sent boarding parties onto other ships, she stayed on the bridge to assess how the boarding was going and to screen people who came to help to make sure they were coalition forces.

The 110s were in an unusual position because the Navy was in charge of them, but not all Navy personnel knew how to use the cutters since they didn't work much with them. The Navy commodore had worked with 110s, but his staff hadn't. Often, the *Aquidneck* would be treated like a bigger ship than it actually was. The question wasn't so much whether Harrison and her crew could do something but how long they could sustain their capability with such a small crew. They were all tired.

The 110-foot cutter is a minimally-manned ship, but the *Aquidneck* operated on an all-hands evolution, which meant that, no matter what they were doing, everyone was involved. The crew's watches were four hours long, followed by eight hours off, but during that time, they could be boarding other vessels. When a sailor's watch was in the middle of the night, he would have to fit his sleep in around operations.

Sleeping was hard for Harrison. Prior to Iraq, she was a deep sleeper. Nothing woke her. On the river, she was sensitive to the tiniest noises. A change in the engines or in the way the ship was riding through the water would wake her. She slept in her uniform with her boots next to her rack so she could step into them and react immediately. She tried to keep up with her sleep so she'd be fresh. She knew that fatigue would dull her mind and that she needed to stay sharp because she never knew when something would happen.

The crew of the *Aquidneck* had been warned to search the fishing dhows for not only people from Saddam's regime who were trying to sneak out of the country, but also for Saddam himself.

In addition, they were supposed to look for any riches, such as gold, that the Iraqis may have been trying to smuggle out with them.

One time, the crew spotted a vessel that was sitting so low that there was only a foot between the water and the top deck of the boat. If this vessel had rolled to either side, it would have capsized. Harrison's crew spotted gold bars strewn all over the deck, so they boarded for a closer look. It turned out that the bars were brass, not gold, but there was no way of knowing that from a distance—at least not without the kind of equipment that a team of Australians had, that determined the essence of such bars. The crew on the dhow said they were taking the shipment to Kuwait. If they had been in U.S. waters, the Coast Guard never would have let the boat leave the pier. It was too unstable. But Harrison did not have the authority to regulate their shipping business. Luckily, the water was calm that day.

After all the dhows had been searched, Harrison's ship began guarding the minesweepers and hunters as they scoured the water for explosives. The sweepers needed protection because they carried lots of equipment and towed sleds under the water. If they came under attack, they wouldn't be able to turn and run quickly. The *Aquidneck* would head up the river first, followed by the sweepers. During one mission, coalition forces seized a barge and tugboat that had mines on rails and rollers ready to deploy. All the Iraqis had to do was open a hatch and release the mines into the water. They found two types of mines on the boats: acoustic mines that sit on the bottom of the ocean and are triggered by the noise and pressure of boats overhead, and floating mines that could detonate anywhere at any time.

They always had to be on the lookout for mines. In 1988, the USS *Samuel B. Roberts* struck a mine while operating in the Persian Gulf, causing major structural damage, flooding, and fire, and injuring sixty-nine. If a mine were to detonate near the *Aquidneck*, the small ship would be torn apart.

In July, after the *Aquidneck* had been in the region for several months, sweepers out of Bahrain found a mine and declared part of the river a mine-danger area. All ships had to stay a mile away. While plotting the position of the mine on their charts, the *Aquidneck*'s quartermaster discovered old marks on the chart indicating that the *Aquidneck* had sailed over the exact spot earlier. Everyone paused for a moment, each reflecting on how lucky they had been. Another time, they were escorting the minesweepers and hunters when a crew member aboard their sister ship, the *Adak*, reported seeing a mine pop up behind the *Adak*.

One of the most stressful nights on the river was when the officer on deck spotted a small vessel on the ship's radar. He immediately notified Harrison. The vessel was moving toward them at a high speed. Harrison had seconds to figure out whether it was friend or foe. Do we open fire or not? They had a way to hail other vessels by flashing a pattern of lights. If the boat was friendly, it would respond with a certain pattern. But this small vessel wasn't responding. It was moving fast, and the *Aquidneck* was tracking it on the radar. Harrison's job requires that she be able to apply intuition and common sense when necessary. As the small vessel got closer, Harrison noticed that it was heading straight at the *Aquidneck*. She hadn't seen anything moving that fast on the river, so it seemed out of place. She thought it could be a coalition ship or maybe an Al Qaeda operative that obtained a speed boat.

Harrison ordered the crew to man its stations. The *Aquidneck* has .50-caliber machine guns all around the ship to cover 360 degrees and a 25-millimeter gun for distance. Then she rolled the dice. She didn't have much information to make a decision one way or the other. The boat speeding toward her didn't fit anything she had seen on the river. She knew Navy SEALs were operating in the area along with British and Australian forces, but there were plenty of other people sneaking around, too.

With her crew's fingers on the triggers, the small vessel veered off and followed the curve of the river. The crew didn't open fire. It turned out the speed boat was operated by SEALs. They weren't playing by the rules that Harrison had been given.

"We came very close to lighting them up, and I can't tell you how bad that would have been," Harrison said. "It's frustrating when they go and do their own thing because there are other forces in the area, and we need to be able to identify them."

As Harrison was finishing her deployment, two oil terminals at the mouth of the river came online. The primary way Iraq makes money is through its oil, which is essential to its reconstruction. Patrolling the waterways near the oil rigs isn't a glamorous job and doesn't get the media attention that soldiers get patrolling the streets of Fallujah or Baghdad. And it may not have a day-to-day impact on the war, but keeping the waterways safe and passable is critical to the overall goal of rebuilding the country. It's a unique part of the war for which the Coast Guard is well suited.

Not long after Harrison left to come home, a fishing dhow got too close to the terminals. Just as a Navy ship carrying a Coast Guard boarding team drove up alongside the dhow, it blew itself up, killing and injuring several people. The Coast Guard believes the dhow was on its way to damage the oil terminals.

At the end of July 2003, the crews from the four 110s were called to a meeting to receive combat action ribbons for operating in a mine environment. To be given this decoration, an individual must have rendered satisfactory performance under enemy fire while actively participating in a ground or surface engagement. At the same meeting, the commodore of the destroyer squadron called on Lt. Cmdr. Sean MacKenzie, the most senior of the four commanding officers of the 110s. Harrison saw an aide holding a medal that looked pink and white and thought how awesome it was that MacKenzie was getting a meritorious service medal. Then the commodore started to read the citation, and Harrison realized it was for a Bronze Star and was surprised. He then presented the same to Lt. Chris Burrows, though the citation was different.

When the commodore called on Harrison, she still wasn't sure what to expect, but she also received the Bronze Star and knew it was special. She also knew that without her crew, none of the things mentioned in the citation would have been accomplished. She looked at the audience and saw her executive officer, Matthew Michaelis, with a big grin on his face. She later learned that he had provided many of the details that justified the citation. He had known about it in advance but didn't let anything slip, so she was completely surprised. That night, Harrison called her mom to tell her about the Bronze Star, and her mother was thrilled. Having been in the Navy, her mom knew the significance of the medal and promptly called or e-mailed the entire family.

Within the next few days, MacKenzie, Burrows, and Harrison turned over command of their cutters and headed back to the States. When they got back, they were called to U.S. Coast Guard Headquarters in Washington, D.C., for an awards ceremony. The commandant, Adm. Thomas Collins, spoke about the sailors' contributions overseas. He was followed by Secretary of Homeland Security Tom Ridge, who said a few words and then "presented" the officers with their medals again.

Harrison felt a bit awkward about receiving the Bronze Star. Though she was responsible for the cutter's missions, it was her crew that executed them. Their selfless dedication, camaraderie, and can-do attitudes were instrumental to the cutter's success. Harrison also realizes that she and her crew were removed from the primary battlefield on land. They didn't interact with the Iraqi people except when boarding their boats. What she did to earn a Bronze Star was quite different from what a Marine or soldier did, for example, in an Iraqi city. She did not feel she experienced the same personal danger as Marines and soldiers who went out on convoys every day. She didn't ride in Humvees and expose herself to lethal improvised explosive devices. On the other hand, her job of patrolling the river was critical to keeping the waterway and oil terminals open and safe—and it was dangerous. If the *Aquidneck* hit a mine, the only thing separating the crew from the mine was an inch-wide hull. Hitting a mine would have been catastrophic to the ship and the crew.

When she came back, Harrison wasn't so much physically exhausted as mentally tired. Family members immediately started calling to talk to her. How was she doing? What had she experienced? When were they going to see her? Harrison is usually one to talk about her adventures, but at the time, she wasn't feeling very chatty. She didn't think she could accurately convey what she and the crew did over there. Words didn't seem to do her experience justice. She could not explain what it was like to someone who was not there. She could tell them how hot, tiring, and challenging it was, but that never seemed enough. Rather than cheapen things, she preferred to keep her explanations short and simple. Her dad never talked much about what happened in Vietnam for what she believed to be the same reason. It wasn't that he didn't want to tell people; he just couldn't do the events justice.

Harrison didn't have much time to dwell on her experiences in the Middle East. She had to focus on getting her household goods packed and shipped to her new job. Once there, she would be able to jump in and focus on learning her new duties. She was assigned as the senior instructor of the Maritime Law Enforcement School in Yorktown, Virginia, for ten months. She then moved with the school to Charleston, South Carolina, to help establish the Coast Guard's new law enforcement academy by combining it with another school from the West Coast. Then she went on the *Legare* for two years as the executive officer. The *Legare* is a 270-foot, medium-endurance cutter and is in one of the Coast Guard's bigger classes of ships. In addition to counter-drug and illegal migrant interdiction patrols in the Caribbean, she sailed the *Legare* to West Africa in 2007.

The tour in Iraq made Harrison more adaptable. While on the *Legare*, she was notified of a ship carrying drugs. It took fourteen days to find the vessel, board it, and tow it. The small vessel was able to stay afloat, but if it ran out of fuel, it would be at the mercy of the waves and likely capsize. The only way to keep the vessel afloat would be to take it in tow while it was underway, before its fuel ran out. Normally, a vessel is taken in tow from a dead stop, but that would not work in this situation. And the seas were getting worse and time running out before it ran out of fuel. This was demanding, but Harrison had been through worse during long hours on the river in Iraq. It didn't seem so insurmountable. The crew quickly brainstormed an innovative plan and safely took the vessel in tow, just minutes before it ran out of fuel. While escorting the vessel, the seas had grown choppy, with ten-foot waves.

She's also not as intimidated by new challenges as she once was. She weighs her options, finds out what skills her crew has and what positions they can fill, and applies her "let's do it" attitude.

"I don't mind a good challenge," she said. "Just because I haven't done it before doesn't mean I can't do it. That doesn't faze me. I enjoy a good challenge."

Her latest challenge: earning a master's degree in public policy at Princeton University to prepare her for more demanding assignments in the Coast Guard.

Rachel McNeill

Out of My Way

ARMY SPECIALIST RACHEL MCNEILL GREW UP IN HOLLANDALE, Wisconsin, a town with fewer than 300 people. As a teenager, her idea of taking a risk was riding thoroughbred horses bareback or jumping off the cliff at Yellowstone Lake near her parent's house. But during her junior year at Pecatonica High School, when she was sitting in history class and learned that terrorists had attacked the United States, McNeill began to redefine her risk-taking threshold.

The terrorist attacks heightened her awareness of world issues. She was reminded of a quote from Abraham Lincoln: "America will never be destroyed from the outside. If we falter and lose our freedoms, it will be because we destroyed ourselves." Was this still true? She had always felt safe in her small town and schools. Now her sense of security had been violated. She wondered what would cause someone to attack America. What can be resolved by war? She had a difficult time imagining that violence was the answer. She realized this was a turning point in history and didn't want to watch from the sidelines. Always the student, McNeill believes in studying something before forming an opinion. If she went to Iraq, she could be a part of history and make up her own mind about war.

One day, she woke up and decided to have a recruiter talk to her parents to convince them that she should go into the military. She joined the Army Reserves in 2002, a year after 9/11. She was seventeen, not even eligible to vote. She trained one weekend a month until she finished high school. After graduating a semester early, she went to Madison Area Technical College for a semester. Then she left for basic training and advanced individual training in July 2003. She started the visual communications program at Madison Tech until she was involuntarily transferred to another reserve unit to prepare to deploy.

At the age of nineteen, McNeill deployed to Iraq as a heavy construction equipment operator with the 983rd Engineer Battalion from Southfield, Michigan, near Detroit. By the end of her deployment, she would be working in a combat role, driving gun trucks through the city of Ramadi, arguably the most dangerous place in the world at that time.

McNeill's thick trendy glasses give her the appearance of being more comfortable among stacks of books in a university library than around military trucks and guns. That's not necessarily the case. She is very comfortable reading a book or getting the news or socializing on the Internet, but nothing in a book or on the Internet could provide her with the answers she sought. She is smart, confident, and willing to take risks; she's a fighter through and through. She went to the battlefield in search of the truth.

Her deployment started in January 2005 at Camp Speicher in Tikrit. From there, she would drive Humvees, or semis with hillbilly armor, fifty kilometers to Samarra to transport mail and equipment. These missions boosted her confidence. She also participated in base improvements, operated heavy construction equipment, and supported the construction of a helipad at a medical station.

At the end of February, while driving a loaded tractor trailer to Samarra, McNeill's leaders took the convoy down several wrong turns. Iraqi civilians along the road glared at the soldiers as their trucks snapped through low power lines. On her return trip to Speicher, McNeill's truck came under small-arms fire. When her passenger leaned forward to look around, she calmly reminded him that the armor protecting his head did no good if he leaned in front of it. At the first *ting* on her truck, McNeill turned on her right blinker to signal the direction of contact. No one was hurt.

Next, McNeill headed toward the Iranian border for a bridge-building mission. To get to her destination, she had to drive to Camp Caldwell near Kirkuk and then to Camp Cobra, a tiny base near the area in which they would be working. After a couple of wrong turns, the convoy got lost in an unfamiliar village. McNeill was in a twenty-ton dump truck. Another female in her platoon had a tractor trailer with equipment on the back. Because the roads weren't built for such big trucks and loads, they would have to climb on top of the cabs and equipment to lift the power lines over their loads as they moved through the old, narrow streets, villages, and crowded markets with no information about their surroundings.

From the front of the convoy, the two-way radio of another semi crackled, "These are high-tension wires, break."

That's no good.

"I don't know what the fuck we're going to do, over," a soldier ahead of them said into his two-way radio.

Keep moving.

The taut wires snapped as they pushed through. A little boy, following the convoy along the road, gathered his friends and pointed to McNeill. The convoy came to a stop. McNeill threw her last MRE to the little boys standing barefoot in sewage. They grinned, sang, and jumped up and down. An Iraqi man asked McNeill's driver if he would trade "that woman on the truck" for a white camel, some chickens, and a horse with good feet.

At the end of March, McNeill was selected to drive in what would be one of the largest rebuilding efforts of the time. For this mission, she was chosen to drive a tractor trailer and haul a five-yard loader. They convoyed from Camp Speicher and eventually met up with others, assisting in the move of the "Mother of All Generators" (MOAG). Vehicles lined up behind the generator, along with explosive ordnance disposal personnel, and various other forces. Some vehicles were placed in front. McNeill's truck was the first to travel through several security checkpoints.

For this mission, McNeill's job was to haul the loader on her semi and offload it to make the checkpoints wide enough for the generator to pass through. The majority of the convoy traveled at seven miles per hour since that was as fast as the generator could travel. At every checkpoint, security pulled out around McNeill's vehicle, and she and her truck commander dropped the trailer and took the chains off of the loader. She guided him down and stayed in the truck while the truck commander pushed the berms of dirt off the road at each checkpoint. Then she guided him back on the trailer, hooked the trailer back up, and moved to the next spot.

On the second night of the mission, the convoy for the generator stayed within a perimeter on the road set up by the infantry. McNeill wasn't sure what was going on, but once the sun went down, everyone put their headlights into blackout drive and moved into the newly created perimeter. The infantry covered them 360 degrees while everyone got fuel from the fuel trucks.

This was the first time McNeill ever used night-vision goggles to drive. Her truck commander got out of the truck and guided her to the fuel trucks. She followed his lead and cranked the wheel to the left. She had to negotiate a steep ditch that led to a flat area. She held her breath as she drove down the hill, keeping the truck as steady as possible. As she drove, the heavy loaded trailer popped as if it had come undone from the steep angle, but she edged forward until her trailer began to straighten out behind her, popping again as the vehicle leveled out. She breathed again as her truck commander led her to the right to pull into a narrow row beside the fuel tankers.

Her truck commander complimented her driving skills. He hadn't driven the semis too much, only the loader. The fueler stepped up to his window. "That takes skill," he said as he handed them a sheet to sign for the fuel. "I didn't think you guys would be able to make it."

"Yeah, that was pretty crazy," McNeill said. The fueler was taken aback by the female voice. McNeill loved introducing guys to the idea that women can do something as well as men. After more blackout driving, they were directed to their place alongside the road in a line of trucks. McNeill set up her sleeping bag on the trailer underneath the loader and hopped down to get an MRE. A random soldier came up and presented them with a bunch of milk boxes and cereal, so she ate that instead.

Since they weren't in a camp, just on the side of the road, they had to pull hour-long guard shifts around the equipment and the people sleeping nearby in case any insurgents were lurking in the area. Mortars landed nearby throughout the evening. The blasts echoed, so McNeill couldn't tell if they were outgoing or incoming. With each one, she rolled over, unable to sleep and chilled to the bone from the cool night air. It didn't help that she had grease from the equipment all over her sleeping bag. After some brief bouts of sleep, she woke before sunrise to get back on the road.

Soon they were on their way, creeping out of the area in blackout until the sun inched up over the horizon. On the last day, after clearing all of the required checkpoints, they waited at the last one for the rest of the elements to pass by and for their rear elements to link back up with them so they could return to Camp Speicher. McNeill had yet to see the MOAG, but as she hung out at the last checkpoint with the Iraqi soldiers, she watched the enormous convoy approach. The massive generator arrived on a truck flying a British flag. With the generator came air support and bullet-ridden black SUVs with men in khaki pants and black polo shirts—Blackwater security personnel, stopping to get out of their armed vehicles. It was the biggest convoy and mission in which McNeill would participate and included various coalition and American forces.

A year later, the Kirkuk power plant became fully operational and increased the national power grid by 325 megawatts. The completed power plant was a $178 million chunk of the $18 billion spent to rebuild.

Before long, McNeill learned she would be moving to a new area of operations in the Anbar Province. Throughout May and into June, she ran missions back and forth between Speicher and Camp Ramadi to move everything. For the first three trips back and forth, she drove her usual tractor trailer with various loads and equipment. During the last few trips, she was on a gun-truck crew, escorting the vehicles. McNeill didn't have a secure radio in her truck. The company had only a few, and they were spread throughout the Humvees in the convoy. Her crew used a walkie-talkie to communicate when they needed to stop to check their loads, have someone tell them they had lost a chain, or whatever the case may be.

One day after stopping on an entry road to a base, the convoy commander decided they weren't going to enter the base, but rather refuel the Humvees outside with fuel cans. Once refueled, the trucks began to turn the tractor-trailers around, one by one. A staff sergeant directed McNeill to turn around in a different area to speed up the process. It was difficult to do in the dark and with a load, but McNeill managed. She backed in and turned around. As she pulled out, another convoy drove by. She assumed her convoy would still be waiting on the other side of the road, but when the trucks passed, her convoy was nowhere in sight. Her truck commander grabbed the walkie-talkie, but all he got was static. McNeill knew where she was but didn't know where everybody else was. She started driving to catch up. She sped through eighteen gears in the hopes of getting in range of the two-way radio before anything happened to her and her passenger, Specialist Ryan Eggleston. She started to worry because the static wasn't clearing. A couple of minutes later, she saw headlights approaching, and someone came through on the radio. It was the gun truck that was supposed to be behind her. The convoy was waiting up ahead for them. It turned out the gun truck told the convoy commander that McNeill wasn't in line, but the convoy commander told him they were and that he had counted them before they headed out.

On Mother's Day, McNeill's battalion took its first casualty. A couple of troops were wounded, one of whom died. Sergeant Andrew Eckart had received the Purple Heart for wounds he got on his face from a roadside bomb that exploded in Samarra on his first deployment. In 2005, he volunteered to go on a mission into the same city. The bomb that killed him went off on the very same block in Samarra, just yards from the one that wounded him in 2003.

In early June, one of McNeill's convoys from Speicher came under attack. She was handing her gunner an energy drink when a bomb went off. As she turned to face the front, she saw a plume of smoke rise from the right side of the road. The gunner dropped the energy drink when he jumped, but that was about the extent of the damage. The gunner for the vehicle closest to the explosion got some burns on his face. They stopped after they got out of the "kill zone." The maintenance team changed a couple of their tires and did their best to fix a fluid leak. After taking almost an hour, they worried that insurgents would be waiting for them up the road.

Soon it was dark. As they traveled down the road, McNeill's driver almost ran over what looked like a sandbag in the road. The gunner was gawking at the debris through his night-vision goggles. McNeill yanked at his legs to tell him to get down.

"There were wires coming out of that thing!" he yelled.

She keyed the mic to warn the convoy, and as soon as she hit the button, an explosion behind her rocked her vehicle.

Orange light flashed through the ballistic windows of the Humvee and a putrid, powdery taste filled her mouth. Over the ringing in her ears, McNeill heard the crackling radio, "Badger 1, this is Badger 4. My gunner is down. SITREP [situation report] will follow."

McNeill never got the memo that *military* radios could trigger IEDs. The only threat they were warned about was walkie-talkies. Either way, the radio likely set off the explosion. When the gunner in the truck behind her regained consciousness, he was disoriented. He probably suffered a mild concussion.

To prevent major injuries in the attacks, the gunners rode at "nametape defilade," which meant their nametape never went above the level of the roof in the hatch. So their heads and shoulders would still be covered by the shields most vehicles had around the turret to protect from deadly shrapnel. If the IED had gone off just seconds before she yelled at her gunner for *not* being at nametape defilade, the damage would have been unbearable.

She knew it was a bomb on the road, and the gunner was ridding himself of a shield to get a closer look. He has kids at home!

After that incident, which could have been a near-death experience for the gunner, McNeill told him that you can't fight an IED—so just stay down the rest of the trip.

"Stay below nametape defilade when we're moving," she said. "The only time you stand up is when we're blocking traffic. I don't want to have to pull you out of that sling with shrapnel in your fuckin' face."

He sighed in his headset as she reminded him why they have rules. He kept reaching for new excuses before finally saying, "Okay! Just don't be mad at me, McNickel. I just don't want you to be mad at me."

"That was fucking close," she said.

He sighed. "I know."

"Do you realize what would have happened to you if that fucking thing blew up *next* to—"

"Yes!" he interrupted. "You're right, McNickel. You're right. I get it. I know. I just wanted to see if it was an IED! That thing had wires coming out of it."

They pulled into a base to assess the damage and determine if they could continue the mission. After they had their trucks refueled, they lined them up on the side of the road next to the fuel point. McNeill got out of the Humvee and headed to the truck behind her. Tar was splattered all over the Humvee, and there were shards of shrapnel everywhere, but the gunner was below nametape defilade, so he didn't get any on his face. The handle on his M249 mounted machine gun was broken, but that was the only visible damage. McNeill wasn't sure which soldier was in the turret during the explosion, but it turned out to be Specialist Josh Bloomfield, who would later become her boyfriend. She didn't know him that well, but she handed him a cigarette to calm his nerves.

After another delay to wait for explosive ordnance disposal to clear a suspected IED site along the route, they pulled in the base with another mission completed. It had been at least fifteen hours since they started their day. As they gained radio contact with headquarters, they were instructed to stop there for a debriefing. Once they were all crammed into a small room with the captain on duty, all the soldiers were scolded for not staying in contact with their command. Their command had received the message that a second IED had gone off, but all follow-up messages failed to arrive. The command knew only that there was a soldier down. After that, the commanders of the area of operations lost contact, and several hours passed before the convoy returned.

When she was out on the road, McNeill rarely worried about what might happen. She always dealt with things as they occurred. "There's no sense worrying about the things you don't know," she'd say. "You can't spend your time fretting away. You'll either live, or you'll die." If she died over there, then it was meant to be. As they headed back to base, McNeill thought about the letter she had started writing to her family. She felt like she should write the letter after her friend, Specialist Julie Blaker, handed her a sealed envelope addressed to her children in North Carolina. She pulled McNeill aside and, in her thick, southern drawl, explained that if she were to die, McNeill was to send it to her family. McNeill looked up to Blaker. She was in her thirties, so she was the oldest female in her platoon and was always watching out for the younger soldiers. McNeill had a hard time writing her own letter. She'd get to "Dear Mother" and couldn't think of anything to write. Or maybe there was just too much to write.

Soon after they had arrived in Iraq, Blaker went on a mission to Samarra and saw combat for the first time. When she got back to base, she recounted the events to McNeill, "And the bullets were just flyin' by us! And nobody's excited . . . everybody's just standin' around—*everybody*!" Blaker had given McNeill her letter after that.

Over time, McNeill started calling family and friends less. To talk on the phone meant to hear someone's voice and yearn to be home for just a day. She found that it was easier not to talk to anyone back home if she didn't have to, so she communicated mostly by e-mail. She didn't feel she had anything to say to them. Or what she did have to say to them she couldn't begin to describe. To give them an idea of her life in Iraq, she made movies and picture slideshows to send home. Her family would send her pictures of her nephew, telling her what new things he had discovered. With each letter, her heart broke a little more.

Gradually the number of letters from her friends dwindled. When she did receive letters, they told her of births, loves, jobs, friends, and family members. She was overcome with guilt for not being there. She would read each letter over and over, wishing that it were just another page longer or that she had one more memory to reflect on. But at the same time, it was as if nothing mattered except the soldiers next to her.

That summer, McNeill went on numerous convoys. One night while serving as the gunner in the second truck, her driver pulled off to block oncoming traffic while the rest of the convoy crossed the highway behind them onto a dirt road. As each vehicle approached, McNeill pointed a spotlight on it and flashed it to signal the drivers to stop. They usually stopped. Many a night while sitting in the gunner's turret, McNeill ran through her head what it would be like to pull the trigger of a machine gun with a human being she couldn't see in her sights. She knew what actions to take—after all, they read over the rules of engagement before every mission, even if it was the second mission of the day—but there were always those situations where the line blurred.

The night it blurred for her was late that summer, heading into September. The vehicle was several hundred meters away when it came into sight. "He doesn't look like he's stopping,"

McNeill said to her crew through the headset. She stood up and continued to flash the light as she had been trained to do.

"You flashing the spotlight?" her truck commander asked.

"Roger," she said.

When the car was about 100 yards away, she prepared to use an escalation of force. The vehicle was approaching quickly, and the semis she was helping protect in the convoy were steadily crossing the highway behind her. *I hope this guy stops.*

She quickly set down the bulky light, angling its beam on her weapon. Now the vehicle was about seventy-five yards out. She gripped the smooth black handles, lifted them up to lower the barrel of the eighty-four-pound .50-caliber M2 machine gun, and took aim at the side of the road in front of the car, updating the crew on her actions as they prepared to exit the vehicle and fire if needed. She placed her thumb on the butterfly trigger and prepared to fire a warning shot after showing her intent. *I would stop if I saw a Ma Deuce pointed in my direction*, she thought as she leaned forward to look through the sight. The car slammed on its brakes and began to reverse as the last gun truck in the convoy passed behind them.

One night in August, McNeill was driving on the outskirts of Ramadi to Camp Corregidor to drop off equipment and people. She was driving a gun truck with a staff sergeant truck commander and a sergeant behind the .50-cal. It was the first time she'd been in a gun truck with either of them. The long route involved driving the semis and Humvees in blackout drive with night-vision goggles as fast as possible for about forty-five minutes on the last part of the route into East Ramadi. Often on this route, they would find IEDs and have to stop and watch their perimeter while waiting hours for explosive ordnance disposal teams to remove the bombs. It was a difficult route, usually limited to the most experienced operators.

Air Force Tech Sergeant Michelle Barefield and her EOD team were blown up in this Joint EOD Response Vehicle (JERV) in Iraq.

Barefield (right) and Staff Sergeant Heidi Leon in front of the Big House that they lived in and worked from at Baghdad International Airport.

A Tactical Movement Team from Bravo Company, 983rd Engineer Battalion (Combat Heavy).

Army Brigadier General Jody Tymeson presents Army Master Sergeant CJ Robison of the 185th Support Battalion (National Guard) with a general's coin and a National Guard coin during the battalion's welcome-home celebration. Robison is joined by her daughter, Amber; son, Ben; mom, Mary; and sister, Sandra Faluri.

Robison with her son and daughter.

Navy Lieutenant Terrell Byrd and Navy Commander Lenora Langlais. Byrd, a chaplain, saved Langlais's life by applying pressure to a neck wound she received on April 7, 2006.

Langlais with her children, from left: Christian, Daniel, Danielle, and Kamielle.

Army Sergeant Jeanna Marrano serves with the Army National Guard 105th Military Police Company. She's shown here on a border mission in Arizona.

Army Sergeants Jeanna Marrano and Amanda Wheeler.

Marine Lance Corporal Shannon Weber poses in front of her vehicle, *Lefty #3*, after returning from an IED call.

Marine Captains Ky
Hunter and Billy Birzell.
Hunter is a Cobra pilot.

Army Sergeant
Michelle Wilmot.

Wilmot in a crashed
Russian helicopter in
Habbaniyah.

Elaine Snavely and Chaplain Kay Reeb celebrate Thanksgiving dinner in Al Asad Airbase in Iraq.

Snavely provides medical coverage during a training exercise at a remote location outside Yuma, Arizona.

Army Captain Sarah Rykowski with her horse, Chappel.

General David Petraeus, commander of the Multi-National Force in Iraq, awards the Purple Heart to Rykowski.

Rykowski is shown here after receiving the Purple Heart. The vehicle she was driving in was blown up by an IED.

Army Specialist Ashley Pullen was with the 617th Military Police Company.

Pullen atop a vehicle in Iraq.

Marine Sergeant Major
Irene O'Neal (second
from right) with some of
her Marines.

O'Neal (far right), her
husband (Master
Gunnery Sergeant
Anthony O'Neal), and
Gunnery Sergeant Anita
Colunga (Ret.) at the
2007 Marine Corps Ball.

Army Sergeant Lisa
Spencer of the 403rd
Transportation Company.

Army Specialist Elainena Filion provides perimeter security around her M915A4 truck outside of Baghdad.

Army Specialist Danielle Hinson, Specialist Elainena Filion, and Private First Class Jessi Allen take a break at Camp Arifjan, Kuwait.

Army Specialist Elainena Filion with her husband, Brian, and son, Brian Jr.

Laura Buckingham.

Army Master Sergeant
Ronda Warrick and
Sara Warrick.

West Point graduate
and Army Captain
Lauren Glaze.

Naval Academy graduate and Marine Captain Elizabeth Okoreeh-Baah, the first female to pilot the Osprey in combat.

1st Lt. Tania Moreno with Iraqi children.

Marine Captain Angela Nelson doing Iraqi weapons familiarization with Regimental Combat Team 2 at Al Asad Airbase, Iraq, prior to heading out on Lioness duty.

Air Force Master Sergeant Denise Malloy served in Afghanistan at Balad Airbase in Iraq and at Camp Victory, Baghdad, where this photo was taken.

Technical Sergeant Lisa Russey covers enlistment options with a potential airman in her Air Force recruiting office in Charleston, South Carolina.

Army Sergeant Heather Rudolph (center) served at Forward Operating Base Speicher (Tikrit, Mosul, Balad).

A young female Marine.
KATARIINA FAGERING

They were wearing old night-vision goggles that didn't stay on well while driving. To solve this problem, they were told that their truck commander would wear the night-vision goggles and direct the driver. What tripped them up that night was razor wire set up in the road. As they drove through the area, they had to weave around it, but most of them knew that it was there from previous trips. The challenge was being able to see the wire with no lights and old night-vision goggles. Sergeant Mike Cepress was driving a gun truck near the front of the convoy with the convoy commander. Cepress asked him to radio back to the other vehicles that there was wire in the road.

"They'll see it," he said, complacently. He was the same convoy commander who left McNeill's semi and said he had accounted for them.

A moment later, the Humvee in front of McNeill's came to a stop. The Humvee that stopped didn't have a radio or a gunner, so no one was sure what happened. McNeill's truck commander radioed up to the convoy commander to halt the convoy, yet the lead element continued to move, disregarding the message. With about a kilometer separating the convoy, they finally stopped, leaving a large gap in the convoy. Many of the soldiers on the convoy that night were green, except for a few, like McNeill, who were providing security. The higher-ups had wanted to spread the duties of convoys to more than just the experienced few. McNeill thought this would have been fine if they had an experienced soldier in each vehicle.

McNeill took off her headset, grabbed her M16, and ran up to the Humvee to see why they had stopped so she could relay the message to the convoy commander and maintenance if needed. Neither soldier in the Humvee had much experience on convoys, especially not driving in blackout. There was razor wire wrapped tightly around the axle and tire. The wire would have to be cut off. McNeill ran back to tell her truck commander to radio it up, and maintenance pulled forward to try to cut it off. Meanwhile, the convoy commander became impatient and left Cepress and his crew to walk back—without a weapon or radio—to the stopped vehicle.

An unfamiliar soldier approached McNeill's truck, and she opened the door. It was a soldier from the infantry unit positioned on the road who saw that the supply convoy stopped and wanted to know what happened. She pointed to the Humvee that got tangled up in the wire and briefly explained. Meanwhile, the water pump went out in one of the semis, and they had to get it hooked up to a wrecker. "It could take awhile," she said. The tractor trailer was fully loaded, so the wrecker driver would be towing a loaded semi in blackout to Camp Corregidor.

When she spoke, she could tell by the soldier's expression that he was surprised to be talking to a female. It was a typical response from someone who worked in a male-segregated unit.

"No shit," he said. "You're a female."

"Yeah, no shit," she said as she stepped out of the vehicle to hear better. "So where do we need to cover?"

An infantry Bradley fighting vehicle creaked up along the side of the road behind him. He gestured where there were men on the ground patrolling. A mosque began blaring a message over the loudspeakers.

"This isn't a good place for you guys to be for too long," he said. "But we'll have you covered 360 in a few minutes."

"We'll do what we can," McNeill said. "Thanks."

She told her truck commander what the tanker said, and he told her that the convoy commander wasn't on the radio and disregarded what she said. He anxiously ordered McNeill to dismount and provide security, without night-vision goggles. She reminded him of the foot patrols in the direction he pointed. He repeated his instructions as she exchanged looks with the gunner. Then he went to the broken-down vehicle and had the female driver of the vehicle get in the prone position. McNeill stood on the side of the truck with her weapon resting on the hood. Neither one of them could even see what they were pointing their guns at. They were staring into darkness. There were houses in front of them, but there were no lights on, and they were just far enough away that the soldiers couldn't see anything but the skyline. To those with experience on this route, being outside the armored vehicle to scan a sector with friendlies in it and without night-vision goggles seemed absurd.

After about an hour, they mounted their vehicles and continued on. McNeill was convinced they needed to get and keep a permanent security team and make sure only experienced drivers traveled the most dangerous routes, even if it meant using the same group of soldiers. She saw no excuse for leaders not getting updated about what to do and what not do at a halt on this route. After she and others brought this up to their command, and after several incidents reinforced their perspective, a few changes were made.

Eventually, about twenty-five soldiers, including McNeill, were assigned permanent convoy security. They were taken from their various platoons and split up, three to a truck, into teams chosen based on the cohesion of each small group that had been used so far; an experienced sergeant first class was placed in charge of the designated Tactical Movement Team (TMT). After completing most convoys as the front vehicle with soldiers from McNeill's platoon, Sergeant Doug McBrierty requested her as a driver for his truck. She was eventually assigned to drive and gun for his team with Bloomfield. McNeill and McBrierty were both certified combat lifesavers and had instructed first-aid training in Camp Atterbury. They were designated as the Aid and Litter Team and carried the medic in their vehicle, usually Specialist Mike Jones. From that point forward, each day and mission blended together. McNeill no longer cared about the small things, such as the day of the week or how bad her hair looked after she let the guys cut it.

In September 2005, when routines began falling into place, McNeill's TMT began formal training under the Marines in Ramadi to take over much-needed convoy security missions in the city on one of the most hostile supply routes in the world. With the increased training, McNeill would be able to drive just fifteen minutes through Ramadi, rather than the twelve-hour moonlight drive around the city. The shorter route was referred to as "The Thunder Run" by some and "The Gauntlet" by others. The primary purpose of the missions was to bring supplies and personnel to East Ramadi, where there were about twenty-five soldiers from construction platoons in her company working on improvements for the Iraqi security forces in the area. Thunder Runs also involved escorting government officials, soldiers, Navy Seabees, supplies, dirt, mail, and equipment along the dangerous route.

In the Marine Corps, a machine gunner is an infantry specialty for crew-served machine guns, and it is not open to females. Yet here they were, teaching McNeill and two other women how to do it all. To drive a Thunder Run, McNeill needed to be able to operate a variety of weapons. There was no question that she would come under fire, so she had to know how to fire whatever weapon was available. Before she deployed to Iraq, McNeill went through brief combat training, which included hands-on training with the M16. To prepare for the Thunder Runs, she became well acquainted with the M249 squad automatic weapon, M60 machine gun, M2 (.50 cal) machine gun, Mk 19 grenade launch, and the AT4 antitank weapon. She would also receive more in-depth training on how to react when they were ambushed and how to call in a medevac. She learned all this in the sweltering afternoon heat at Camp Ramadi.

After learning everything and being individually tested, the convoys began to take the short route through the city on a regular basis during the day. McNeill was reminded of the destruction that had taken place within the city. Bullet holes had marked nearly every inch of the buildings along the way; others had collapsed, and many of them had informants and snipers—both enemy and friendly—scattered among their crumbling rooftops. When they were attacked, they couldn't stop and look for a triggerman. They were told to keep driving. It seemed strange to McNeill to duck and run, but they had always been told to do just that.

On September 22, McNeill ventured out for her first Thunder Run with the cavalry unit that had been doing operations in the area. After a thorough briefing from the lieutenant, they headed into the Gauntlet. The mission went smoothly from Camp Ramadi to Corregidor and onto Combat Outpost, the Law College, and Camp Tiger. Despite all the warnings about the dangers and a virtual guarantee of an attack, nothing happened that day. This was good since they were trying to familiarize themselves with the routes and potential obstacles.

Their last mission with the cavalry was on September 25. The threat level was high as usual, but they were ready to go. On the way to Camp Corregidor, McNeill saw what looked like pieces of track from a tank stacked like a Jenga tower with various gas cans and other items sitting on the pieces jutting from the stack. After reporting it, they were told that it was nothing to worry about. Apparently, it had always been there. On the way back to Camp Ramadi, though, they experienced their first Gauntlet attack. McNeill was near the middle of the convoy when the trucks all came to a stop. Stopping on this road was never a good option. It meant there was trouble up front. They started moving again and situations were being reported over the phone. Young kids on the side of the road were giving McNeill's truck the thumbs down as they passed, and others pointed in the direction they were heading. As they moved farther up the road, local teenagers had bottles with gasoline and rags that they ignited and threw at the trucks. Another female in the convoy reported that Molotov cocktails were being thrown at the truck she commanded. While they aimed for the turret, the bottles shattered on the side of her armored Humvee traveling ahead of McNeill. As soon as they threw the bombs, the kids took off into the alleys. Farther up the road, the stack of tank tracks and fuel jugs exploded. As she felt the concussion, McNeill saw a thick plume of black smoke rise between buildings up ahead of the long convoy. The vehicles came to a stop. The radio chirped with updates.

When they started moving, they hauled ass. McNeill drove through the smoky, blackened area where the IED had exploded. Shrapnel and concrete were scattered around the smoldering black hole in the middle of the road, the only remnants of the IED. After making it safely back onto base, they saw that one of the bigger trucks had a flat tire and some shrapnel. A large piece of shrapnel had burst completely through the ballistic glass windshield in one of the Humvees. The shrapnel hit the driver's helmet, but failed to injure him severely.

McNeill's TMT was cleared to provide security without escorts through the city. As the attacks became more frequent, McNeill gained a strong spiritual grounding, even though she considers herself an agnostic. When she prayed, she held on to a small star charm with a saint in it that her godmother gave her before she left. She hoped for protection and guidance. She read from the Bible and from the Koran. She engaged in conversations with people of many religions and carried a set of prayer beads given to her by a Pakistani truck driver over tea while waiting to leave on a convoy. She carried several lucky relics with her.

One morning in early October, the deafening scream of her alarm clock broke the silence, and McNeill reluctantly woke up after four hours of sleep. It was three in the morning. Her bed almost felt comfortable now that she had to get out of it. She put her hair up into a bun and grabbed a bottle of water to brush her teeth. Outside, she poured the water over her toothbrush, cringing once she brushed her teeth. She grabbed lemonade instead of water. It would have to do, because she still wanted to clean her weapons, which were finicky and had to be cleaned often. Still in the dark, she fumbled with the laces to her boots and felt under her bed for her M16 and the M60 for her truck. Cutting through the humming of the generator and air conditioners, area mosques began echoing a call to prayer on megaphones throughout Ramadi.

By now, McNeill had been overseas for about nine months, and units in the area were taking steady casualties. TMT was doing as many as three Thunder Runs a week in addition to continuing night missions to other bases. Despite the risks they took when they cleared for departure, McNeill continued to be focused and calm, feeling nearly invincible despite the war going on around her. Perhaps that was what gave her the ability to be one of the few drivers able to negotiate the route.

Prior to departure, they received an intelligence briefing. The route was red. Since the high risk for an attack was nothing new, they prepared to depart. McNeill drove in the second gun truck; on the radio, her team was "Badger 6." Jones, the medic who usually rode in her truck, wasn't on the convoy. Two other medics were sent in his place. It was the first mission outside the wire for the medic who rode with them, and the Aid and Litter Team would be the first to respond if they took any casualties. Following the convoy briefing, everyone, religious or not, bowed their heads while the chaplain led them in prayer. He was a captain, soft-spoken and genuine. Every time they prepared to leave the home base, he met them.

The rocks in the lot clambered beneath the soldiers' boots as they dashed to their vehicles to begin the mission. McNeill took her place in the olive-drab driver's seat of a gun truck and turned the switch to start the engine. Once everyone was in the truck, she fell into position in the line of armored semis and dump trucks preparing to leave.

Before the soldiers headed out on Thunder Runs, they cranked up the music. One of their favorite songs to jam to was "Out of My Way" by Seether: *Out of my way! / Out of my . . . way!*

As they drove on the gravel road leading to the exit gate, McNeill watched the sun break the horizon. She cursed it for taking away the camouflage of a dark, moonless night. The tank blocking the exit creaked and scraped backwards after clearing the convoy to go outside the wire. After passing over the murky Euphrates River, the westernmost of the two great rivers that define Mesopotamia, they began their descent into the city. Throughout the prior week, McNeill remembers hearing about eight soldiers and Marines being killed in Ramadi.

Everyone concentrated on their surroundings. As they crawled through the usually bustling marketplace, the sidewalks were empty. They approached the Great Mosque and crossed over the median by a water tower when an explosion erupted near a truck in front of her. The familiar blast of an IED rang in her ears. Fortunately, no one was hurt, so they resumed driving.

After they arrived in Camp Corregidor, the gun trucks moved away from the convoy to an area behind a hollowed-out cement and brick building referred to as "Full Metal Jacket" by those who call it home. They waited until the supplies were unloaded from the semis. McNeill and her team would be there until they got clearance from higher-ups for their return trip. It was possible they would have to stay there for the night and sleep outside by their trucks because space was limited in Full Metal Jacket. McNeill walked to the chow hall with her crew to eat breakfast and calm her early-morning adrenaline rush. She always chose the omelets along with a couple of Red Bull energy drinks.

Following breakfast, McNeill gathered with other soldiers inside Full Metal Jacket to escape the heat and hang out for a while. She joined a conversation soldiers were having about whether they thought they'd be able to leave that day or have to spend the night. Moments later, a sentence was cut short by the impact of rockets that shook the building's cement walls.

Two more rockets slammed outside Full Metal Jacket. Pieces of shrapnel and rocks cracked against the stone walls. McNeill ran down the open stairwell to go outside. The last time she was outside, most of the soldiers were in or around the trucks. As her eyes adjusted to the glaring sunlight, soldiers were moving frantically around the vehicles, and the only sound she could distinguish above the piercing warning siren was a medic screaming that three soldiers had been wounded. Bloomfield ran to their truck to move it out of the area. McNeill saw two gaping holes in the ground smoldering from the rockets and smoke lingering in the sky. The antifreeze smelled sweet as it poured from one of the trucks into the blackened sand, which was littered with fragments of shredded tires.

McNeill moved toward one of their gunners, Specialist Trevor Baize, lying in the sand beside a truck. Bright red blood was caked on his thigh, and shrapnel wounds peppered the entire right side of his body. The more experienced medic was already working to stop the bleeding. McNeill looked for other wounds and assisted the medic by telling the wounded soldier not to worry.

As the medic got up to check on their convoy commander, who was also wounded, McNeill heard the faint shrill scream of more incoming rockets. She was sweating profusely, but a chill washed over her. She imagined the wounded soldiers being hit with more shrapnel. As he took cover, the medic screamed, "Incoming!" McNeill could hardly hear over the ringing in her ears.

Events seemed to move in slow motion as the rounds cut through the smoke hanging just above them. McNeill struggled to move her body to cover the gunner's head and to determine the trajectory of the shrapnel. The gunner had gone into shock. To McNeill, those few seconds felt like they would never pass.

The other inexperienced and frantic medic stepped on her back as he jumped into the open door of the Humvee beside McNeill. She looked back as the armored door slammed shut with the medic safely inside. McNeill braced herself as more rockets landed on the other side of Full Metal Jacket. The other medic returned with the corpsman who had arrived to help move Baize into the field ambulance. Their convoy commander was already in the ambulance.

McNeill's training was automatic. She jumped into the truck, and as Bloomfield drove toward the gate, McNeill pushed open the hatch and mounted the M60 into the turret. They were escorting the ambulance and medics to the medevac site across the street where a chopper would pick up the wounded and transport them to a hospital in Baghdad. As they blew through the gate, McNeill flipped open the feed tray cover to lock and load a belt of ammunition. The powder tasted like salt as it blew into her face. Sweat rolled into her eyes from the 140-degree heat.

"Stay down," Bloomfield shouted, frantically reminding McNeill that there could be snipers around. He hated it when she was in the turret in this area.

"I know where we are," she said as she spun the turret to her rear.

They were rounding the barricades and heading toward the landing zone when they saw an Iraqi National Guardsman shouting and waving them over to his position. The front end of a van had smashed into one of the cement barricades when a rocket exploded nearby. An Iraqi civilian was trapped inside the van. The driver's door wouldn't budge despite the pulls of the soldiers. McBrierty jumped out to attach the tow strap from their truck to the door. Bloomfield hit the gas once and the strap yanked the door off. Inside the van, the civilian struggled for his life. The soldiers put him on a stretcher, but he died moments later.

On the short drive back to Corregidor, a somber silence drowned out everything except for the roaring diesel engine. The civilian was lying on the stretcher inside the field ambulance. He wouldn't see his family again, and to his family right now, he was still alive. How long would it be before they found out what McNeill already knew?

At Corregidor, McNeill learned that several others had minor shrapnel wounds, and three vehicles were disabled. With the help of soldiers at Camp Outpost, ballistic glass and tires were acquired within two hours, and the maintenance team had two of the Humvees running. With the third vehicle loaded on a trailer, they were prepared to complete the mission with two fewer soldiers.

The next morning, McNeill awoke with her body aching from the previous day's adrenaline. It was hard to get up again and move. While she relaxed and unwound for the day, heavy violence was plaguing the Anbar Province. Over the next week, six soldiers in the 3rd Infantry Division were killed in Ramadi when IEDs destroyed two Bradley fighting vehicles. Moments after driving by the Government Center on a Thunder Run on October 18, McNeill heard over the radio that armed gunmen had just opened fire on the building. The deputy governor had been assassinated less than two blocks away from them. On Halloween, word arrived that another soldier who had been wounded in the same attack had died in the States. Both soldiers were engaged to female soldiers in the same unit and would carry on with their duties despite such a tremendous loss.

The next morning, McNeill and her team lined up for yet another Thunder Run. The threat level was high, and there was talk that they might leave before the road was "swept" for IEDs. They were also hearing that there were a few IEDs daisy-chained together at one point on the route, so when they reached that location, they were to drive as far to the opposite side as possible. The convoy commander called up to headquarters to make sure their convoy was still cleared to go. The decision makers were taking too long. The soldiers in McNeill's truck worried the sun would come up before they got out of the gate.

Because there was so much back-and-forth between the convoy commander and headquarters, a Buffalo mine-protected vehicle had time to drive out in advance of the convoy to sweep the road. While the soldiers waited in a staging area near the gate to leave, the Buffalo turned onto the main route and was hit with a vehicle-borne IED—a suicide bomber. The explosion ripped the Buffalo in half. After waiting around for three hours, to the soldiers' relief and frustration, the mission was postponed until the next day. Ninety-six service members were killed in Iraq in October.

The next day they headed out, hoping that with the end of Ramadan would come an end to the elevated level of attacks. No such luck. One of the Humvees hit an IED on the way to Corregidor. It seemed that no one had been wounded beyond the usual concussion, but the shrapnel left spiderwebs in the ballistic glass windshield of the wrecker, which had been added to the hillbilly-armed truck only days before. Rockets were fired into the base around lunchtime. They stayed inside Full Metal Jacket until the attack was over. The rockets had become a routine part of their days. As soon as the soldiers were able, they headed back through the Gauntlet toward Camp Ramadi. As they rounded a corner, their truck started taking AK-47 fire. To McNeill's left was an Iraqi man standing with his children shielding him at his feet. The man was firing his AK-47 at McNeill's truck. She felt safe behind the armor. As they rolled by, everyone was anxiously yelling instructions to the gunner. He took aim at the man but didn't get clearance to shoot. There were too many people around.

Around this time, soldiers in McNeill's unit were informed of the opportunity to extend their tours and stay at Camp Ramadi. This was something McNeill was interested in doing. She knew that it would take nine months before she could pick up where she left off in college. In the meantime, why not get a full two years of active duty time out of the way so it wouldn't interrupt her education? Plus, she was familiar with operations and was one of the few left in her group who still wanted to go outside the wire on missions.

After some confusion, she was denied the extension. Her platoon sergeant told her that he thought she should go home. "You've been on a lot of missions, McNeill," he said. "You've taken a lot of risks, and it might not be a good idea to keep testing your luck." She didn't stop inquiring until her first sergeant told her there were no slots available for females to extend.

With McNeill's time to leave rapidly approaching, she and her team trained their replacements while continuing missions. By the beginning of December, Ramadi was entering the "eye of the storm." On her last few Thunder Runs, cement barricades were placed all over the city, and strict curfews were put in place. There was hardly a soul on the streets during those last few missions, and no civilian traffic was allowed on the Thunder Run route. The United States was preparing an offensive to dismantle the stronghold of Ramadi to bring about a sense of control. On

December 1, ten Marines were killed in a single IED attack in Fallujah, and another soldier died in Ramadi. People were suffering. Children were begging. McNeill felt death all around her. She always felt victory in Ramadi was without definition and always just out of their reach. Without more troops in the city, the situation would only deteriorate.

Also coming to an end was McNeill's "study abroad program" on the battlefield. She went to Iraq to help rebuild a struggling nation and found a beautiful country with strong and hopeful people in a state of total chaos and fear. She was uncertain of her place but was determined to have a positive impact. Every person in the war was an enemy to someone, but she could never tell who or why they were fighting when she faced them. The resistance fighters believed the Americans were trying to destroy the Arab and Muslim identity by occupying their country without improving living conditions after the fall of Saddam. Some were citizens of Iraq; others were foreign fighters and Al Qaeda in Iraq, a group which wasn't active before the U.S. invasion of Iraq. The members of Iraq's Army under Saddam fought Americans because of Paul Bremer's decision to disband their army without pay as part of the flawed debaathification effort even as they wished to fight for George W. Bush and help rebuild. And the Americans fought whoever fought them. All of these aspects made understanding the identity of McNeill's friends and enemies more difficult.

McNeill was given hope when she met Kurdish soldiers happy to be rid of Saddam and glad to be free; however, they admitted that their quality of life was better under his rule and said they remained optimistic that it would soon change. She was given hope when Iraqis showed enthusiasm and pride in voting. Early in her deployment, she felt she had made a contribution to the rebuilding efforts when she participated in a convoy to move the Mother of All Generators that eventually increased the amount of electricity produced.

But she felt more despair than hope for the service members and civilians involved in Iraq. Contractors like KBR provided the soldiers of Camp Ramadi and other bases in Iraq with shower water that was not disinfected with chlorine or properly filtered; it was concentrated waste stream. Providing water that was not disinfected was not only against military regulations on water for bathing, but it would require a permit to dump the water which McNeill and other soldiers showered in. They would have had cleaner water if they had bathed in the Euphrates River, even after the city dumped its sewage less than a mile away. She wonders what exactly the contractors spent the money on since it wasn't used on water purification or chlorine. She didn't learn about the exposure until she returned home and saw the problem exposed in the film *Iraq for Sale: War Profiteers*. In March 2008, the Army's Inspector General released a report confirming the exposure to contaminated water, calling it a "near miss" that could have resulted in "mass sickness or death."

By supplying the soldiers with water that was not disinfected and filtered, the contractors carelessly exposed troops from the moment they took over operations on Camp Ramadi and other bases across Iraq to E. coli, typhoid fever, and hepatitis. The troops showered in that water every day they were there. Some people brushed their teeth with the contaminated water. Both the military and KBR previously claimed that nothing serious had occurred, but McNeill and those she served with had grown used to an upset stomach and the smell of sulfur in the showers.

McNeill also contemplated the effectiveness of the armor that tax dollars were buying—or *not* buying. She carried a new M16 that was missing a part, so it wasn't a reliable weapon. She carried a gas mask with a "training" canister rather than the type that would actually work in an attack.

Many of her missions to East Ramadi involved supplying the base with improvements for the Iraqi Security Forces. When sol-

diers in her company completed the renovations of almost sixty
rooms in a two-floor barracks facility near Corregidor, it was
turned over to the Iraqi Security Forces, who chose to defecate in
every single room without even glancing at the fully functional
western-style bathrooms that had been installed. They also looted
the air conditioners and stripped other electrical work the elec-
tricians had installed. After all these things sunk in and she discovered the fruit of the soldiers' labor in East Ramadi, McNeill
was left wondering if it was worth the risks they endured to complete the upgrades? And was it worth the nightmares, post-traumatic stress disorder, and other wounds from which many she
served beside now suffer? While she believes the soldiers greatly
improved the quality of life and force protection at American and
Iraqi camps, she knows the key element causing the chaos was not
having enough soldiers on the ground in Ramadi to maintain stability.

The mission to remodel the barracks was a small part of a
push for Iraqi forces to take more responsibility so that coalition
forces could draw down the number of troops in Iraq. To
McNeill, however, it seemed inefficient and costly to delay the
large surge of troops in Iraq necessary to regain control and perform stability operations. Iraqi security forces were operating in
the area with little or no body armor, driving small, unarmored
pickup trucks and troop carriers. McNeill believes that the result
of inadequate protection in some of the most unstable areas of
the country contributed to the deaths of more than 3,500 international security forces in the year she was in Iraq, almost enough
to man a brigade.

As the December offensive in Ramadi began and McNeill got
ready to head home, her thoughts shifted from the battlefield to
Wisconsin. She was overcome with a gut-wrenching feeling that
life had gone on without her. She thought about all the people

back home who had known everything about her only a year before. Suddenly, she felt they knew nothing about her. She wished they could understand her without words as they once did. McNeill was bothered by the idea that some people would not be moved by her experiences. Complacency kills. The reality of war is so different from what American civilians experience when they turn on their television or open a newspaper. She worried they wouldn't understand the complexity of the stories of daily tragedies and the gravity of those experiences when those soldiers return home.

When McNeill returned from Iraq as a twenty-one-year-old female veteran, she got quite an education on the aftermath of war. Like so many veterans, she came back with her share of physical and emotional challenges. But she was fortunate because between her inner strength and the support of family and friends, she was able to work through her challenges without significant disruption to her readjustment. She was resilient. The same couldn't be said for her boyfriend, Bloomfield. The demons he faced overwhelmed him and were too much for him to deal with on his own. McNeill was about to embark on another stage of war—the consequences—as she fought to take care of herself, Bloomfield, and their relationship. She would learn that the transition home can be just as deadly and emotionally intense as war itself.

McNeill spent just over a week at Camp Atterbury in Edinburgh, Indiana, before seeing her family in Wisconsin for Christmas. Bloomfield returned to his home state of Ohio. McNeill was feeling good. It was the holiday season, and she was happy to be back around family and friends. The new year was fast approaching. However, she missed Bloomfield, who was now a six-hour drive away. Granted, it was a short drive compared with some of their convoys in Iraq, but it was a long distance for two people who were used to seeing each other every day on the battlefield, often multiple times a day.

Back in Ohio, Bloomfield wasn't coping well. He felt more comfortable and stable when he visited McNeill in Wisconsin than he did when he was home. He spent time with his friends and family but would get anxious when he was in crowds. When he went to bars with his friends, he'd get paranoid. Many nights, he would return home to sit in his bedroom, alone, drinking tequila to help him fall asleep. When McNeill asked him a direct question over the phone—like "What are you doing tonight?"—he'd become evasive. He didn't want her to know that he was drinking because he thought she would get mad at him.

Late the night before Christmas Eve, Bloomfield was drinking at a friend's house and got a DUI after leaving the party to move his car across the street so it wouldn't get towed. He didn't plan on drinking so much. He wasn't even twenty-one yet. He doesn't remember moving the car; he blacked out. He only remembers that he had been at the police station and got a ticket for drunk driving. The police dropped him off at his car with his keys, and he slept in a friend's car until morning. Not only did he have to serve time in jail and attend classes, but he also lost his driver's license. Now he would have to take a bus or train to see McNeill.

Bloomfield wasn't the only soldier-friend of McNeill's who was struggling. As soon as the newness of being home faded, many of those McNeill fought beside began to fall apart. Some got divorced, lost their jobs, or lost interest in their jobs. Some were recovering from physical wounds, and many were trying to cope with post-traumatic stress disorder. She'd spend evenings talking to soldiers who were there with her and sometimes their girl-friends, and by the end of the night, the conversation would drift to nightmares or feeling anxious in crowds. But McNeill couldn't worry about everyone else.

Within the first month of returning, McNeill began coughing
and having difficulty breathing, which she had previously attributed to the desert sand. She was constantly coughing to clean out
her lungs. She went to urgent care at the University of Wisconsin
hospital and was eventually diagnosed with asthma.

A couple of months later, she started going to William S. Mid-
dleton VA hospital to treat her asthma and other symptoms. In
Iraq, she had noticed she was losing her peripheral vision but had
attributed it to lack of sleep and other environmental factors. She
became concerned when she got home and it didn't improve.
She had hearing loss and constant ringing in her ears, a condition known as tinnitus. Sometimes, she felt lightheaded and dizzy
and got headaches. She lost almost twenty pounds during her
first few months home. Every night, the insomnia that had begun
in Iraq kept her up. Her VA doctor attributed most of her physical ailments to stress—not the stress of combat, but of the civilian
life she was enjoying outside of her health issues. She submitted a
disability claim with the VA, and months later, when she called to
check the status of her claim, the VA could find no record of it.
With the help of Disabled American Veterans, she completed
another claim.

In the meantime, Bloomfield's drinking had increased.
McNeill didn't know this since they were living in different states,
nor did she realize how clumsy, off balance, and anxious he had
become. She only knew that he was reckless, unlike his usual self.
In February 2006, she received a frantic phone call from Bloomfield while she was on the East Coast visiting a friend. He was in
the bathroom of a friend's house but told her he was in the emergency room. McNeill could only understand that he had broken
his leg; otherwise, he was too upset to be understood, and he
hung up the phone. Her heart sank. *This is the part of me my friends
will never understand.*

After learning that Bloomfield jumped out of his friend's car that was moving forty-five miles per hour and only vaguely remembered the events of the night before, McNeill encouraged him to see a counselor at the VA hospital in Toledo, Ohio. He never did. McNeill thinks he was too overwhelmed to figure out the VA process and do the paperwork. He went to a civilian doctor once or twice, then stopped going because he didn't think there was anything they could do. He felt completely alone. He tried to cope on his own. He lied to McNeill about small things and became uncharacteristically defensive.

In July, Bloomfield moved in with McNeill and a couple of her friends. She was happy to have him around. Like McNeill, Bloomfield was active and energetic. He enjoyed getting out and doing things, although some days his post-traumatic stress disorder made it hard for him to be interested in doing much of anything. While he could no longer do some things that he used to do, such as ride his motorcycle and skateboard, because of problems he was having with his balance and coordination, in time he was able to find other things to replace them.

Bloomfield was funny and outgoing and got along well with McNeill's family and friends. They were opposites in many ways but had common interests in music, history, and the Army. "Josh was the kid who always wanted to be a soldier when he grew up," McNeill said.

McNeill became more aware of Bloomfield's post-traumatic stress disorder when he moved in with her. As they'd prepare to go out with friends, he'd get increasingly anxious and paranoid, as if they were getting ready for their next mission. They started arguing, which was uncharacteristic for them but difficult to avoid. Usually, after everything was said and done, McNeill was confused by the arguments. They were never about anything major, but

Bloomfield would get angry and frustrated easily, and she grew more concerned.

Bloomfield was having trouble getting a job and wanted to start counseling so that he could feel better about working again or attending college. Later that summer, he went to the VA in Madison and was told he couldn't be seen for two months. The VA system as a whole wasn't prepared to deal with the veterans when they came home. There was a waitlist for services that were supposed to be "readily available" to them. An article by Rick Rogers of the *San Diego Union-Tribune* stated that the Department of Veterans Affairs expected to handle 2,900 cases of post-traumatic stress disorder in 2006. As of June, it had already seen more than 34,000. Bloomfield walked out of his initial VA appointment with a prescription for Lithium and medication for other symptoms the doctor associated with bipolar disorder and depression.

The idea was that Lithium would help control Bloomfield's mood swings, but his growing symptoms of post-traumatic stress disorder and traumatic brain injury were overlooked. After a few weeks on medication, Bloomfield's health continued to decline. No one at the VA knew this because he didn't show up for his appointments, and no one from the VA called to check on him. Bloomfield told McNeill the medication was "messing him up." He couldn't remember anything and was slurring his speech.

As planned, McNeill re-enrolled in Madison Area Technical College in the fall while juggling her and Bloomfield's medical appointments. She also returned to the 826th Ordnance Company and was promoted to sergeant. Bloomfield enrolled in the college, but the additional stress of being around other students made his symptoms worse. Plus, he was having memory problems. He'd get in his car and start driving, forget where he was going, and call McNeill.

"Where are you going?" he'd ask her.

"I'm on my way to school."

"Am I supposed to be in school?"

"No, you're supposed to be going to . . ."

One day in October, Bloomfield woke from a dream in the middle of the afternoon. At the sound of breaking glass, McNeill walked downstairs. Bloomfield was gone. The bed was upside down. The wooden slats were broken into pieces. Shattered glass shimmered across the living room carpet. Clothes were spread across the floor. Some were packed in a green Army duffel bag in the corner. She looked out the open window at the tree line behind the house. Bloomfield was crouched in the woods and sitting perfectly still. It had been exactly a year since their worst month in Iraq.

"What just happened?" he asked and looked behind him. He was breathing nervously and felt like he was having a panic attack.

"What do you mean?" McNeill asked, unsure what to think or do.

A confused look spread across his face. He had no idea what was going on but was shaking in anger as he looked skeptically at McNeill. He wished he'd died in Iraq. McNeill couldn't do anything to help him. There was no question at this point that he needed help—now. Nothing she had suggested, from the VA to the Army, had worked. Every time McNeill brought up Bloomfield to the VA, they suggested McNeill think about herself and end the relationship, even though she and the relationship were helping keep Bloomfield alive.

Finally, McNeill called her mom. She was upset and bothered that there was apparently nothing anyone in the VA was able to do for Bloomfield and the thousands of other soldiers in the same situation. Her mother called McNeill's reserve unit to talk to her first sergeant. It was clear that Bloomfield needed more than medication. The first sergeant called the VA to set up a meeting between someone on the medical staff and Bloomfield. McNeill had been assured they would be properly greeted, and Bloomfield would be pointed in the right direction to be admitted into an in-patient program. When Bloomfield started to panic and change his mind about going, McNeill reassured him that he was going to be taken care of. After calming down, Bloomfield told McNeill he felt like killing himself. He was a ticking time bomb.

When they walked through the deserted VA Hospital toward the emergency room, McNeill felt relief and then concern. As soon as they reached the ER, it became evident that no one was waiting for them or had any idea they were coming. Bloomfield checked in, and then they waited two hours to speak to the psychiatrist. After a series of questions, the psychiatrist told Bloomfield he had seen worse, and if they checked him in, he would probably feel like he didn't belong there. When Bloomfield said that he was reckless and suicidal, the psychiatrist told him the incident of jumping out of the moving car was in the past and no longer an issue. In other words, he was no longer a threat to himself, and it wasn't necessary for him to stay there. After some time had elapsed with no results, Bloomfield got irritated. The doctor cornered him and asked, "What, are you getting angry?" The doctor repeated it, and Bloomfield left the room and walked out of the hospital.

The psychiatrist called the VA police. They found Bloomfield outside smoking a cigarette. McNeill couldn't believe what she had just witnessed. Bloomfield had post-traumatic stress disorder and felt suicidal, and this psychiatrist was acting as though it was in the past? It was getting worse. She wanted to scream at him, *What kind of a doctor are you?* She walked out of the room as Bloomfield came back inside. She didn't know whom to be angry at, but she was at the end of her rope. She couldn't have Bloomfield's chaos around the house, but he couldn't not be there if he was that unstable.

She didn't go back in the room with him. She stayed in the hallway and talked to the security guards.

"How can they not let him stay here?" she asked.

"Can't one of you stay with your family?" he asked.

"We are not the problem. The problem is that he has PTSD and needs help *now*, and the VA is doing nothing but giving him pills, and he's losing his mind," McNeill said. "I can't deal with it, and I don't know what to do." She was in tears.

"Sometimes, you have to do things for *you* and not someone else," a guard said. "If you can't deal with it, as hard as it is, it might be better for you to not be with him." He explained that it takes time to get help at the VA. "I see guys in here on wheelchairs breathing with respirators waiting hours for an appointment." She wasn't sure if the words were supposed to comfort her, but she felt defeated. Money she felt was so freely wasted in Iraq could easily have been used for adequate and timely healthcare for veterans of the war.

Bloomfield was finally allowed to check into the hospital and by midnight had been locked up in the psychiatric ward. He was allowed visitors—except for McNeill—and was not permitted to smoke by himself or, after the first day, to talk to McNeill on the phone. None of these conditions was made known before he checked in.

His last call was to McNeill, and he asked her to come see him. Her mom and sister went with her. When they got there, they were told that Bloomfield was too "fragile" for visitors and suggested that Bloomfield hadn't called McNeill. She insisted that he had called her and said she could wait until he was well enough to have visitors. The doctor called the VA police to make sure they left.

Bloomfield doesn't recall feeling "fragile" as the doctor described. They never told him McNeill had stopped by; he thought she didn't want to see him. Other than sitting in his room, he played Bingo with severely mentally ill patients. He doubted that listening to one patient talk about killing children in Vietnam would improve his condition any. A day after he arrived, when Bloomfield realized they weren't going to treat him, he asked to leave. He was told he couldn't leave until the third day. When he asked about post-traumatic stress disorder care, he was told the waitlist for intensive in-patient treatment programs was more than eight months long.

McNeill contacted Bloomfield's squad leader at the reserve unit in Madison to let her know he had PTSD and needed some time to deal with it. His squad leader responded that many soldiers with PTSD managed to go to school *and* make it to drill on the weekends. McNeill was not in the mood for more obstacles. She explained the medications he was on and his hospitalization. McNeill was going crazy dealing with all of these people on her own.

She got in touch with Wisconsin Congresswoman Tammy Baldwin's caseworker, who promised to get Bloomfield into a treatment program and said that the seven-week program at the VA Center in Cincinnati, Ohio, was the best in the nation. Everything was supposed to have been coordinated between the VA systems to make it happen. Bloomfield didn't want to ride back to Ohio with his family because they would ask too many questions and he'd get overwhelmed. So McNeill drove him, and they followed his mother and sister back to Ohio, where he would check into the program the following day. She dropped him off and was heading back to Wisconsin when Bloomfield called. It would be two weeks before they could get him in for an assessment. This was the third time he was denied entrance into a program, and he was now eight hours from home, at his sister's house a couple of hours from Cleveland.

Four days later, Bloomfield called McNeill and said he needed help right away. She reminded him to call the point of contact that the VA gave him. He did, and she told him that it was possible there were waiting lists he could get on and assured him help was available.

"Ma'am," he said, "that's why soldiers commit suicide."

He ended the call and dialed McNeill's number to tell her what he found out.

"You know," he said, "they can bring you home from the war, but I don't think you really come home, you know?"

McNeill called Tammy Baldwin's caseworker and told her that Bloomfield didn't get into the program and that it would be the end of the month before he was "assessed." By the end of the day, Bloomfield was informed that he could check into a program in Fort Thomas, Kentucky, the next morning. A patient who was supposed to enter the program had apparently not shown up. When he arrived, they checked him in as planned. It was October 7, 2006.

Throughout the seven-week program, Bloomfield struggled with eleven other veterans, most of whom served in Vietnam. They received daily individual counseling as well as regular group therapy and activities. Both together and individually, they re-experienced the traumatic days of their time in combat. A military history buff, Bloomfield saw another side of the Vietnam War. He saw how the Vietnam veterans had suffered over the years with divorces and alcohol and substance abuse. The Vietnam veterans saw hope that Bloomfield was there, relieved that he would receive help sooner than they did. The program helped Bloomfield learn where his anger was coming from and how to control it better. The other veterans explained how anger had taken control of their lives.

Although their experiences in combat were in different countries at different times, they all shared a common struggle when they came home. When Bloomfield finished the program and headed back to Wisconsin, he felt really good, like he could finally start to feel normal again.

Several months later, Bloomfield received a letter from the VA stating that during his recent visit to the VA, he had screened positive for a traumatic brain injury. The letter instructed him to call the phone number listed within fourteen days to follow up or they would assume he was receiving care elsewhere. When he called the number, he always reached the voicemail. No one returned his calls. He hadn't been to the VA since finishing the program. Unbeknownst to him at the time, the VA in Wisconsin had decided that he would no longer need follow-up care in Madison because he had moved to Ohio.

A few months later, Bloomfield called Military OneSource to inquire about the letter he received from the VA to find out what he needed to do. After Military OneSource called the phone number on Bloomfield's behalf, the VA returned his phone call. He was told to schedule an appointment at the Madison VA, and after the process of reestablishing his primary care at the Madison VA, another year passed before Bloomfield was first examined for traumatic brain injury. Testing confirmed he had an injury from the roadside bomb that knocked him unconscious in June 2005.

The same month, McNeill received a response for the VA claim she filed. She was granted service-connection disability for asthma, tinnitus, and a sleep disorder; it was not granted, however, for peripheral vision loss and other health effects she had identified after she returned. Because she was still awaiting diagnosis or treatment for the vision at the VA, she waited to appeal the decision.

After being diagnosed with traumatic brain injury in January 2008, Bloomfield went to physical therapy and was given a palm pilot and GPS to help with his cognitive issues. When he requested individual counseling sessions to help him maintain control of his post-traumatic stress disorder symptoms, he was offered compensation for completing a medication trial, which he declined. He was offered group cognitive processing therapy but didn't want to talk to a group of people about his problems. He wanted to talk to a psychiatrist.

Over the next several months, Bloomfield began struggling with depression. He rarely attended training with his unit. He wasn't sure what medicine he should be taking, and most of it had run out. After making so much progress, McNeill now worried about his depression. He wasn't communicating with his friends or family. In July 2008, Bloomfield told her he felt suicidal sometimes and began acting more out of character, McNeill contacted his commander. She expressed her concern that if the military or VA didn't get him into counseling, his condition could further deteriorate. Beyond that, she felt that because these issues stemmed from combat, the military had an obligation to help him.

McNeill and Bloomfield had served with his commander in Iraq. He was Bloomfield's platoon leader and spent a lot of time in Corregidor. He called around and was eventually given information about the Army's warrior transition program where soldiers receive comprehensive care. There was only one problem. Soldiers are supposed to enter this program within six months of returning home, so the unit would have to request an exception to the policy. McNeill and Bloomfield didn't receive physicals before being released from active duty, so much of the medical paperwork he needed as documentation hadn't been completed.

Since there was no guarantee of Bloomfield getting help from the warrior transition program, once again McNeill got on the phone and contacted the Madison VA to find out how Bloomfield could get into counseling. She was told something different each time she called. She contacted Iraq & Afghanistan Veterans of America, which suggested more points of contact to try to get help for him. A couple weeks later, she contacted Senator Russ Feingold's office for assistance. By mid-August, several VA employees had gotten in touch with Bloomfield to explain all the reasons why he had fallen through the cracks of their changing system. By the end of the month, he had been reestablished for primary care at the VA, and as McNeill started school in the fall, Bloomfield was regaining his footing with the help of the VA. He began regular individual counseling, and treatment for previously unaddressed high blood pressure and residual effects from the traumatic brain injury.

Bloomfield still doesn't sleep well, is at times hypersensitive and defensive, and has trouble interpreting what people are saying or feeling, but the improved care he's received has helped him maintain stability. He has 60 percent service-connected disability for post-traumatic stress disorder, traumatic brain injury, and labrythitis, the cause of his balance problems. He is still waiting to hear more from the military about the warrior transition program and his retention in the military. His initial application for the program was rejected in November 2008. He has appealed that decision.

While completing the paperwork to receive her education benefits for the semester, McNeill found out that a medical profile hadn't yet been processed for the asthma she developed in 2005. Without a profile, she couldn't perform an authorized alternative aerobic activity. She could not longer complete the timed run on the fitness test and was "flagged" for failing a run. Even after asthma was addressed during an Army physical, the appropriate and expected paperwork hadn't been initiated.

Because of a medical flag, she was unable to complete the mandatory training for her rank and job classification. It was the end of 2008, her unit was preparing to deploy to Afghanistan in early 2009, and she had no idea if asthma would affect her retention in the military or if she would deploy with her unit. Only after McNeill contacted Congresswoman Tammy Baldwin's office in September 2008 was the issue addressed matter-of-factly by the military. In the meantime, she had gathered more medical documentation about her problems with vision and appealed the VA's initial decision on her disability claim. A few days later, she traveled to Fort Knox, Kentucky, for a fit-for-duty medical evaluation in response to the congressional inquiry in which a doctor determined that McNeill did not meet Army retention standards and recommended a medical evaluation board.

She returned to Fort Knox and saw a doctor at the Army hospital for her board, and he determined that she has multiple sclerosis and traumatic brain injury, both of which are service-connected. The MS diagnosis has since been revised to a type of nervous disorder. The next step is two physicals, after which her medical information will go before an informal physical evaluation board. She could appear before a formal board, where her military disability rating would be determined as well as her future with the Army.

Her physical-evaluation-board liaison officer, who serves as her advocate during the process, told McNeill that often asthma results in placement on the temporary disability retired list. This would mean her condition wasn't yet stable, and she would need to return for an exam every twelve to eighteen months for up to five years before she would be permanently retired. If her health improves during that time period, she would return to duty.

She continues to drill with her reserve unit in Wisconsin, but only one weekend a month. She will drill at least until the medical board process is over and it's determined whether or not she will stay in the Army.

Having to handle her affairs as well as Bloomfield's affairs has taken a toll on McNeill. "I had no life for a very long time," she said. She was a student. She was editor-in-chief and graphic designer for her college newspaper. Those are the expected activities of a young woman her age. She also went to drill and spoke at a Senate Democratic Policy Committee meeting in Washington, D.C., on contractor misconduct and the electrocution deaths of American soldiers in Iraq. When she had free time, she spent the majority of it on the telephone with the VA, scanning medical records and paperwork for the VA and military, going to appointments, writing and sending e-mails, and following up on paperwork for education benefits.

Also putting a strain on McNeill was her and Bloomfield's dwindling finances. At first, Bloomfield worked in construction, but that became more difficult to do when his balance started to affect him and he was no longer comfortable working. He stopped working. If he went to school, he would have gotten extra money through his education benefits, but after a couple of attempts, that wasn't an option, either, because of his memory loss and the frustration that ensued. When he stopped getting a check, McNeill helped him, but she didn't want to go in the hole, too. After about a year, they couldn't afford much. She was making extra money through her education benefits and by working for the newspaper, but that wasn't enough to support the two of them.

After three years of being home, McNeill is doing everything in her power to get on with her life. She continues to prove to family, friends, and strangers that she is capable of doing anything she wants to do, from Thunder Runs to tackling the VA. She has dealt with her medical problems head on. She will graduate in May 2009 from Madison Area Technical College with an associate's degree in visual communications at the age of twenty four and then plans to transfer to a four-year college to study political communications, followed by law or public policy. It turns out she is as comfortable among bookcases in a college library as she was on the battlefield. While she wouldn't trade her experience in Iraq for anything, she's ready to move on from the military to serve her country in other ways.

Army Sergeant Jeanna Marrano

ARMY SERGEANT JEANNA MARRANO IS AN MP WITH THE ARMY National Guard 105th Military Police Company in Buffalo, New York. She deployed to Iraq from April 2003 to April 2004. During the deployment, the company's mission usually changed weekly. One week, the company would drive up and down the main supply route and search for IEDs and anything else that posed a threat to American troops. The next week, it would provide perimeter security and make sure no one came on base who wasn't supposed to.

Being in combat was the worst—and the best—experience Marrano has ever had. "Every day, I had to fight to get up, and I had to fight back the tears," she said. "But it made me stronger because now I know I can do anything."

Two soldiers from the 105th were killed while Marrano was in Iraq. The company was ambushed more than 150 times, and Marrano got shot at four times: three times by Americans and once by Iraqi celebratory fire. She said the thought that a comrade could have ended her life was very disturbing, but unfortunately, those things do happen.

When she returned from Iraq, Marrano wanted to sleep and drink with friends for about the first month. Then she realized that what doesn't kill you makes you stronger, and she's definitely stronger. "I didn't want to be another military statistic and waste away my life," she said. "I knew in time the depression and stress would go away or get easier."

Since returning home, she has earned her bachelor's degree in criminal justice and is working at the Monroe County Medical Examiner's Office in Rochester, New York. On November 8, 2008, she married a Marine she met shortly after returning from Iraq.

Shannon (Weber) Evans with her son, Cayden

PHOTO BY DRUSILLA ELLIOTT

A Fresh Start

WHY DID YOU JOIN THE MILITARY?

It was the same innocuous question I asked every female serv-ice member I interviewed, and 99 percent of the time the answer was predictable. This time was different. This was the other 1 per-cent, when the driving force to be a Marine had nothing to do with following in a father's footsteps, educational benefits, or patriotism.

At seventeen, Shannon Weber (now Evans) was living in Hamilton, Ohio, with her father. She had moved out of her mom's house when she was ten because her mom, Lisa, was living with an abusive man and Shannon couldn't take listening to the chokings and beatings. The relationship between Lisa and her fiancé, Frankie, lasted seven turbulent years. Time and time again, Lisa left Frankie, and time and again, she returned to him. But on Mother's Day 1998, when Frankie was away, Lisa packed her bags and left her abuser for the last time. Like in the movie *Sleeping with the Enemy*, Lisa started a new life by moving to another town and getting a new job at a pharmaceutical company. Shannon watched all of this with a great sense of relief. Everything got better—until Frankie tracked Lisa down and started stalking her. When Lisa left work at the end of the day, Frankie would be waiting for her. He'd

169

stand outside his car or pace back and forth beside it. He hoped that she would come over and talk to him, but Lisa was beyond talking. She had learned that talking eventually led to hitting, choking, and more threats on her and her children's lives.

Then one day Frankie showed up with no intention of going away. Lisa and her son, Justin (Shannon's brother), were leaving work for the day. They worked together but drove separate cars. As they took off down the street, Lisa was in the first car, followed by Justin, and then Frankie behind both of them. Lisa turned onto an industrial road in an area that was being built up. The road was used by construction workers but was empty now because most workers had already gone home for the day. Since she hadn't been working for the company long, Lisa wasn't famil-iar with the side streets. As Frankie chased her, she didn't know where to go. She turned down a road that was a dead end. Frankie pulled ahead of Justin and rammed his car into Lisa's vehicle. Justin stepped on the gas, crashing into Frankie's car in the hopes of seriously wounding him. No such luck.

Earlier that day, Lisa called Frankie's cousins and urged them to come to her workplace and talk some sense into him. They were there when the three cars pulled out of Lisa's workplace, and they followed the vehicles to the crash site. Lisa and Justin got out of their cars and ran to the cousins' car. Frankie grabbed his shotgun from his car and headed toward Lisa. As she ran, Lisa fell. When Frankie reached her, Lisa begged him not to hurt her. He grabbed her hair and dragged her to his cousins' car. He kicked them out, pushed Lisa in, and drove away. Justin ran to the closest building to call 911. Frankie drove about 1,000 yards north of the crash site until the road ended in a wooded area. That's where the trail of Lisa's belongings began.

While all this was happening, Shannon was returning home from a friend's graduation party. She ran out of gas and had to walk the rest of the way home. She hadn't been home long when the phone rang. The caller ID showed that someone was calling from the Babbling Oil Company.

"Shannon, it's Justin," he said frantically. "Something terrible has happened. The police are here. You need to come pick me up right now. Don't turn on the news. Don't do anything. Mom is here. Frankie has her."

Shannon yelled upstairs to her father.

"We have to go NOW!"

"What's wrong?"

"Frankie has mom."

Her dad grabbed his .45 rifle and put it in the car.

"If I see him, I'm going to kill him," he said.

By the time they got to the crime scene, the area was crawling with police officers from three different townships, a SWAT team, and police dogs and trainers. Helicopters flew overhead. Shannon overheard the police talking to one another. One said two shots had been fired. The officers talked about delaying going into the dense woods to find Lisa because it was getting dark and Frankie was armed. There was no telling whom he would shoot next if he was still there.

The police chief told Shannon and her family to go home. He would call them with any news. She thought he was kidding. She couldn't believe it. *Her* mom was in the woods, either dying or dead. *Her* mother! And she was supposed to just walk away. She began to hyperventilate. When the police chief said they didn't know what was happening, Shannon dropped to her knees and sobbed uncontrollably. She couldn't breathe. The lack of hope and reassurance was suffocating her.

Since their maternal grandmother lived just fifteen minutes away, they drove there and turned on the news. Soon it was confirmed on the news that an unidentified woman had been shot twice in the neck, and her ex-fiancé was still at large. Frankie had told Shannon's mom many times that if she ever left him, he would go after her and her kids. He knew where they lived. But he didn't go after them. Instead, Frankie ran to his cousin's house, showered, washed his clothes, and turned himself in the next day. Lisa died just a few weeks after Mother's Day. She was thirty-eight.

It was unbelievable to hear Shannon tell this story ten years after it happened. She was sitting in front of me in Cleo's restaurant in San Diego and was as cute as could be, with freckles, shoulder-length hair, and puffy cheeks. She was still losing weight after giving birth to her son, Cayden. As Shannon spoke about that traumatic time in her life, it was obvious that it had been rough, but it was also clear that she wasn't living in the past. She had found a way to move on with her life. After her mother died, though, life got markedly worse before it got better.

Shannon had post-traumatic stress disorder and didn't know it. She had no idea how to cope with the violent death of her mother. She missed lots of school during her senior year for court appearances as Frankie was tried for aggravated murder in the first degree, kidnapping in the first degree, and weapons under disability in the fifth degree. She got into drugs and alcohol, experimenting with anything she could get her hands on, anything to make her feel better.

After Shannon graduated from high school, she continued to live with her father for a while. Justin occasionally called home to see how she was doing and to find out what she planned to do with her life. She had no idea. He had joined a Marine Corps reserve unit out of Dayton, Ohio. A career in the Marine Corps was the farthest thing from Shannon's mind until Justin came home in his uniform and with his gear. He blew her away. He seemed like a completely different person—so strong and full of confidence. She wanted to be like him.

But the pictures in her mind of Justin in his Marine uniform faded as she moved two hours away to Columbus, Ohio, and tried to get on with her life. She got two jobs—one at a day care center and another at a hair, skin care, and body company—and enrolled in college. She started out strong, working and going to school, but the stress of two jobs, tuition and monthly bills, studying for classes, and the memories of her mom's murder eventually got the best of her.

She started replaying the old negative tapes in her mind. The ones that said, *Who was she to think she could make it in life?* She was a failure, and she should just accept her lot in life. Life would be so much easier if she realized now that she wasn't going to amount to anything. Think of all the future disappointments she could prevent. It wasn't unusual for the women in her family to be downtrodden. Her mom was a perfect example, choosing an abusive relationship over being alone. She had told Shannon that change is good for people because it teaches them how to adapt, but look where that got her. When her mom tried to change her situation once and for all, her ex-fiancé killed her. Shannon feared similar repercussions; she felt that any risks she took would fall short. Part of her believed only bad things would come from trying to make a better life for herself. Her defeatist thoughts became a self-fulfilling prophecy.

She found a new apartment, job, and friends in Columbus, but not knowing how to cope with stress caused her to fall back on old habits. When the going got tough, she turned to alcohol for relief. She thought that being in a different environment would somehow automatically change her when, in fact, she was the same. At first, alcohol made dealing with this reality easy.

Then she started drinking heavily and blacking out again and again. She'd go out with a friend after work—just for dinner and a couple of drinks, they'd tell each another. That's how it always started, dinner and drinks. Then they'd get to talking about their problems, and the next thing Shannon knew, she was drinking double shots of Bacardi 151, Everclear, tequila, and vodka. She'd wake up the next morning on her apartment floor in the same clothes she had been wearing the night before, with the door wide open. She wouldn't remember driving home. That was a typical night.

She put her bar tab, which ran up to $400 a night, on her credit card. *Oh well*, she thought when her credit card statement arrived in the mail, *what can I do? The damage is done.* Then a couple of days later she'd go out and do the same thing all over again. Eventually, she accumulated $15,000 in debt just from alcohol. Credit card companies threatened to close her accounts. She wanted to pay them back on her own but was earning just enough to pay her rent, food, and car payment. She had no health insurance. One day, she decided to talk to a recruiter. She told the recruiter her brother was a Marine and she wanted to be like him.

Shannon turned twenty-four at Marine Corps Recruit Depot Parris Island. After graduating from boot camp, she went to military police (MP) school in Fort Leonard Wood, Missouri, and finally the Marine Wing Support Squadron (MWSS-373) in Miramar, California.

In July 2005, Shannon met Marine Lance Corporal Henry Evans at a friend's party. Evans is six feet tall, with brown hair and bluish green eyes, and is always tan. While he was cute, charming, and upbeat, Shannon didn't think this surfer from Pensacola, Florida, was her type. She gravitated to bad boys. He seemed too good for her. He was polished and clearly cared about his appearance. At first, they would see each other when they went out with mutual friends. Then he asked her to dinner. After that, they were inseparable. Henry knew within two months of meeting Shannon that she was the one he wanted to spend the rest of his life with. Shannon didn't know what to expect. As soon as things between them started to get serious, she found out that she was going to deploy to Iraq. Both lived in the barracks and began spending every waking moment together.

Six months later, on January 12, 2006, Henry dropped by Shannon's room and invited her to dinner. "Let's go to the Olive Garden," he said. When he picked her up later that afternoon, he handed her a small bouquet of flowers. He had mentioned that he wanted to stop somewhere prior to dinner. She didn't ask where. She assumed he had an errand to run. No big deal. They ended up at La Jolla Cove, a small beach tucked between adjacent sandstone cliffs, one of the most photographed beaches in southern California. Henry had picked out a spot that would overlook the setting sun. He pulled out a bottle of wine and two glasses. As the sun was setting, Henry told Shannon that he thought she was great and that what they had was special. Then he said there was something he wanted to ask her. He pulled an engagement ring out of his pocket, got down on one knee, and proposed to her. "I'm a smart gal, but I was completely dumbfounded," she said, recalling that moment.

Many Marines and soldiers squeeze in marriages before a partner deploys because they can make more money that way. Married couples get family separation pay—an extra $250 a month—for being apart, and that money is not taxed if one is deployed. Couples also receive a basic allowance for housing, $1,850. Since many move into smaller apartments, the amount they receive is more than their monthly rent or mortgage payment. Many are able to pocket the extra money. "It wasn't about money for us," Shannon said. "It was about trying to do the right thing." They planned to get married when Shannon returned. Five weeks later, Marine Sergeant Shannon Weber, an MP, deployed to Iraq.

Two security teams provided protection for the Explosive Ordnance Disposal (EOD) technicians attached to MWSS-374, a Marine wing-support squadron. Shannon was an MP for one of those security teams. The EODs covered an area between Al Taqaddum and Ramadi, west of Baghdad. If someone spotted a weapons' cache, roadside IED, or vehicle-born IED, the EODs would respond, with Shannon's team securing the perimeter. It was a busy job.

Ideally, each team would work two days, then have two days off. But if one team was already out on a call, the other team would have to go on call. And when the nearby Ramadi security team needed extra help, one of the teams from MWSS-374 would pitch in. When they weren't on calls, the MPs helped with station beautification, attended training sessions, did weapons maintenance and physical training, and tried to stay hydrated. Adding to Shannon's hectic schedule were the two online classes she signed up for. She had hoped to take seven classes while in Iraq, one a month, but as soon as she arrived, she realized she would have to readjust her academic goals. The two classes she did finish moved her closer to her goal of earning a bachelor's degree in secondary education with an emphasis in history. She'd never forgotten how she'd told her high school civics teacher that she was going to have her job one day. The classes were a positive distraction during those few waking hours when she wasn't working.

One day, she was taking a quiz in information literacy and report-writing through National University. She had answered ten of the twenty questions on the quiz when a Marine walked into the internet café and said, "9-line." That's the Marines' way of telling each other that they need to get their gear and roll. 9-line refers to the nine lines of information they are given to put their mission in action, such as grids, radio frequency, type of IED, and the call sign of the team out there.

Shit, Shannon thought as she closed out the quiz, grabbed her ID, and went to work. No matter where she was or what she was doing, the mission always came first. Fortunately, the internet cafe was right next to where her MP detachment was based. That mission kept the security team out all night. When she returned to the internet cafe the next evening, Shannon e-mailed her professor and explained that she was in Iraq, got called out, and couldn't complete the quiz. Could she retake it? He said yes.

One of the MPs on Shannon's team was Sergeant Marco Franco of Omaha, Nebraska. They were good friends. Franco is five feet, six inches tall, Hispanic, and so outgoing that he could always make Shannon smile, even when she was having a bad day. He rarely let anything get to him. Shannon met him at MWSS-373 when the squadron was gearing up for Iraq. They fed off each other because both were sarcastic and enjoyed each other's sense of humor.

Some of Shannon's most memorable moments in Iraq involved Franco, like the day he found a copper wire and the two of them decided to test its authenticity—is it an IED?—instead of asking the EOD techs for help. On this day, Shannon's security team went out on a call with EOD. They were stopped on the side of the road, and the techs were defusing an IED up ahead while the MPs patrolled the area in between their trucks to make sure there were no secondary IEDs. After looking around for a minute, Franco said to Shannon, "Come here and look at this."

She looked where he was pointing and saw copper wires sticking out of the ground. It usually means trouble when wires are sticking out of the ground. It doesn't necessarily indicate an IED is on the other end, but it could. Shannon had no interest in getting any closer to the wire than she needed to.

MPs are trained how to spot an IED, and Franco didn't want to call the EOD techs over if it was nothing. It didn't look like the wires went deep. If the dirt is packed hard, that often means the wires run deep and are attached to an IED. The dirt was loose near this wire. Franco didn't want to make something out of nothing.

They decided to test the wires themselves.

Franco got on one side, Shannon on the other. Franco said that if he was going to die, he wasn't going to die alone. Shannon thought, *Well, I'm your sister-in-arms. This is what I'm here for. Let's just pull the wire. What's the worst that can happen? Boom—and we're gone?*

When she picked up the wire, Shannon felt a little tension. She thought that if it was hooked to an explosive, there would have been more tension. If there had been more tension, they would not have pulled the wires. They would have notified the EODs.

On the count of three, each was going to pull their end of the copper wire.

One.

Two.

Three.

Weber closed her eyes and pulled.

Nothing.

It turned out to be a long spool of wire.

So why would a man with a wife and three kids at home and a woman with a fiancé at home take such a risk? If that wire had been attached to explosives, their Marine buddies would have been picking up their body parts from the ground. They believed they were taking a calculated risk. They knew what they were doing. There may have been a little cockiness involved in the decision making since they were halfway through their deployment and less patient than they were on their first few missions. They didn't want to have to wait for the EOD techs to respond. They were already busy with one call. If they had another, it could add hours to the mission.

Shannon's mom was killed June 9, 1998. When the anniversary of her mom's death rolls around each year, Shannon feels a sense of calm take hold of her. Her best friend sends her a card telling her how proud she is of Shannon and how proud Shannon's mother would be. Her mom was a month shy of her thirty-ninth birthday when she tried to start a new life. Much like her mom, Shannon had wiped the slate clean and begun fresh by joining the Marine Corps and then by choosing Henry, who was not a bad boy, as her fiancé.

Before Shannon deployed, she heard other Marines who had already served in Iraq talking about all the downtime they had over there. So she figured that once she got settled in at Al Taqaddum, she could spend her free time shopping for wedding dresses online and looking for wedding and reception locations in Pensacola, Florida. Lots of people watch movies and TV or read in their spare time. What's wrong with planning a wedding?

But there was no way she could do it. She was too busy, and planning a big wedding didn't feel right when her mom wasn't alive to help her. After much thought, Shannon decided she didn't want a big wedding. The absence of her mom would have been too much to bear. She didn't want to be reminded of that enormous loss, of the fact that she wouldn't have her mom there to straighten her veil, zip her dress, and give her approval. "It wasn't even about me," Shannon said. "It was about my mom. Granted, it was going to be my biggest day, but it should have been my mom's biggest day, too. She would have been giving her only daughter away."

During the second half of her deployment, Shannon picked up another mission. Her first mission was to provide security for EOD teams, and now she was also to patrol the areas where convoys would be traveling. Her security team would go out on the roads prior to a convoy, recon the area, and make sure it was safe. If they found anything suspicious, they would call for an EOD team. Once they had determined that an area was safe, they would give the all-clear to the convoy and sit and wait for the line of trucks to drive through. Then they would stay in that area until the convoy returned. Shannon and her team often left base in the afternoon and didn't return until nine or ten the next morning.

No one, including Shannon, wanted to be out on the roads at night; that's when things are the most dangerous. Shannon couldn't see the enemy, but the enemy could see her. The Marines and soldiers have night-vision goggles, but it's still easier to see in the daytime. The small red beam of a flashlight can't compare with the light of day.

On August 19, 2006, two security teams, each made up of three trucks, went out on patrol. Shannon was on one of those teams. She sat in the back seat of the lead vehicle. As the truck rolled down the road, she shined her flashlight out her window, kept an M-249 SAW (squad automatic weapon) propped between her legs, and manned the radio on the seat beside her. Her team had just cleared a strip of road along MSR (Main Supply Route) Long Island, twenty miles outside Al Taqaddum.

The road was notoriously dangerous. There had been so many IED blasts in the area they were driving that it didn't even feel like a road. Truck drivers had to constantly swerve to avoid pot holes. Shannon had to get out of the truck every few yards to check holes already created by IED explosions and make sure they were clear of active IEDs. These holes, one to two feet deep, were full of chemical sticks. When the sticks are broken in half, they light up. Marines would throw them in the holes to illuminate the area and potential IEDs. Some holes had accumulated fifty or sixty chem sticks from previous patrols.

It was a nuisance getting in and out of the truck every few minutes, so Shannon would sometimes walk alongside the vehicle as it moved. That was risky, though, because of sniper fire. It was so dark out that the Marines often drove in blackout conditions; if Shannon walked fifteen or twenty feet from her vehicle, she would not be able to find her way back. That explains how an insurgent could hide an IED fifty feet away and not be noticed or how a sniper could fire without being seen.

Shannon and the rest of the security team had turned around to backtrack over an area on MSR Long Island that they had just cleared five minutes earlier, a stretch of road with small hills on either side. Apparently, before they turned around, when the Iraqis could see their taillights fading in the dark of night, they planted two IEDs.

Shannon was shining her flashlight out the truck's window and looking down, but never saw the two 155 mortar rounds and three rocket warheads buried on the side of the road. The pressure plate detonated as the rear tire on the passenger's side rolled over it. She never heard the blast from the IED that hit her truck. The explosion shook her vehicle and the one behind it, spraying parts of her truck everywhere.

Franco was driving the truck behind Shannon, and he was certain the blast had killed her. There was no way she could have survived that explosion. When the smoke cleared, the back of Shannon's truck was missing; it had been blown off. The back tires had been shredded. Franco raced to Shannon's truck and found that her door had been blown off. Shannon was slumped over the metal ammo cans beside her. Her Kevlar had been blown off from the blast and was in the seat next to her. The doc checked on one of the other Marines in the truck, and Franco stayed with Shannon.

"Shannon, Shannon, Shannon. It's me, Marco."

When she gained consciousness, Shannon saw Franco yelling at her. His lips were moving, but she couldn't hear him. The vehicle commander was talking to her, but she couldn't hear him either.

She remembers reaching for the radio and saying, "Lucky Three, this is Chevy." That means everything is okay, that they're still moving. But everything *wasn't* all right, and they *weren't* still moving. According to Franco, she never made that call; she imagined it. If she had made that call, he would have heard it.

When Franco tried to help her out of the truck, she screamed, "Don't touch me. Don't touch me."

"You need to get out of the vehicle now."

She reached down for her weapon and pulled it up to her chest.

"Give me your weapon. Give me your weapon."

"No! It's my weapon. It's my job."

She attempted to roll out of the vehicle.

When the doc reached her, he asked her what was wrong. She said she couldn't feel her arm.

"Can you move it?"

"I don't want to move it. I can't feel it right now." She kept her other hand over it.

Her face was covered with a thick layer of soot from the blast.

The doc pulled her to the front of the vehicle and took off her vest to get a better look at her arm. While she was being checked out, an MP located another IED just eight inches in front of the second vehicle. What a mess: Marines wounded, a vehicle down, another live IED. The first vehicle couldn't move because it had been damaged, and the second vehicle couldn't go anywhere for fear of another explosion and because of the hole created by the first blast.

Someone called for a ground medevac. The Marines relocated to a distance 300 yards away from the second IED to be safe. Shannon still couldn't move her arm. The doc guessed that Shannon got tossed around in the vehicle during the explosion, injuring her arm.

Another convoy approached and offered to provide security. A corporal from that convoy walked up to Shannon and said, "Holy shit! What the hell happened?"

"We just got blown up."

"No shit! I could see that blast from miles away." It looked like a fireworks celebration because all the chem lights they were carrying exploded.

When she arrived at the Surgical Shock Trauma Platoon (SSTP), Shannon spotted her sergeant major and commanding officer just outside the door. She walked by them, hunched over because she was sore, and said, "Good evening, gentlemen."

"Did she just say, 'Good evening, gentlemen'?"

She looked like a chimney sweeper who had just put in a full day's work. A doctor used wipes to clean her face—one swipe of her face and a wipe turned completely black. The medical staff took X-rays but couldn't find anything wrong with her arm. They wanted to send Shannon to Germany to do more tests, but she fought it. She didn't want to go, so she spent another day at the SSTP for observation. There were three male Marines in the vehicle when it exploded. Two went to the SSTP with her. One had a busted eardrum, and the other had a hard time hearing. The driver walked away. Since the explosion happened just a month before Shannon was to go home, she was put on light duty. No more heavy lifting or going on missions.

When Shannon returned to San Diego on September 21, 2006, she hit the ground running. The next day, she went to work while her fiancé, Henry, shopped for wedding dresses. He picked out one dress in two different sizes at Macy's that morning and met Shannon at lunchtime. She tried them on and chose the one that fit. That evening, after Shannon got off work, they got in their car and drove four hours to Vegas, where they checked into the Venetian Resort, Hotel, and Casino and took an evening stroll. The next morning, they drove to the Little Chapel of the Flowers.

While Shannon was still in Iraq, she'd researched chapels in Vegas on the Internet. Even though she was eloping, she'd put a great deal of thought into where they would exchange their vows and make their lifelong commitment. She wanted the service to feel as traditional and sophisticated as possible, something they could be proud of, but not too fancy. She and Henry spend the majority of their time in flip-flops; they're no-frills kind of people. She definitely didn't want purple velvet, lace, and an Elvis impersonator as her minister. After looking at about thirty chapels, she knew Little Flower was the one.

Things can be deceiving on the Internet. Buyers don't always know what the product they have purchased is really going to look like. When Shannon and Henry drove up to the chapel, Shannon immediately started to second-guess herself. *Oh geez, I made a bad decision.* Would the chapel with the small gazebo and bridge out in front live up to its billing on the Internet and meet her expectations? Had she chosen wisely? *I really hope this works out.*

It worked out perfectly.

The package cost about $600 for the ceremony, wedding certificate, DVD, and pictures, plus $40 for the minister. They even got a military discount. The ceremony started at ten o'clock in the morning. They walked down the aisle together, lit the unity candle, and exchanged vows. Shannon's favorite part was lighting the unity candle, as that symbolized that it was no longer about being individuals; it was about being a married couple. They ate lunch at Jimmy Buffet's Margaritaville Café, spent the rest of the day walking around in Vegas, and drove back to San Diego that night.

"I wouldn't have had it any other way," Shannon said. "No cake. No flowers. No frills. Nothing fancy. Just us."

The day after they were married, Shannon and Henry went shopping to furnish their new apartment. Henry found the apartment for them while Shannon was in Iraq, and he moved in two weeks before she returned. Within seventy-two hours of returning from Iraq—which causes enough stress itself—Shannon had gotten married, moved, and furnished a new home. It's enough to make anyone's head spin.

Henry and Shannon settled down into married life. This was hard for both of them at first for several reasons. After the excitement of the wedding, Shannon became distant; she wasn't as affectionate as Henry might have liked. War changes people. Shannon had been affected by her experiences on the battlefield. Since Henry hadn't changed, it seemed to fall on him to get to know the new Shannon. "I didn't understand that at the time, even as a Marine," he said. "Why isn't she exactly the same? It was hard because I didn't go to Iraq, so I didn't see why she had to be different."

Like so many other Marines returning from the battlefield, Shannon wanted to be with her buddies, with the people she had been with in Iraq, after the dust settled. The distance hurt Henry. Why on earth would she be more excited to go back to work with her Marine buddies than be with her husband? There is no bond like the one created in war among Marines and soldiers. She didn't have to explain anything to them. They knew what she had been through because their experiences were the same. Shannon knew she was being distant toward her husband, but it wasn't intentional.

Henry and Shannon argued. Henry felt Iraq was more important to Shannon than he was, and Shannon knew that was true at first. So much happened over there, and she couldn't just come home and forget it. That's one of many things she had to work through. She also had to relearn how to ride in and drive a car in the States. Henry would be driving down the road with her in the passenger's seat, and her mind would return to Iraq. She drove in the middle of the road for weeks after she returned for fear that she would hit an IED.

It was almost like her emotions were on a dimmer switch. When she got back from Iraq, that switch was on its dimmest setting. As she adjusted, the light gradually became brighter. "You don't come home thinking it's great to be home," Shannon said. Even now, with a husband and nine-month-old son, Shannon says she would go back to Iraq. She's been home a year and feels worthless working in the rear.

Shannon was also trying to figure out how to be a wife by preparing meals, doing romantic things, and basically being a woman again instead of GI Jane. None of her female friends in Iraq wore makeup. They were women, but their femininity was buried beneath dirt and grime from sixteen-hour patrols and infrequent showers. It was refreshing to come home, shower daily with clean water, wear makeup, and get her hair colored.

Shannon was the first female with MWSS-373 to rate a Purple Heart. She still wakes up every morning and can't feel her right arm. For the first two to four hours of the day, it's numb from her shoulder to her finger tips. Doctors have done X-rays, MRIs, and electroshock therapy to test the nerves. The last medical treatment she had was electroshock, and it showed that the nerve endings in her pinky and ring finger were weak and unresponsive. The next step is pain management and injecting steroids into her shoulder to stimulate nerve movement. She writes left-handed but uses her right hand for everything else. Since her right arm was wounded, she had to learn to hold the phone with her left hand, vacuum with her left hand, everything.

About five months after returning from Iraq, she had to requalify on the pistol and M16. To fire the rifle, she had to put its butt into the pocket of her hurt shoulder. Her whole body shook from the pain. She didn't think she'd be able to qualify, but she earned sharpshooter.

If anyone could self-identify PTSD, it would be Shannon after what she went through following her mom's murder. Shannon doesn't think she has suffered much post-traumatic stress disorder since she's been back and is happy about that. It's not something that most Marines will freely admit to having, she says, and she wouldn't want that diagnosis to follow her. There are service members coming home from the battlefield who are much worse off.

There are similarities, however, between Shannon's reaction to her mom's death and her response to returning from war that are symptomatic of PTSD. Both left her empty. What now? What's next? Both required a complete readjustment. Nothing can soften the blow of losing a parent or of returning from deployment. You just have to go through it. Her way of getting through the early post-deployment period was to do what she needed to do to get by and deal with deployment issues later. "I'm okay. I'm back home."

She can't change the past but thinks she has learned from it and been able to make good decisions. "I look at what I have now and how I can make it better. It's the Marine way—adapt and overcome." There isn't a day that goes by that Shannon doesn't think about her mother. She knows her mom would be proud of her. But she also thinks about her buddies in Iraq every day.

In early 2007, Shannon was handpicked by Master Gunnery Sergeant John Hood to compete for the NCO of the Quarter Board for the best noncommissioned officer (corporal or sergeant) at Miramar. To win the board, Marines have to know Marine Corps history, sword manual, and basic skills, and they are interviewed by a panel of Marines. She won that board. Then she competed in the Meritorious Sergeant Board for Marine Corps Installations West and won that as well. In July 2007, she was meritoriously promoted to sergeant. Major General Michael Lehnert promoted her, and Sergeant Major Barbara Titus presented her with an NCO sword. She also served as grand marshal in the July 4 parade in Mera Mesa, California.

Shannon plans to leave the Marine Corps in October 2009. She, Henry, and their son, Cayden, are moving to Pensacola, Florida, where Henry grew up. Shannon wants to teach ninth-grade civics. Henry finished his Marine Corps career in 2007 and became a 911 operator for the fire department at Miramar Air Station. He plans to take over his dad's business and become an underground utility contractor.

Prior to the Marine Corps, Shannon couldn't go to school without having a drink before, after, or both. If she hadn't enlisted in the Marine Corps, she thinks she would still be drinking at a bar somewhere. But she did join the Corps, and her drinking days are a distant memory. It's true she sometimes can't believe the drastic changes that have occurred in her life. When she thinks about her Marine Corps career, she feels like she is dreaming. "I think about where I was and where I am now. I know that I wouldn't be here today if it wasn't for the Corps. The Corps stands firm on commitment and dedication and honor to Corps and self. I wasn't treating myself and others around me the way I should."

Cayden was born February 7, 2008, about a year and a half after Shannon came back from Iraq. He changed her world. He helps make her life more complete. Everything is about being a mother, about being able to find more love within herself to give to Cayden. He is the most important thing in her life. "When I pick him up from the babysitter, he kicks his feet and smiles. That's the best part of my day. He knows how to hug now. When he hugs me, it's like all the stress from my workday melts away. It's just me and my son in that moment."

Michelle Wilmot

Quixote in Ramadi

"The truth is that when his mind was completely gone, he had the strangest thought any lunatic in the world ever had, which was that it seemed reasonable and necessary to him, both for the sake of his honor and as a service to the nation, to become a knight errant and travel the world with his armor and his horse to seek adventures and engage in everything he had read that knights errant engaged in, righting all manner of wrongs and, by seizing the opportunity and placing himself in danger and ending those wrongs, winning eternal renown and everlasting fame."

—**Don Quixote**

MICHELLE WILMOT COULDN'T BELIEVE HER EARS.

The twenty-four-year-old Army sergeant had recently returned from a year in Camp Ramadi, Iraq, and was sitting in a college philosophy class. The students were discussing different views of war throughout history, and another female student spoke up. She said that what American soldiers were doing in Iraq was wrong, that they all deserved to die.

"Excuse me?" Wilmot said. "I was in Iraq for a year, so I should be fucking dead? Really? Why don't you come over here and fucking kill me? Come on. Do it!"

Wilmot was a college student when she received orders to deploy to Iraq. Within a month of returning from the desert, she re-enrolled at the University of North Florida in Jacksonville, changed her major from psychology to international studies/political science, and started classes. The classroom environment hadn't changed, but Wilmot had. Like so many other veterans re-entering academia, Wilmot chose to blend in and not draw attention to her veteran status. If she was going to talk about the war, she preferred to discuss it with people who had been on the battlefield and gone through similar experiences.

Up to this point, Wilmot seemed to fit in with her classmates. Other than being a few years older than the other co-eds, she fashioned herself like the other female students. Her straight brown hair was streaked with highlights and fell just below her shoulders. She accented her eyes with shadow and black eyeliner and her lips with a natural lip liner and cappuccino gloss. But after her outburst, she could no longer hide that she was a veteran. Now they knew. Emotionally and mentally, she had little, if anything, in common with her classmates. They were oceans apart. The students had learned in a flash that although Wilmot was only five feet, three inches tall, she could grow to six feet tall in an instant when she gets angry. Since returning from deployment, she often takes on the appearance of a giant.

Her first semester back at college was a disaster. She couldn't concentrate. When students said they knew what was wrong with the war in Iraq and Wilmot attempted to set the record straight, she often felt silenced. No one seemed to want to hear what she had to say, even though she had been there and had firsthand experience. Wilmot reached her breaking point in the philosophy class with about a dozen eighteen- and nineteen-year-old students.

"Well, we didn't belong in Iraq in the first place," the other student said.

Wilmot told the student that she agreed with her that the United States shouldn't have gone into Iraq, but now that the American soldiers were there, they couldn't just pick up and leave. That would be a disservice to the Iraqis. "We have to fix it. We have to make things right before we leave."

Usually, when Wilmot spoke up in the classroom, she stayed in student mode, which meant she could be articulate without swearing. But she couldn't maintain that reaction when she heard something that went against her beliefs. That's when she reverted to her role as sergeant, and the person she was talking to became a private.

"You don't know what the fuck you're talking about," she said, unleashing her rage on the student. "At least I've been there. Where the fuck were you? What have you ever worked for in your life?"

Wilmot felt her entire year on the battlefield being invalidated by this student and the others, including the instructor, who remained silent. At seventeen, she joined the Army. She had already served her country for seven years and had worked for everything she had. Now teenagers living off their moms and dads were telling her how life worked.

Wilmot was working at the 345th Combat Support Hospital in Jacksonville, Florida, when she learned she was deploying to Iraq. The Army was selecting soldiers from various commands to fill slots for deploying units. Initially, she was supposed to go to Iraq with a transportation battalion, but a month later, she was issued new orders to transfer to a different medical unit, one focusing on combat stress control. She would deploy with a company of soldiers whom she had never met.

Her journey began with two weeks of annual training, followed by predeployment training. From the start, Wilmot felt unwelcomed by a small segment of her unit. This wasn't a total surprise since she had already spent a lifetime defending her slightly brown skin, almond eyes, gender, and Catholic faith. At a young age, she was forced to develop thick skin. The strength and layers of that skin would be put to the test.

She prefers that her race not be the first thing you ask her about, but if you are curious and sincere, she will gladly tell you that her mother is a Chamorro from Saipan, an island about 100 miles north of Guam in the Western Pacific. Her father is Irish-Catholic and hails from Boston. She's many other things, too, so don't try to put her in a box. She hates labels. Hate is a harsh word, but she's earned the right to it. She has spent a quarter of a century bearing the brunt of hatred disguised as racism. She grew up with the Irish side of her family not accepting the Chamorro side. Her father was in the military, so her family constantly moved. Wilmot attended seven different schools in Florida, Alabama, Hawaii, Guam, and California between kindergarten and twelfth grade. In elementary school in Alabama, she ran from a boy with scissors as he yelled, "Go back to your country!" She was fourteen when her half sister was driving her to a homecoming dance in Guam. They got in an accident, and her sister abandoned Wilmot inside their wrecked car. Wilmot attributes this unthinkable act to jealousy. In Guam, she was considered a haughty *mestiza*, a half-breed, exotic.

People accepted one side of her or the other, either the Chamorro or Irish. She received half the dignity, half the respect, and half the love throughout her life because she looked multiracial. This torment followed her into adulthood, into the Army. As far as she's concerned, all you need to know is that she's American and that she loves her country.

Wilmot's loyalty comes honestly. In World War II, the Allies needed to capture the Marianas Islands to put Tokyo well within the range of the U.S. military's new B-29 Superfortress long-range bomber. Prior to the arrival of American troops, the Japanese occupied Saipan and were brutal to the Chamorro people. Wilmot's grandfather, Enrique Santos, who Wilmot calls Tata, barely survived these times. He came so close to death that he was standing in line to be beheaded after being accused by the Japanese of concealing the whereabouts of American soldiers. Tata witnessed heads rolling on the ground in the execution line in front of him in Marpi, Saipan, and the scrambling of Japanese troops as American troops landed to capture and liberate the island.

Wilmot, then, is proud to fight on America's behalf. Yet nowhere did she find racism more rampant than in the military, and nowhere did the sting of prejudice hurt more than in Iraq, where Wilmot, a mental health worker and medic, cared for her fellow soldiers.

Prior to deploying to Iraq, Wilmot went through annual training at Fort Benjamin Harrison in Indianapolis and then predeployment training at Fort Benning, Georgia. All soldiers reporting to annual training had to take a physical training test. Some soldiers had excuses for either not taking or not completing the test. Wilmot was getting over pneumonia, and she didn't feel great but took the test to get it over with. She threw up and was coughing up blood while running. She failed the test. A couple of mornings later, she went running in the snow. Still weak, she blacked out and fell, and a sergeant, realizing how sick Wilmot was, told her to go back to her room. As she was walking back, she crossed paths with the first sergeant. This was Wilmot's first week with the unit and her initial meeting with the first sergeant, a senior enlisted leader.

"What the hell are you doing?" he shouted. "How dare you drop out of formation?"

As he yelled, two white females who had already skipped physical training several times walked by. *So they were able to get out of PT feigning sore ankles, but having pneumonia wasn't a good enough excuse. Where the fuck is this coming from? Why is this happening to me?* Wilmot shrugged it off, thinking this would be an isolated incident.

"Well, what do you have to say for yourself?" he asked.

"Nothing, first sergeant," she said. "Not a thing." She just wanted him to stop shouting.

The first sergeant and others in her chain of command seemed to be forming an incorrect first impression about Wilmot's integrity. If they had looked at her personnel record from her previous unit, they would have seen that she was a good soldier, maybe even great. She had been the retention noncommissioned officer for the 345th Combat Support Hospital, which is like a recruiter, but instead of enlisting civilians, she focused on retaining soldiers who were already in the Army by getting them to sign re-enlistment contracts and offering bonuses and incentives to stay in the service longer. Yet anytime there was a heavy lifting detail, she was chosen to do it. She felt like their patsy, their workhorse, while the white girls sat out.

When she arrived at Fort Benning for predeployment training, Wilmot's female captain took an immediate dislike to her. On their first encounter, the captain snapped at Wilmot for what appeared to be no reason. Wilmot began to think she had "Fuck You" written on her forehead. She couldn't understand why she was being treated unjustly. During one exercise, she asked her captain if there was anything she could help with. The captain suggested Wilmot learn how to make a cot. "Just get out of my face." *What? What the hell did I do to this woman?*

Wilmot came from a combat support hospital, where her job revolved around putting up tents and making cots. Any time she went in the field, she had to build a hospital. Obviously, the captain hadn't read Wilmot's personnel record to find out what kind of skills she had. The captain and others were making first impressions based on her appearance and not on her work experience. But what was it about her appearance they didn't like? As a soldier, she was good to go. Her uniform was always starched, and she carried around a nail clipper in case she had any small hanging threads. But that's what good noncommissioned officers do.

So it couldn't have been her uniform. It couldn't have been her actions because she had just gotten there. It couldn't have been her attitude because she had barely opened her mouth, and when she did, it was to offer her help. She had just met these soldiers. It must be her race, the color of her skin.

Wilmot likens herself to Miguel de Cervantes's classic character Don Quixote, who read all sorts of fantastic tales about being a knight and then went off with his romantic ideas to improve society. She was the same way. She read war stories like *The Odyssey* and *The Things They Carried* and deployed to Iraq with the goal of doing great things. While Quixote got on his horse, Wilmot rode in a Humvee. Quixote got toyed with and humiliated, which led to disillusionment and, ultimately, his death. Wilmot got harassed, which led to cynicism and a broken spirit. Like Quixote, she looked forward to "seizing the opportunity" and placing herself "in danger and ending these wrongs."

When she arrived in Camp Ramadi, Wilmot's primary job was to provide mental health counseling to the troops. She also worked in the Lioness Program, searching Iraqi women and children. These were roles that she trained for and that she liked to do. What she hadn't anticipated was getting sucked into a personal war with about a dozen other soldiers in a company of approximately eighty.

Wilmot was stationed at Camp Ramadi with a few other soldiers from her company. She stayed in touch with her command in Baghdad primarily through e-mail, but that form of communication was erratic on the battlefield. This led to increasing frustration on both ends. When someone was wounded or killed, the company went into a communication blackout, which meant no one could send or receive e-mails or call one another. This made it much more difficult for Wilmot and her team to receive or respond to orders. The situation was stressful, and to make matters even worse, they were getting rained on by mortars every day;

often, those blasts would disrupt Internet service. Wilmot's staff tried to explain to the command that if they didn't respond, it wasn't personal. It was because there was a war going on. Wilmot's command, however, became convinced that the soldiers in Camp Ramadi were intentionally avoiding them.

Eventually, Wilmot started to take her command's accusations personally. Were they conspiring against her? And if so, how much of it had to do with her race? She would ask for night-vision goggles for evening convoys. Instead of getting the goggles, she was told to stop doing convoys. So she was supposed to stop helping wounded soldiers? It's a violation of every medic's code to refuse to give care. She asked for a radio for her truck but never got one from her command. If she had broken down or gotten lost on a convoy, she would not have been able to communicate with the other soldiers. Time after time, Wilmot's requests for much-needed supplies were denied. This went on for several months. Finally, she submitted an equal opportunity complaint based on racial, religious, and gender infractions. She never got a response.

In mid-April, mental-health soldiers, including Wilmot, traveled to Baghdad for a suicide prevention class. The class wouldn't start for a few days because they were waiting for soldiers to arrive from Balad and other forward operating bases. Two nights after she arrived, Wilmot was talking with the staff sergeant in charge of processing her equal opportunity complaint. Wilmot was informed that her captain had told the staff sergeant not to file the complaint. Wilmot couldn't believe it. You don't just stop processing an equal opportunity complaint because someone doesn't feel right about it. The discussion was cut short by the sound of a Humvee speeding down the road and coming to a screeching halt in front of their building.

"Medic! Medic! Medic!" voices shouted from the street.

"What the hell?" Wilmot and the staff sergeant got up and ran outside. "What's going on?"

"We've got a wounded soldier."

The soldiers were from the 3rd Infantry Division, and their wounded soldier was a female. Wilmot wasn't at a hospital. She was at a mental-health clinic. They didn't have medical equipment there to treat the physically wounded. But the soldiers who had just driven up weren't from the area and didn't know how to get to the hospital. The medical company signs were more visible than the hospital signs at the time.

Some of the soldiers who had gathered for the suicide prevention class were medics. They pulled the wounded soldier out of the Humvee, put her on a litter, and started running down the street toward the Baghdad hospital emergency room.

"Wait, where are you going? Wilmot yelled. "Put her down!"

They had to tie the soldier's tourniquets. Otherwise, she would bleed to death on the way to the hospital. The patient was already bad off. She was pale, barely breathing, and slipping into shock. Her pupils were dilated, and she didn't seem to be aware of her surroundings. Wilmot and the other soldiers screamed for more help.

"Hey! Everybody from the clinic get out here! Get out here!"

At the time, Baghdad and Camp Ramadi were the only teams there. All except two soldiers ran outside. The commander took over and did CPR, and a psychiatric nurse did compressions. Wilmot was at the patient's head, keeping her airway open and stabilized. Others started an IV and got a breather bag.

The MP who saw the female soldier get blown up by an IED was there. He and other 3rd Infantry Division soldiers were screaming and crying. "Don't let her die! Don't let her die." The mental-health staff was trying to save the patient and calm the soldiers at the same time.

"Can you hear me?" Wilmot said, talking to the patient.

The patient moved her eyes and exhaled but couldn't respond verbally. She had already lost a lot of blood. Someone replaced Wilmot so she could run inside and call the hospital. A soldier had tried to get in touch with the hospital, couldn't get through, and gave up. Wilmot was livid.

"What are you thinking?" she said. "Get back on the fucking phone."

It took forty minutes for the medevac to arrive. By that time, the patient had been bleeding for an hour. Wilmot and several others from the mental-health staff accompanied the patient and 3rd Infantry Division soldiers to the hospital to provide support. The wounded female died at the hospital after having both of her legs amputated. The soldiers, including Wilmot, were traumatized. Wilmot had to put her own feelings aside and bury them for the time being, so she could help the other soldiers. Her job was to give the soldiers enough mental and emotional support so they wouldn't feel the need to go off and hurt themselves or someone else. They needed someone to talk to; the worse thing they could do was hold it in.

Wilmot had seen wounded male soldiers before, but this was the first time she had seen a maimed female soldier. She returned, shaken up, to her company. She wasn't feeling like herself. She had been in Iraq for four months now. She thought she had seen it all. She thought that she had learned how to block out her fear of death, that she was able to look past it, that she was invincible. But this death penetrated all those defenses. This hit home: a woman soldier with her legs ripped off.

Her battle buddy, Specialist Miranda Mattingly, was waiting for her when she pulled up. Wilmot had been thinking of Mattingly while holding the female patient because they looked alike. *What if this were Mattingly? Or me?* Wilmot got upset when she saw wounded male soldiers, but she had an even more intense reaction to a female soldier. She was reminded of her own mortality. She and Mattingly talked. Mattingly went inside and came back out right away and said, "Hister wants to talk to you."

She and Hister hadn't gotten along since they met back in the States. He seemed to think that being white ensured him a certain sense of entitlement. When someone made a racist remark in front of him and Wilmot corrected the individual, he made his feelings apparent by rolling his eyes.

In December, before they deployed, Hister was a private first class. He got promoted three times over the next four months. One back-to-back promotion isn't unusual, but multiple ones are highly suspicious. In the meantime, Wilmot's promotional material kept disappearing.

Also, the requests that she made to her command via e-mail went through Hister. Wilmot had been sending him e-mails questioning why he and their command were not responding to her requests. Instead of directly addressing the requests in her e-mails, Hister would respond with snarky little comments, such as, "I don't need to respond to you." She thought the responses were childish. She wrote that if he didn't want to help, fine. She didn't care.

So he was racist, he was unduly promoted, he didn't help her get the supplies she needed, and while she was getting mortared in Camp Ramadi and on Lioness patrols in Ramadi and Fallujah, he was eating Lucky Charms in Saddam's palace.

"Tell him I'll talk to him tomorrow." Wilmot didn't feel like talking to anyone at that moment, least of all Hister. She was way too upset.

"All right, I'll tell him," Mattingly said.

She went back inside and told him. Hister yelled at her to get Wilmot. She did. Wilmot went into his office and told him, "Hey, you know a lot of shit has happened tonight. Let's talk tomorrow. I'll give you all the time you want in the morning, but right now, I need to head to bed."

"No, you need to come in here and sit down."

"I don't know who you think you are, talking to like that, but I just saw somebody die tonight," Wilmot said. She didn't mention that she knew he hid in his room while others treated the wounded soldier. "I'm going to bed. I can't even think right now."

"No, you need to sit down."

"Stop," she said. "Hold up right there."

"No, you stop," he said, putting his hand very close to her face.

Wilmot was raised that if someone puts a hand near your head, that person is asking for it. That person has a death wish. She looked at him. Her rifle was slung over her shoulder. She took her rifle out and had it in butt-stroke mode; she was prepared to hit him in the face with the bottom of her rifle.

He had some nerve. While she was trying to grieve over the loss of a fellow female soldier, he was trying to pick a fight with her. What was he thinking?

You should die, she thought. *And I'm gonna kill you.*

Before she could point her rifle at him, two soldiers pulled her away. She fought them.

"Let me go! Let me go! You coward! You need to cut off your balls and give them to somebody who can use them! You are a fucking piece of shit. You should die." She screamed at him in every language she knew, including English, Chamorro, and Spanish. He escaped and ran up the stairs to his commander's room.

The next morning, there was a knock on Wilmot's door. "You need to come see the commander and chaplain." When she arrived, the commander, captain, company chaplain, and first sergeant were already there. At first, Wilmot felt as though she had an ally in the first sergeant. He said he understood her reaction to Hister. He said it was wrong for Hister to pick a fight with her.

When Wilmot tried to defend her actions, her female commander responded, "Well, where you come from, this might be okay."

"What is that supposed to mean?" she asked.

"Well, Hister comes from a small town in Wisconsin."

Wilmot wanted to know what Wisconsin had to do with anything. Is the commander implying that this has something to do with race?

"You need to treat him with dignity and respect. He's special. He's a special boy."

So I'm Chamorro. Does that make me chopped liver?

She was listening to the conversation, but it was so ridiculous that it seemed surreal. She was waiting for someone to pop out and say, "Gotcha!"

Then the chaplain started to defend Hister. "In your culture, it might be okay to be a little rough," he said.

Do you even know what I am?

All of these soldiers were part of the command in Baghdad. They threatened to discipline Wilmot on the grounds of character assassination if she so much as said anything else to hurt Hister's feelings. Here Wilmot thought she was the victim, and everyone felt sorry for Hister. *Are you fucking kidding me? I have to treat this sergeant with respect?* This was the same sergeant who ensured that the unit had TVs and that all the offices had brand new desks, yet she drove around Iraq in a truck with no radio. She couldn't believe it. Surely, if she was white this wouldn't be happening.

In July, Lieutenant Colonel Kathy Platoni, clinical psychologist, deputy commander for clinical services in Iraq, and officer-in-charge of Team Ramadi, joined Wilmot in Camp Ramadi. Wilmot first met Platoni at predeployment training in Indianapolis. She had heard that Platoni had been stationed at Guantanamo Bay for a year and Wilmot was eager to talk to her and find out what it was like there.

Platoni is under five feet tall, but she is a ball of energy. She has more get-up-and-go than most, even though she only sleeps about four hours a night. She selflessly expends that vigor while motivating others; she encouraged Wilmot to finish her bachelor's degree so she could go on to earn a master's degree and a doctorate. Wilmot described Platoni as someone who is always on and doesn't do anything to spite anyone. She's very positive.

Part Jewish and part Italian, Platoni had experienced racism throughout her life and could empathize with Wilmot. She had been with the command in Baghdad for five months and wasn't impressed.

When Platoni arrived in Camp Ramadi, relations continued to deteriorate and all requests were ignored. In July, a soldier in Baghdad contacted Wilmot and said, "Hey, I heard you guys filed an IG [Inspector General] complaint."

Typically, when soldiers file an equal opportunity complaint, the command has sixty days to respond to it. Wilmot had never gotten a response. The next step was to file a complaint with the Office of the Army Inspector General. Wilmot hadn't filed a complaint, but she and Platoni had contacted the IG's office about some questionable activities.

In August, Wilmot and Platoni sent an e-mail to Baghdad to find out when Platoni would be going on R&R. They had repeatedly asked for dates. All requests, for R&R and everything else, continued to be ignored.

They called Baghdad. "Hey, what's going on? Are you having problems there?"

"No, we're not having problems."

"Then what's going on?"

Her requests were being ignored.

Then, in late August, Wilmot received an e-mail from Captain Custer in Baghdad. Addressed to all noncommissioned officers, the letter was requesting dates for R&R. Wilmot wrote back, "Once again Ramadi was in the dark, but thanks for the info." She got an e-mail back from her first sergeant in Baghdad telling her to stand down, the equivalent of back off. She also got a call from her commander and her first sergeant charging her with mutiny, conspiracy to overthrow existing authority. Wilmot was furious. She couldn't let their responses go unanswered. Stand down? Are you serious? She'd been asking for R&R dates for months and not getting a response on that or any other requests. Now she gets an e-mail asking for R&R dates like it's the first time the subject has come up. It was the last straw.

Replying in full force, this knight sat down to "right all manners of wrong." She composed a four-page, single-spaced e-mail highlighting all the injustices that she and others in Ramadi had experienced over the past nine months and explaining why she felt they had been left in the dark. She wrote that her intent was not to disrespect anyone of rank. It was, instead, to show why she and the others in her unit felt out of touch and abandoned. She cited much-needed supplies that her unit never received. She mentioned how the Marines and National Guard soldiers would scrounge up supplies for her and how she never had an answer when they asked her why her command wasn't supportive. She wrote of equal opportunity complaints that went unanswered. She wrote about feeling unsafe and wanting more security.

Wilmot always had her rifle on her, but now she also had to carry her knife when she went to the Port-a-John because a soldier had been stabbed by one of the third-country national workers in the middle of the night. Their chow hall had gotten blown up in the very corner where she normally sat for lunch.

Wilmot felt that the soldiers' physical, emotional, and mental needs were being ignored. They were sick and tired of being mistreated, and they needed someone to do something about it. Wilmot wanted all the soldiers to know they weren't alone in their gripes and complaints. Her goal in writing the letter was to get more support from her command in Baghdad. It was a final attempt to explain the concerns of the soldiers with whom she worked in Camp Ramadi and those spread out at different bases throughout the battlefield.

Wilmot e-mailed the letter to her entire company, which was made up of about eighty soldiers. Platoni agreed with Wilmot's correspondence and even called Baghdad and reiterated their frustration. Other soldiers agreed with her e-mail, but no one else came forward. If they all stood together and admitted the truth, she doesn't think she would have gotten into so much trouble.

To an outsider, it seems unfathomable that the soldiers' concerns weren't being addressed. One would think that the responsibility of the command is to make sure the soldiers get what they need to do their jobs. So what's the benefit of not helping the soldiers? Wilmot answers the question with more questions. "Why does rape happen? Why does assault happen? It's not just about sexuality. It's not just about rape. It's about use and abuse of power."

In addition to their needs not being met, there were unethical things going on in her unit. If one person got caught, Wilmot feared they would all get into trouble. A private blog that Wilmot wrote after she returned home shed some light on this unethical behavior. She wrote: "God forbid if you questioned events"—why it was okay for officers to mail weapons home illegally; why it was okay for married officers and noncommissioned officers to have affairs; why alcohol flowed through the Green Zone despite the Army's anti-alcohol policy in theater; why her team was punished for providing desperately-needed medical support for infantry units; why soldiers were promoted based on favoritism and not on ability; why her command expressed disappointment when she showed up to the clinic with a cross drawn in ashes on her forehead for Ash Wednesday; why her objectivity as a female was questioned; why the unit's female leaders attacked others for holding soldiers to a high standard; why she was instructed to give white soldiers special treatment or face punishment.

No one was saying anything about any of these infractions. "All I'm saying is that if something's going on that's wrong, you're supposed to speak up, whether you're an officer or not. But I guess I'm the asshole who actually believed that."

At the end of August, Wilmot got a call that a female soldier had been sexually assaulted by an Iraqi special forces soldier at Camp Corregidor. The soldier was stationed at Habbaniyah. Platoni had finally gotten her R&R, so she was gone at the time. Wilmot contacted her commander in Baghdad and was ordered not to go. She was told it wasn't her concern. Wilmot felt differently; as a medic and mental-health provider, she thought it was her duty to respond. The female soldier's brigade commander had authorized Wilmot's assistance, and this was a lawful order; her commander's order from Baghdad was not. She went against her commanding officer's orders and told a few soldiers from her unit that she was going. She proceeded to stow away in the back of seven-ton truck with about a dozen Marines. It was a three-hour drive.

It took her a couple of days, but she finally found the soldier eating in the chow hall at Habbaniyah. Wilmot sat down with the soldier and introduced herself. She explained that she worked for a combat stress team. The female soldier thought it was a coincidence that she had been attacked and now someone was there from combat stress to talk to her. Wilmot explained that she was there because she had heard about the attack and wanted to make sure she was okay.

The assault victim described what had happened. An Iraqi soldier had grabbed her hand and started groping her. He then tried to pin her wrists against the wall. He fought to get her to the ground, and she struggled to get free. He got her part way to the ground, but fortunately, he wasn't that big. She was able to get away.

The soldier said she was doing okay, aside from not wanting to be left alone again. She promised Wilmot that if she did have any problems, she would seek professional help.

When Wilmot first arrived in Habbaniyah, she called back to her clinic in Camp Ramadi and told one of her soldiers to make up some excuse about her whereabouts if her commanders in Baghdad called. Instead, the soldier told his chain of command exactly where she was. To add insult to injury, while Wilmot was gone, a fellow soldier threw all her gear and food in a trash can. He knew she was in a heap of trouble and took pleasure in adding to her adversity.

When she returned to Ramadi on September 4, Wilmot's commander accused her of violating her orders. Platoni was still on R&R when Wilmot was ordered to pack her bags for Baghdad, where she would receive a military escort to jail. Wilmot believes that the order had more to do with her e-mails than her trip to Habbaniyah and that her command waited until Platoni was gone to have her shipped out.

During her flight from Ramadi to Baghdad, Wilmot had time to reflect on her romantic ideals of war. Those ideals no longer existed; they had been shattered. She was a sad pathetic knight in broken armor, a knight who had now been pushed to the edge. As Ramadi faded, she thought about all the hours she had invested in the Army and in her mental-health clinic and how they—the powers that be—were trying to strip her of her dignity. She gripped her M16 rifle for comfort and protection against her enemy—who happened to be certain other soldiers. Her mind raced as she thought about ways to do the unthinkable, to kill them. She'd been pushed around long enough by her command. She wasn't going to take it anymore, and she wasn't going to go down without a fight.

I'm gonna fucking hurt them as soon as I get there.

As the aircraft neared Fallujah, it started to descend fast. Wilmot was so preoccupied that she didn't realize they were making an emergency landing until the C-9 hit the ground with a thud and she heard the *clank clank clank* of metal parts. They had landed on a grassy field in Fallujah.

She asked one of the crew members what was going on.

"Get out! Get out! Get out! Get out!"

The helicopter had broken down.

It took a week for Wilmot to get another flight to Baghdad, but the layover didn't do much to quell her anger. When she finally got to Baghdad, her housing was a fluorescent teal room for transients. As she sat alone in the room, she thought about all the times she searched Iraqi women and children, counseled soldiers and Marines, conducted pain-management classes for troops who survived explosions, drove in convoys, and intervened in suicide and homicide cases. Didn't this amount to anything?

Holding a bullet in one hand and her rifle in the other, Wilmot's rage escalated. Her heart had become as still and dark and cold as a desert night. They had broken her. As a medic, her job was to save lives. She had been raised with the teaching "Thou shall not kill." Now she felt like wounding people.

What now? Who were these people eager to destroy her world, her peace of mind, simply because she wasn't white? It didn't matter. She didn't want to ask any more questions, of herself or God. She heard and felt a loud, sharp ringing in her ears as she began to quake in anger. Tears streamed down her cheeks. Maybe she wasn't a person after all; maybe she was just an exotic animal placed in a fluorescent teal room in order to be observed. Never mind her character, personality, intelligence, or interests. The first questions from most people were about her ethnicity— who she was and where she was from—because there was no way she could be American. Wilmot no longer saw herself in the mirror the same way. In her reflection, she saw an empty vessel. They had cheated her, and she was desperate to make the sharp pain in her head go away.

The morning after she arrived in Baghdad, Wilmot attended her first hearing in front of her commander and first sergeant. She accepted ownership of her e-mails. She meant what she wrote. But she wouldn't admit to the other charges, such as mutiny and disrespecting an officer. A controversial e-mail could land her an Article 15, which meant a possible reduction in pay, demotion, or forty-five days of extra duty. Mutiny and disrespecting an officer were another story.

Also in attendance at her initial hearing was Platoni, who was on her way back from R&R. She was awaiting a flight from Baghdad to Camp Ramadi. She empathized with Wilmot and urged their command to put an end to the racism and to the suffering that went along with it. "This needs to stop," she said. "It's gone on too long." The hearing brought Platoni to tears. Wilmot was moved that the clinical psychologist would put herself out there for her.

Wilmot had another hearing the next morning with just the first sergeant. He counseled her again for picking on Hister. "You need to be nice to him," he said. "He's a special boy." He accused Wilmot of being racist toward Hister because he is white. "I don't think so," Wilmot said. "I think you guys are being racist towards me." She had never brought up the fact that Hister was white. She told them that she thought they were obsessed with racism.

"Oh, you need to stand down," the sergeant said.

A black female sergeant standing by nodded her head in agreement.

"You're telling me this shit, and you expect me to stand down? I've heard Catholic this and minority that and woman this and all this other shit, and I'm the one who needs to stand down?"

Afterwards, back in the teal room, Wilmot cried tears of anger. *I'm gonna fucking do this right now. I'm just gonna go in there, and I don't care who's in there. I'm just gonna light it up like a Christmas tree and I don't give a fuck.* Platoni walked into her room and saw that Wilmot looked like hell. She sat with Wilmot and validated what she was feeling. Everything was coming to a head.

As they were sitting there, the black sergeant came into the room and started consoling Wilmot. "Get the fuck out of my room!" Wilmot told her. "You were there! You were condoning this shit! If this happened to a black person, you would be all over it. You wouldn't let this shit happen to you. Since they're not picking on you, you're kissing their asses."

Platoni returned to Camp Ramadi, and Wilmot was sent to Camp Stryker, a tent city in Baghdad. Reassigning Wilmot to Camp Stryker was meant to be punishment, but the conditions weren't that bad. She did have to live in a tent, but she wasn't exposed to daily rocket and mortar attacks, and she wasn't searching Iraqi women and children. She would stay at Camp Stryker from the beginning of October until her unit left Iraq in mid-November. She worked very little between trips to Baghdad for hearings.

On October 10, Wilmot returned to Baghdad for a hearing with the 6th Combat Support Hospital to decide her fate. If she denied the Article 15, she would face a court-martial. At this point, she didn't care anymore. She had given up on the Army and her dream of becoming a career soldier. She threatened the command with thirty-nine single-spaced pages of documentation of abuse. She would send it to reporters at CNN, FOX, and the all major networks who were staying at a local hotel. They knew she was serious. Again, they ordered her to stand down.

When she finally stood in front of the colonel and sergeant major of the 6th Combat Support Hospital, she lost it. They asked her if she really believed her superiors were racist. Wilmot compared it with asking a rape victim in front of her attacker if she thought the accused had really intended to rape her. She said it was her experience. They told her that was her perception. *It was my perception that they called me names, tried to damage my reputation, and denied me of all my protective gear?* It was her word against theirs, and the legal system sided with her command. She got an Article 15 and was told not to disrespect officers next time. Her punishment was a forty-five day probationary period and two weeks of extra duty in the internet cafe.

What does it say about the leadership in Wilmot's reserve unit when there are five Article 15s and disciplinary problems? In Wilmot's opinion, there are no bad soldiers; there are only bad noncommissioned officers and officers. If she had a bad soldier under her, it was her fault and her problem. The military she had joined in 1998 had morphed into something else. The justice system and leadership were corrupt, tainted with self-interest and vanity.

Her whole experience in Iraq felt like one big nightmare. Along with the Article 15 and everything it encompassed, she had friends who died over there. Her battle buddy was medically evacuated from Iraq. One member of the bomb-disposal team who had lived on the compound with her had lost his eyesight, while another had lost his hands. She'd be eating chow with soldiers one day, and the next day, they'd be dead or medically evacuated.

By the time she arrived back in the States, Wilmot had reached the end of her rope. She was hanging on for dear life. The soldiers in her reserve unit dispersed while she returned to the 345th Combat Support Hospital in Jacksonville, Florida. When she got there, most of the soldiers in her unit hadn't even deployed.

She came home with an intense desire to seek revenge on the soldiers who she felt had wronged her, who had harassed her daily. She began profiling them and devoting a large amount of time getting personal information on them. It was her way of coping. She knew they lived in Ohio, Indiana, and Virginia. She knew how many children they had. She knew their social security numbers, their blood types, and their spouse's names. If anyone ever did anything horrible to her again—and she had a sense they would—it would be okay because she knew where their kids went to school.

Fantasizing was another tactic she used to cope and stay in control of her life. Before falling off to sleep at night, Wilmot would dream up situations in her mind where she'd meet the soldiers face to face, perhaps in an empty parking lot, and finish what they started. Visualizing revenge made her feel a little better about things. She never intends to act on her fantasies but still thinks about them three years after returning home.

Knowing that revenge was a sign of post-traumatic stress disorder (PTSD) and not a healthy way to deal with her anger, Wilmot went to see a civilian priest in Jacksonville, Florida. It was Christmas, and she was Catholic. While Catholics aren't required to go to confession during Advent, more are likely to do so during the holiday season, especially if they have done or were contemplating something for which they want to be absolved.

The priest hearing the confessions that afternoon was an angry old Irish priest Wilmot knew. Of all the priests to be working that day . . . She was sure that he would tell her that her thoughts of revenge were going to send her straight to hell. Instead, he listened . . . and listened . . . and listened.

"Bless me, Father, for I have sinned," she told the priest. "Something happened to me in Iraq. I experienced a lot racism and sexism, and discrimination because of my religion. It drove me to a boiling point, and I wanted to kill, and that feeling hasn't left me. I'm really disturbed by it." She told him in detail what she planned to do, what she almost did, and how she felt about it.

When she finally stopped talking, there was a long silence before the priest began to speak. He didn't respond the way she thought he would. She thought this priest was kind of an asshole, so she expected a hard-hearted response. She thought he would yell at her and tell her to get out. She was wrong.

"You know," he said, "I've talked to a lot of people who served in Vietnam. What you're feeling is totally normal."

Here she thought she got the one priest who wouldn't understand her, and he totally got it.

"You'll get through it," he said.

He encouraged her to pray and meditate about it. Pray for her enemies and let God seek justice for her. Don't allow wrath to blind her, however justified it is. Talking it out was the best way to get through, he said. Seek out other vets with similar experiences to help mend the wounds within your soul. She walked out of the church knowing she wasn't alone.

Wilmot's PTSD symptoms include insomnia, little to no short-term memory, and depression. When she thinks back on her experiences in Iraq, she can't sleep. Her short-term memory is shot. She has to write everything she plans to do for the day. She writes down her dreams, the day's events, and emotional triggers so she can't forget them. She can recall everything from the battlefield, however, from the scent of charred human bodies to what Ramadi looked like, what she kept under her bed, and where her fellow soldiers were born.

Her depression comes and goes. As a member of the mental-health profession, it's not easy for her to admit when she has a problem. But she knows what to do. She doesn't take drugs. Instead, when she's feeling down, she'll reach out to a battle buddy or to Platoni. She knows soldiers who are much worse off than she is. In terms of racism, she had it bad, but she wasn't wounded physically.

It's not unusual for soldiers to return with feelings of aggression. Each has her own way of releasing her excess anger and energy. For an emotional and mental release, Wilmot frequently wrote in a journal in Iraq. She continues to write everything down to keep track of her behavior. For a more physical release, she works out on weights and cardiovascular machines at the gym.

Wilmot describes herself as easy going. Prior to going to war, she likened herself to Ferdinand the Bull, the storybook character who would rather smell flowers than fight in bullfights. Ferdinand would sit in the middle of the bull-ring failing to take heed of any provocations of the matador and others to fight. Wilmot was never one to start fights, but once they started, she would be the one to end them. She'd rather sit around and smell the flowers, uninterested in everything else and daydreaming. But once she got stung, someone was going to get gored.

The conversation in the philosophy classroom certainly made her much angrier than she would have been had she not been a soldier on the battlefield. After the heated exchange in the classroom, Wilmot couldn't sleep. She'd wake up five times a night. She got chronic stomach aches and had allergies all the time. She stopped going to class. She couldn't look at any of the students, the one she argued with or the ones who sat by silently. They were just as complicit in their ignorance and betrayal. It was Camp Ramadi all over again. Wilmot believes in being a Good Samaritan. If you see an injustice being committed, you have an obligation to intervene. If someone is being hurt, she is not going to sit by and watch.

It sickened her to look at her classmates. They were pathetic. When she did look at them she tensed up, shook, and turned red. Her body and mind returned to Iraq and the weak soldiers who made false accusations against her. Her mind shifted from philosophy to killing in seconds. If she had to listen to any more students talk about the war as if they knew what was going on, she would get up and smash a desk over their heads. She couldn't deal with it. She couldn't be there. But she didn't feel comfortable anywhere.

With the encouragement of an officer she met in Camp Stryker, Wilmot applied to the Harvard Public Policy and Leadership Conference. She didn't have an interest in political science before she went to Iraq, but her experiences on the battlefield changed that. She was invited to attend the conference, which is hosted annually by the Kennedy School of Government to create a diverse student body for graduate school. She went there for a weekend in February 2006 thinking that she would have a lot to say and that people would be interested in what she had to say because of her firsthand experience as a female soldier in Iraq. Her idealism was short-lived.

The first workshop she attended dealt with racial diversity. The professor was talking about diversity as if it were just a black-and-white issue, with some references to Asian and Hispanic cultures. Wilmot thought he was limiting the discussion by only talking about a few groups, and she simply wanted the professor to accept her premise that diversity is complicated.

The professor said Asians and Pacific Islanders are in the same group.

"No, they're not," Wilmot argued. "It's racist for you to even say that. We need to talk about everyone and not just one or two groups."

After the lecture, Wilmot told the coordinator the conference was bullshit, but the coordinator urged her to attend another workshop. The next workshop was also about diversity and taught by a former female U.S. ambassador to Yemen and Iraq who spent a lot of time in the Green Zone with the Coalition Provisional Authority. She made a comment that the United States military is more misogynistic than Arab men.

"I was in the Army for eight years and in Iraq for one," Wilmot told the lecturer. "I had an AK-47 pointed at my chest by an Iraqi soldier who said he was just cleaning his fucking weapon. I've had more passes made at me by Iraqi men than by American soldiers who I lived with. So if you're going to make that stereotype, I think you're wrong. I think you have it backwards."

"I was in the Green Zone," the lecturer said.

"I was in Ramadi," Wilmot shot back. "Did you even leave the Green Zone?"

"No."

"What the hell do you know about Iraq outside the Emerald City? What do you know? They have yoga and Arabic classes and patisseries. They have porcelain toilets that are cleaned by Iraqis."

The lecturer said she talked with special forces soldiers, who are highly trained to conduct specialized operations such as reconnaissance. After that, Wilmot kept raising her hand, but the lecturer wouldn't call on her. Wilmot got up and left in the middle of the speech.

Wilmot was released from the 66th Medical Company–Combat Stress Control on December 31, 2005, and she returned to her old unit in Jacksonville, Florida. She didn't leave the Army Reserves until September 2006. She was denied benefits upon discharge because she was in the reserves and not active duty. When she joined the Army she had been told that when she got out, she would still be eligible for the GI Bill. That wasn't the case; she lost the GI Bill, along with tuition assistance and medical coverage.

In addition to the emotional and mental challenges she faced in Iraq, Wilmot also experienced physical trauma from IED and mortar explosions, one as close as twenty-five feet. She experiences dizziness and vertigo, gastrointestinal problems, traumatic brain injury, sleep apnea, and hearing loss. She contacted the VA while still in the reserves and was told she wasn't covered.

She contacted the VA in Gainesville, Florida, for locations where she could have some of her symptoms examined. A doctor from Gainesville returned her call. Wilmot had moved with her Marine husband to Jacksonville, North Carolina. The closest VA is in Wilmington, an hour south, and she was told she would have to fill out paperwork there and then go to Fayetteville to fill out more paperwork. She doesn't know if she wants to go through all that; she doesn't want to put herself in a situation that will cause more stress.

She started off idealistic, like Quixote. From there, it was all downhill, her romanticism tumbling and perishing along the way. She had no idea that she could get so detached from her command, that they could care so little about her well-being. She never imagined that someone could charge her with something as serious as mutiny. At the moment, she's taken a more serious look into pursuing a career in writing, particularly about the darker moments of her deployment and the ongoing crises in military mental health.

"I went out and did a lot of dangerous shit voluntarily," Wilmot said. "I went to combat outposts. I didn't think twice about getting hurt. I pretended it wasn't happening and told myself that I would deal with it when I got home."

At home, she and her husband, Donny, have made plans to settle in the Northeast. Wilmot is optimistic about her personal life. She looks forward to spending her time painting murals, drinking tea, smoking hookah, and relaxing with family and friends.

Lisa Spencer

LISA SPENCER JOINED THE ARMY AT SEVENTEEN, BECAME A MECHANIC, and went to Turkey during the first Gulf War. She joined the reserves and eventually got out of the Army and earned associate's and bachelor's degrees. After 9/11, she re-enlisted at the age of forty and went to Iraq for a year in 2003–04 with the 403rd Transportation Company out of Fort Bragg, North Carolina.

Her company split up, and she was sent with the 3rd Platoon to Camp Cedar 2 near Tallil Airbase, which is about halfway between Kuwait and Baghdad. She offloaded and delivered supplies to troops throughout the camp. Sometimes, she supervised the missions by checking the vehicles to make sure they were in working order. She also pulled guard duty and rode on convoys.

Spencer spent most of her time inside the wire, but in her case, the enemy was also on the airbase. She had a young male squad leader and was in a platoon made up primarily of young male soldiers. She felt like she was a victim of discrimination mainly because of her age. Her platoon sergeant had it in for her because she was older than the rest of the soldiers in the platoon. He was constantly screaming at her. It was stressful enough working on an airbase that was mortared nearly every night; his attitude made things much worse.

"When we first got to Iraq, we were all down about being there," Spencer said. "Church services were held every Sunday, and I went. It helped. I'm a religious person. I truly believe in God getting me through everything. I also love to sing. We got a choir together. My platoon sergeant said I could go to church, but if I did, he was going to make my life miserable. It wasn't the Iraqis that were the problem; it was some of my fellow soldiers."

The platoon sergeant told Spencer she wasn't a good noncommissioned officer because she was too soft and too old. She needed to be a bitch and drop soldiers. Spencer believes there are times when you need to be tough, but there are also times when you need to listen and encourage soldiers.

As soon as she got back home in February 2004, Spencer was told that she would be returning to Iraq in six months. She started to get depressed. It wasn't so much the idea of going back and being in danger; she had enlisted in the Army after 9/11 and expected to deploy. She just couldn't handle returning to Iraq with the same platoon. If she had been with the soldiers she deployed with during the first Gulf War, she would have been happy to go to Iraq any number of times because they cared about the troops and treated them well.

She started to have panic attacks and wound up in the hospital emergency room several times. She'd drive down the road and, for a good two minutes, wouldn't know where she was. It was scary. One time, she drove her car over cement steps at battalion headquarters on Fort Bragg. While shopping at farmer's markets and department stores, she'd hear noises that would put her right back in Iraq and made it difficult for her to breathe. At night, when soldiers were firing at the practice range, her sister often found Spencer in the closet trying to get away from the noise.

Her company commander and executive officer assured Spencer's mother that they would take care of her, but instead, they got on her for not being able to do her job. They spoke one way to the family and another way to her. Spencer got out of the Army not because she wanted to, but because she felt like she wasn't getting any support. She gave the military eighteen years, and in return, she got a "you're not good enough for this man's army."

She started going to the VA for her combat-related physical and emotional wounds and ended up fighting a battle that was much more costly that the one in Iraq. "I felt like they didn't care," she said. At first, her doctor seemed genuinely concerned and willing to help her. "Now it's what can I do to get you out of my office so I can see the other twenty people I need to see today." At one appointment with her primary-care physician, Spencer was told she would have to choose what symptom she wanted to be treated for as he did not have time to check them all out.

She went to the VA for counseling for post-traumatic stress disorder when she got out of the Army in late 2004. It wasn't until three years later that she was diagnosed with it and got an eye appointment. "You just fall between the cracks." Spencer has since been rated 100 percent disability for post-traumatic stress disorder and other physical findings from the VA.

Elaine Snavely

The World as She Knows It

WHEN THE UNITED STATES WAS ATTACKED ON 9/11, ELAINE Snavely was a corpsman stationed on the newly-commissioned destroyer USS *Winston Churchill.* The ship had been at sea for more than a month and was deployed off the coast of Portsmouth, England. Medical and senior staff carried handheld radios to communicate with one another at all times. Snavely was sitting at a computer working on the medical supply inventory when a message came across the radio from the bridge to the commanding officer (CO). It was a flash message—extremely urgent.

The CO responded that he was on his way. Within minutes, he got on the ship's intercom system and announced that a plane had flown into one of the Twin Towers. While still on the intercom, the staff received another flash message. The CO announced that the second tower had been hit. Then another message: the Pentagon had also been struck.

Snavely, a twenty-seven-year-old native of Houston, Texas, sat at her computer and wondered if the world would survive these attacks.

By now, Snavely had been in the Navy eight years and was on her third cruise and second ship. She had joined the Navy right after high school. Enlisting was an easy decision. While she was growing up, the people who meant the most to her were either in the military or had ties to the military. A couple of years before Snavely graduated from high school, she spent a summer with her aunt and worked for a physical therapist to see if that was something she'd be interested in doing. She joined the Navy because she didn't have the money to pay for college. She planned to use her educational benefits to transition from corpsman to physical therapy technician later.

The ship was taken down to a skeleton crew so that officers and enlisted personnel could go to their respective mess and chow halls to listen to reports on BBC radio. Snavely did not get much sleep over the next five or so days. Maybe because she was older than many of the sailors, maybe because she was a corpsman, whatever the reason, Snavely was chosen to help console the sailors who had lost family and friends.

There were lots of frayed nerves on the ship, including hers. On the *Winston Churchill*, sailors of all ages were discovering that the world as they knew it no longer existed. It's a harsh lesson, but one Snavely had learned seven years earlier in Bosnia. The attacks triggered memories of her first deployment in 1994, when she was part of a fleet hospital in Bosnia during the war in Sarajevo. She started having flashbacks of her experiences in Bosnia—a sniper opening fire on a five-year-old boy, bodies torn apart by landmines. She was restricted to the airfield in Bosnia. A sign warned personnel not to walk on the grass. There were landmines everywhere.

Two years after 9/11, Snavely deployed to Iraq for the first time as a corpsman attached to Marine Wing Support Squadron (MWSS-372). She was a pharmacy tech who had been dispensing medicine to patients at Marine Corps Base Camp Pendleton forty-five miles north of San Diego. At Al Taqaddum Airbase, she responded to flight-line emergencies and assisted with several mass casualties.

In 2007, Snavely deployed again, this time to Al Asad Airbase. Prior to leaving, the squadron's mission changed. MWSS-372 would take over a low-altitude air defense position. Instead of providing medical coverage for the flight line, Snavely would provide care for the base and assist with security patrols.

She had been in Al Asad for several months when, on November 28, 2007, she was sent out on a security patrol. On the way to her destination, the now-thirty-four-year-old petty officer second class would have another experience that would significantly alter her world.

Snavely rolled out of bed for a convoy brief at 3 A.M. She knew she would be getting ready in the dark and hadn't wanted to wake her roommate, so she got her gear and clothes ready the night before. Her uniform was hanging on her locker door. Draped over her uniform were her T-shirt, bra, and underwear. She had already filled her backpack with some necessary items: gloves; a neck gator, which was like a sock that kept her neck warm and that she could pull up over her mouth and nose to keep the dust out; a beanie; a can of Campbell's soup (her soup de jour was cream of chicken); a couple packages of Gold Fish; and a can of Arizona sweet tea. Later in the morning, she planned to put the can of soup on the floorboard of the Humvee and let the engine heat it up. She also brought her MP3 player, on which she listened to anything but gangster rap. She walked about a half mile from the can (i.e., her sleeping quarters) to the rendezvous area.

The convoy was made up of four Humvees, about fifteen Marines, and Snavely. During the brief, everyone found out what equipment they would need and what vehicle they would ride in. Snavely was assigned to the fourth vehicle with three Marines whom she didn't know very well. Her job on the convoy was to provide medical support for Marines and any locals who needed help.

She doesn't remember where they were heading that morning. She vaguely recalls the convoy stopping at a security halt and starting up again. Then something caused her Humvee to flip. The turret gunner, Corporal Allen Roberts, was thrown out of the turret and landed close enough to the truck that when it rolled over, the vehicle crushed his head. The vehicle commander, who was riding in the front passenger seat, was thrown out the side of the vehicle. The driver got bumped around but wasn't severely wounded. Snavely was sitting in the rear passenger seat when she was ejected through the turret. She and Roberts were medevaced to the hospital in Al Asad.

At the hospital, the medical staff took X-rays and did a CAT scan of Snavely. The tests showed that she had broken two vertebrae in her neck: C2, the axis that turns the head, and C3. This type of break is called a hangman's fracture and is similar to actor Christopher Reeve's paralyzing injury, though his fracture was lower. If Snavely's fracture had been lower, she would have been paralyzed or dead.

Once the medical staff saw that Snavely had several fractures—the two vertebrae, her left upper arm, her ribs, her pelvis in two places—and had sustained a concussion with loss of consciousness, they immediately had her medevaced to the hospital in Balad, where she could get a higher level of care.

Snavely has trauma-induced amnesia. She doesn't remember the accident and has only a flash of memory of seeing Chief Jonathon Wells in the ER in Balad and then being loaded onto an airplane. Her next memory is of waking up in a hospital room and being greeted by a female officer.

"Who are you?"

"I'm the charge nurse in the ICU."

"What ICU?"

"You're at Landstuhl."

"I'm in Germany? Are you kidding me?"

"No, I'm not kidding you."

"What happened?"

"You had a small accident in your Humvee two days ago."

"Oh shit. . . . Where is everyone else?"

Snavely was the only one who had been transported to Germany. All the lieutenant commander knew or could tell her was that she was seriously wounded and someone had died. If Snavely had the energy, she "would have beaten the woman who delivered the bad news with the end of my IV pole." She was frustrated and angered by the lack of information and details. She had no idea what had happened, who had been hurt, what was going on. It took her a couple of days to process what had happened. She didn't cry. She said her body wasn't strong enough to allow her to cry.

On her second day in ICU, the medical staff operated on Snavely's neck. They couldn't go in through the back of her neck because it was too "jacked up," a common military expression these days, so she was sliced open horizontally from the front of her neck, below her left ear, where her left carotid artery is located. A cadaver bone was inserted between C2 and C3 so the bone fragments—six in all—would fuse together. Then a metal plate was put in front of her spine at the neck and four screws were attached to the plate.

Two days later, more X-rays were taken to make sure Snavely's neck was aligned properly and to see how her left arm was doing. It turned out that she had a greenstick fracture in her arm. When she moved it, she could feel the broken ends of the bones rubbing together. Her humorus had broken into nine pieces. She compared it with taking two ends of a chicken bone and twisting it until it shatters. She was happy to be right handed. The fractures of her pelvis in two places and a rib on the left side close to her spine were considered stable, so there was no reason to operate on them.

Before the operation on her arm, Snavely asked the anesthesiologist not to put the biggest breathing tube they had down her throat. During the first surgery on her neck, the surgeon had to push her trachea and esophagus to the right leaving her with an extremely sore throat. She felt like she had pneumonia and strep at the same time. She also asked the medical staff to avoid putting her in a heavy arm cast because the weight would put a strain on her neck. During the surgery, the doctor sliced her from the back of her armpit down to below her elbow and inserted a plate and nine screws to stabilize the small pieces of bone and ensure nothing moved around. She woke with no cast on her arm.

Snavely had been horizontal for nearly a week when Chief Petty Officer Todd Curtis came into her room and told her it was time to start walking. She thought he was crazy. After much deliberation (and some name-calling on her part), he got her to sit up and then to stand. Standing made her dizzy, so he was content with just having her stand on her own two feet for a while. She worked her way up to shifting her weight from her left to right foot, as if she were slow-dancing with her husband.

Snavely met her husband, Jason, at Naval Air Station Oceana in Virginia Beach, Virginia. He was working as a search-and-rescue corpsman. She was working in the hospital pharmacy. Snavely was asked to be on the color guard committee for the naval hospital corps' birthday since she had worked on it the previous year and knew what needed to be done. Jason, who is six feet, two inches tall and weighs only 150 pounds, was assigned to the committee because he was trim and looked good in the uniform.

Once a week, they drove from Oceana to the naval hospital in Portsmouth for color guard training at one o'clock. As they got to know each other, Snavely and Jason started leaving work early to grab lunch before training. Following training, they would stop off at the White Horse pub to throw darts or at the Purple Cow restaurant for a hamburger.

After Snavely returned from her fifth deployment, this time to Bahrain on a casualty-receiving team, she and Jason went to Cancun, Mexico, for a week. A year later, on February 7, 2004, they eloped in Virginia Beach, with only one witness and their black Labrador retriever, Gunner, as the best man.

They moved to California, where Snavely continued her career in the Navy. After serving as a corpsman for a tour with 1st Marine Division outside Fallujah, Jason got out of the Navy and enrolled at Palomar Community College to complete his general requirements to become a physician's assistant before transferring to a four-year college to earn a bachelor's degree.

Just hours before she was wounded, Snavely called Jason to wish him a happy birthday. After she was wounded, Chief Wells telephoned Jason while Snavely was being flown to Balad. There was very little in the way of details about her wounds or the accident. It was only days later that Jason learned the full extent of her wounds, including her broken neck. During their first phone call, Snavely was "out of it."

Chief Wells, whom she had seen at the hospital in Al Asad, called Snavely at Landstuhl and left a message. She called him back to find out "why the hell am I in pieces and in the hospital?" He asked her if she was going to remember this time. It seems he had answered that question several times already while she was in the ER in Al Asad. As she came in and out of consciousness, she would ask him what happened, he would tell her, and then she would forget.

He told her the Humvee flipped; one Marine was wounded, and Roberts had died. Snavely was upset to learn that Roberts didn't make it although she hadn't known him that well. He was an augmentee who worked at a different command but was temporarily attached to her unit for the deployment. Still, he was a Marine, and they were all in this fight together. She had known one of the other Marines for several years and was grateful he survived. Before they had started the patrol, the Marine told her that just that morning, he learned he had custody of his nine-month-old daughter.

Four days after the surgery on her arm, Snavely was flown to Andrews Air Force Base in Maryland, where she spent the night. It was her first opportunity to interact with civilians after the accident. Members of the VFW greeted the "wounded warriors" and told them they were grateful that they were alive. The patients were put into hospital wards, two per room. The staff checked on them to make sure they were doing okay and that they weren't in too much pain. There was a sitting area with comfortable chairs, a TV, and lots of food. Snavely, who had graduated from a liquid diet to semisoft food, ate a bowl of cream of broccoli soup and some Reese's Peanut Butter Cups.

At this early stage in her recovery, there wasn't much Snavely could do about her physical health, but she knew she could control her attitude. So instead of becoming depressed over her misfortune or lashing out at people, she chose to rely on her wit. After looking at her X-rays and realizing how close she had come to being paralyzed and finding out that someone else in her truck had been killed, she considered it a miracle that she was alive, that she could feel her toes and fingers, that she could walk. All she could do was be grateful. For the first time in fourteen years, she prayed and thanked God.

Snavely weighed 145 pounds before she left for Iraq. When she returned, she had shrunk to 122 pounds. She also thinks she lost an inch in her five-foot-three-inch frame when she was thrown from her vehicle and landed on her head. She has a couple of scars from the surgeries—one on the left side of her neck between her ear and shoulder and another that stretches from her armpit to the end of her elbow. She described everything else as bumps, bruises, and cracks.

Her mom, De De Snavely, a computer programmer who works for American General Life Insurance in Houston, and her aunt, Patricia Payton, drove from Texas to southern California to be there when Snavely arrived and to spend a few days with her and Jason. His seriously-wounded wife and the visiting family presented a challenge to Jason, who was preparing for finals. When Snavely left for Iraq, Jason turned their house on Camp Pendleton into a bachelor's pad and began a diet of corn dogs and coffee. Before his wife and in-laws arrived, he went to Costco and spent a couple hundred dollars on groceries. He bought Snavely cases of Ensure and Coke and would later make her the garlic mashed potatoes she asked for, only to have his mother-in-law say "there's no food in this house."

It took a day and a half for Snavely to get from Andrews to Balboa Hospital in San Diego because of all the stops the aircraft had to make between Maryland and California. She landed around eleven in the morning at Miramar Air Station and was driven to Balboa. In the meantime, Jason was running around Balboa trying to figure out where they had taken his wife. He waited by the ER until around 3:30, and no one had come to talk to him. It turned out that Snavely had been there since noon.

Snavely stayed at Balboa for two days so the staff could monitor her and ensure that she was stable. Before she left the hospital, her neurologist, Dr. Matthew Gluf, determined that the neck brace wasn't giving Snavely enough support, so he put her in a different brace called the Minerva jacket, a plastic body brace incorporating the head and trunk that is usually worn by someone who has fractured her cervical spine. Her arm was in half a splint and a sling. She could barely walk. She shuffled and used a cane to guide her.

Since Jason was getting ready for finals, he squeezed in study time whenever he could. Fortunately, his professors worked around his schedule. He was able to take all his finals—anatomy, English, and math—the morning Snavely was discharged from the hospital.

Snavely's world as she knew it had changed. She would have to work hard to get it back on an even keel.

When she arrived home on December 10, 2007, it was beautiful outside, but Snavely wouldn't have an opportunity to enjoy it. Not yet, at least. She walked into her home and sat down on the reclining chair. Her 125-pound Great Dane, Belle, and the 115-pound black lab, Gunner, stayed next door until she got settled. She didn't want them jumping on her. Fortunately, when the dogs came in about thirty minutes later, they were more interested in their food than in Snavely. They were excited to see her, but it wasn't chaotic.

Jason had already rearranged the furniture in the living room to make it more comfortable for his wife. Snavely couldn't walk up the stairs with a fractured pelvis, so Jason brought the futon down from the second floor. Just walking to the kitchen or bathroom was a chore, never mind walking upstairs to the bedroom or shower. She felt like someone had taken a baseball bat and hit her in the torso repeatedly. She slept downstairs for about a week.

One of Snavely's biggest challenges early on was getting her physical needs met. Sense of touch was paramount. Growing up, she was showered with hugs and kisses from her single mom. To this day, when Snavely is hurt, she wants to be held. But now it hurt too much to be held. She had made a habit of literally laying her head on Jason's shoulder when she got back from a deployment, but this time she couldn't do that. Jason could lie down beside her on the futon, but he tossed and turned, so after about an hour, he would move over to the couch or the recliner. Plus, she was wearing her neck brace and that made it difficult for him to hold her. She couldn't even lean back against her husband's chest.

So the speed at which they usually reconnected after a deployment was slowed. Having a wounded spouse was also hard on Jason. He was feeling somewhat helpless because there wasn't much he could do to make his wife feel better. He could do things to make her more comfortable, like help her sit up, eat, and dress, but those things didn't necessarily make her feel better.

About this time, Snavely started feeling overwhelmed. When she was moving about and had something to focus on, it wasn't bad. But when it was quiet and the only sounds were the two dogs snoring, her emotions would get the best of her. That's when she wanted more than anything to be held. The silence gave her one more reason to be pissed.

There's no doubt that Jason's experience as a Navy corpsman who had served in Iraq was helpful. Snavely didn't have to spend a lot of time explaining what was going on with her physically and emotionally. He got it. He understood what she was going through. When she had a nightmare, he didn't drill her about it. He'd just hug her, wipe her tears, and tell her that it was okay for her to cry, that it wasn't a sign of weakness.

Her world as she knew it was small at first. She was used to going wherever she wanted to go, whether by foot or car, whenever she wanted. Initially, she had to settle with shuffling from the reclining chair to the couch. She watched lots of TV and movies and slept. She was exhausted and taking Percocet.

As her health improved, her world expanded. She began walking upstairs with one hand on each rail to guide and support her. When she had her neck brace on, she would pause a little longer on the second step to kiss Jason without moving her neck.

As she proceeded up the steps, she'd take a step and then pull the rest of herself up. She could handle putting her foot up but not putting her weight on it. Once she got to the landing, she had to stand there for about ten minutes to catch her breath.

Being able to do the little things in life made Snavely grateful, like sitting up without her husband's help, tying her shoes, taking the dogs out, starting a pot of coffee, feeding the dogs, waking Jason so he could drive her to rehab, cooking dinner for the two of them, and having the dogs sit on her lap. "It's stuff you don't realize you could miss until they're gone," she said.

She started going to occupational therapy for her wounds above the waist and physical therapy for the wounds below. In the months ahead, her walking and endurance improved. Snavely started working out on the elliptical machine and strengthening her shoulders by lifting light weights and swimming. The biggest problem she continues to have is turning her neck when she is backing up in her car. She now has about a 95 percent range of motion in her neck. Sometimes, it gets stiff, and she feels like she has a permanent crick in her neck. "It's tough," she said, "but I know I could be paralyzed or dead, so the little range of motion that I don't have in my neck is okay."

Snavely was motivated to get better in part by her memory of Roberts, the Marine who didn't make it. She wouldn't be doing service to his memory by wallowing in her pain. As many wounded service members have said, pain is a good thing. It means you're alive. She needed to make her recovery a positive experience. When she felt like giving up, she imagined Roberts standing beside her and kicking her to go on.

Snavely returned to full duty in the fall of 2008 at the pharmacy at Naval Hospital Camp Pendleton. In April 2009, she was scheduled to go to work at a small clinic in the Naval Hospital at Coronado.

She still has good days and bad days. "The good days outnumber the bad days, and the bad days just serve to remind me how far I have come in the past year," she said.

She thinks about her future frequently, especially about how she can use her experiences in Iraq and back home to help other wounded soldiers returning from the battlefield. While Snavely was hospitalized at Balboa, she heard a guest speaker from Disabled American Veterans and Disabled Veterans Sports talk about all-expenses-paid minivacations for wounded soldiers and their spouses.

Wounded soldiers are flown to different locations and taught how to ski, hike, or scuba dive using the necessary adaptive equipment. When she gets out of the Navy, Snavely plans to go to school and get a massage-therapy license. Maybe she can go on those minivacations and train the wounded veterans on the use of the adaptive equipment and put her massage-therapy skills to good use.

Within a year of returning home, Snavely got a tattoo of a phoenix on her right hip as a reminder of Iraq. The phoenix, which represents death and rebirth, is shedding four tears and has three feather plumes. The four tears are for the four wounded in her Humvee. The three plumes are for the survivors.

Sarah Rykowski

Thirty-Five Days

It was Sarah Rykowski's senior year in high school, and she was riding her horse, Chappel, in the Washtenaw County 4-H Youth Show in southeastern Michigan. The day's top two winners would advance to the state finals. But before the competition even started, it didn't look good for the twenty-year-old Chappel. The mercury was rising on the thermometer. They had been at the fair all week. Chappel was hot and weary and feeling his years.

This was Rykowski's eighth year riding Chappel. Her parents bought the horse when she was ten and Chappel was twelve. Rykowski had taken one look at him and said, "That's the one I want." Granted, she was just beginning her riding career, whereas Chappel, in quarter-horse years, was already washed up. But for a young girl who needed a starter horse, something sturdy and dependable, he was perfect. He is black with a white blaze down the front of his nose and white socks on each of his hooves. He has short legs and a wide-barreled back that make it hard to fall off. This mature horse was perfect for a girl who dreamed of earning her share of blue ribbons but wasn't necessarily driven by a desire to be the best.

Thursday at the county fair was Western Day. Western refers to the saddle used, which is made to distribute weight more evenly over the horse's back so that the horse and rider could counter-balance the weight of a cowboy on the range. In the western pleasure competition, the horses had to walk, jog, lope, stop, and reverse, and the class was judged primarily on the horse's ability to complete the maneuvers.

Rykowski was competing against two other girls whom she respected. They were two of the top riders in the state, and their horses were much younger and more valuable monetarily than the aging Chappel. The top two performers in the western competition would compete that night, with the winners advancing to the state finals. If Chappel had a good day and Rykowski did everything right, they had a chance. The worse they could do was place third.

Chappel's part of the competition started. He walked wonderfully. When asked, he followed up with his signature championship jog. As the rider, Rykowski didn't have to do anything but sit still. When it came time to lope, Chappel nailed it. So far, so good. The problem with a horse like Chappel, who has been around for so long, is that he knew everything. He knew they were getting ready to stop and turn around, but he had other plans. Perhaps because he was old and hot, Chappel seemed more eager than usual to get through the competition, so much so that he decided to speed things up and turn around in the middle of his lope. *No, no, no,* Rykowski thought. She tapped him with her spurs to go straight. He went straight, but he also started to jog when he was supposed to walk—that championship jog that was so beautiful but so inappropriate at that moment. *Don't do this to me.* Rykowski eventually calmed him down, turned him around at the correct time, and enjoyed a championship jog and lope. They both rode their hearts out. When Chappel incorrectly jogged to the middle, she let it go. He was tired. It had been a long day and an even longer show. *We'll take what we get.* They stood in the middle of the ring and waited for the results. As they waited, the judge walked over. The judge never walks over in a competition. It's unheard of.

"How old is your horse?" the judge asked.

"He's in his early twenties," Rykowski answered.

"I thought so," said the judge, who recalled seeing Chappel many years earlier. "You and I know how long he's been around. I like that you didn't take it out on him when he didn't do what he was supposed to do. I want you to know you were winning that class until he refused to walk. You rode a great class today and did your best. It wasn't his day. Take him back to his stall, scrub him down, give him a big carrot, and an even bigger hug."

Army Captain Sarah Rykowski was nervous.

The Judge Advocate officer was trying to catch a flight from Kalsu to Iskandariyah to meet with Iraqi nationals about their legal claims. There were no flights available that day so she would have to do something she had been dreading. She would have to travel in a convoy for the first time since she arrived in Iraq over a month ago.

Rykowski attended Saint Mary's College, a small all-female liberal arts school situated across the street from the University of Notre Dame in Indiana. She had planned to study veterinary medicine because she always liked biology, but only as it related to animals, particularly equine science. When she discovered she would have to learn all kinds of other sciences to get to the equine science, she decided to explore other career paths. Studying political science gave her the opportunity to take some pre-law classes to see if she would be interested in law school. In her first political science class, she met Shanna Conner Cronin, who introduced her to the idea of U.S. Army Judge Advocate General's Corps (JAG). Rykowski graduated from Saint Mary's in three years and entered the University of Michigan Law School. Even though

Rykowski was a serious student, law school was still tough. When she got her first bad grade, she didn't tell her mom for days. Instead, she walked out to the barn and told Chappel. Just being with him was a comfort. When she was with Chappel, she forgot about her troubles for a while.

She entered the Army on September 11, 2005, to further her career as a lawyer. Rykowski's parents, Jenny and Rick, were surprised when their only daughter joined the Army because outside of riding her horse and a one-year stint playing soccer in tenth grade, she rarely showed an interest in the outdoors. She preferred indoor activities such as reading, writing, and playing the piano. But Rykowski wanted to prosecute criminal cases and saw the military as a stepping stone for a career with the federal government. She chose the Army because she thought it would offer her a good balance between lawyer and soldier. She sent her application to the Army JAG Corps. After receiving her commission, she was medically disqualified because of a childhood condition and denied a medical waiver three times. When she learned that she had been turned down a third time, Rykowski visited Chappel. It wasn't until she reached his stall that Rykowski let herself cry. She buried her face in his mane. *I don't know what they want, what their problem is.*

Rykowski sent paperwork and another note from her doctor to the JAG surgeon, even though she was told there was little chance he would change his mind, and she called her congressman's office. Her family jokes that the first legal case she ever won was the one to get into the Army. Within two weeks, she was headed to Fort Lee, Virginia, to complete the Judge Advocate Officer Basic Course. Then she spent ten weeks in Charlottesville at the Judge Advocate General's Legal Center and School, also known as the JAG School, before traveling to Fort Wainwright, Alaska, in December 2005. Those close to Rykowski praise her legal ability and say she's trainable as a soldier. Unlike the stereotypical soldier who is stoic and serious, she is as amiable as they come, as well as chatty. Captain Julia Doran, Rykowski's roommate in Kalsu, recalls many evenings falling asleep while Rykowski was talking.

When she traveled outside Kalsu, Rykowski's paralegal was always by her side. Corporal Coty Phelps was her righthand man. He joined the Army in 2004 and was assigned to the 725th Brigade Support Battalion, 4th Brigade Combat Team, 25th Infantry Division in Fort Richardson, Alaska. He and Rykowski knew each other peripherally before Rykowski traveled to Iraq because she had been stationed at Fort Wainwright in Fairbanks, Alaska. They both worked for the same chief of military justice and staff judge advocate and communicated about interoffice business, and sometimes, Rykowski flew to Fort Richardson to help facilitate courts-martials. The twenty-year-old soldier had been in Iraq for about six months when Rykowski arrived.

Rykowski, twenty-six, is five feet, four inches tall with curly light brown hair down to her shoulders when it isn't knotted in a bun and tucked under her Kevlar. Phelps was a slender young man who stood just over six feet. He was one of those guys who, no matter how much he ate and worked out, never gained weight. He was always moving or eating. To compensate for being so tall and lean, Phelps would slouch to appear smaller.

Rykowski worked with Phelps day in and day out for just over a month. He helped her with paperwork, accompanied her on meetings with soldiers and Iraqi clients, and interacted with their interpreter. Without him, processing a legal claim would have been much more difficult. Phelps taught her the ropes and helped her make a seamless transition from the states to the battlefield.

On May 17, 2007, Rykowski and Phelps stopped by the chow hall for a bite to eat and went to the restroom one last time before joining the convoy to Iskandariyah. As they walked, it was obvious to Phelps that Rykowski was uncomfortable with having to ride in the convoy. Rykowski was talking more than usual.

"Ma'am," he said, looking over at her. "You have nothing to worry about. I'm going to take care of you. I'm going to be your PSD [personal security detail]."

Rykowski cracked a joke. Captains didn't rate PSDs. They were usually reserved for colonels and above.

"I truly don't rate that," she said.

"Yeah, you do," he answered. "Ride with me, ma'am, and I'll take care of you."

When they reached the convoy, they met its commander, Staff Sergeant Jesse Albrecht. The thirty-one-year-old from Hager City, Wisconsin, was a motor transport operator who had joined the Army in 1993.

"What vehicle do you want us in?"

Albrecht said they could ride with him. "You ride with me, ma'am, and you'll be safe." Phelps sat behind the driver, Specialist Donald Robitson. Rykowski sat next to Phelps with her M16 rifle and 9-millimeter handgun. As soon as they left the base, they locked and loaded their weapons. Iskandariyah was a fifteen-minute flight but could take as long as an hour and a half by truck. The longer they were on the road, the greater the chance of driving into a firefight or over an IED. Rykowski stayed alert, looking out her window for anything suspicious. The greater the distance between the convoy and the base, the more real it became to her that they were in the middle of nowhere and anything could happen.

Despite her fear, Rykowski felt good about herself and her preparation. She started off in basic training as one of the greenest soldiers but finished strong. Early in rifle training, the soldiers had to lie down behind sandbags and fire at targets off in the distance. The object was to shoot over the sandbags. As Rykowski was shooting, the force from the recoil of the rifle kept pushing her farther and farther back. Eventually, she ended up shooting so close to the top of the sandbag that the bullets singed the bag on their way to the targets. When they finished shooting, the officers searched their areas for debris. Rykowski noticed the still-smoking hole in her sandbag and spent rounds nearby, thus earning her the nickname Sandbag Sniper.

A friend at the Judge Advocate Officer Basic Course, perhaps sensing her fear of the unknown, reminded Rykowski that it was okay to be afraid—just don't let your fear be known. This was a lesson she had learned at a young age while riding Chappel and would relearn throughout her life. When something spooked her horse and he would try to buck her off, Rykowski had to appear undaunted. She couldn't let her nervousness seep through to her hands and body because the horse would sense it. Whenever he bucked her off, Rykowski always got back on.

At the basic course, she suppressed her fear while completing a three-day field training exercise that included a two-mile run with a rucksack on her back. It was a challenging run, but she didn't fall out. She was hurting and wanted to quit, but officers on either side of Rykowski encouraged her. She also led a mission during the same field training exercise, where she learned three things. First, she discovered her "killer face" and a great set of lungs. Second, she should trust her subordinates. And third, missions never go according to plan. She met or exceeded all of the basic requirements of being an officer, and now, driving down the road in a convoy in Iraq, she felt she had good muzzle awareness.

As they continued to drive down the road, Phelps asked for a drink of Rykowski's water. Just as he handed the bottle back to her, there was a huge explosion. The Humvee had been struck by an explosively formed projectile, a more lethal version of the traditional IED.

Oh shit, Rykowski thought. *This is not happening to me.*

Her greatest fear had become a reality. Debris—shrapnel and dirt—sprayed everywhere. The whole convoy came to a sudden stop.

Okay, now what?

Dead silence inside the truck.

It's okay to be afraid.

Soldiers started swearing and moving into action. Out of the corners of her eyes, Rykowski thought she saw Robitson and Albrecht get out of the vehicle. She assumed they were fine.

That's good. People are going to be okay.

Rykowski glanced over at Phelps, who was curled up against the door. He looked as though he was sleeping. She figured he had been knocked unconscious by the explosion and was going to be okay. From her angle, he seemed completely normal.

The gunner in the vehicle was twenty-three-year-old Specialist Victor Fontanilla from Stockton, California. He was a motor transport operator who joined the Army in 2005 and was assigned to Fort Richardson the following April. The force of the explosion severely wounded him, and he ended up on the seat between Rykowski and Phelps.

"I can't feel my legs!" he shouted. "I can't feel my legs!"

"Don't look down," Rykowski said. She had heard of soldiers seeing their wounds and giving up. She didn't want him to give up. She grabbed his hands. "Hang in there. Hang in there."

He threw a tourniquet to her, but she couldn't do anything with it. There were no legs to attach it to.

Just don't let your fear be known.

Rykowski felt something running down her mouth and could taste blood but didn't know where it was coming from. It could have been Fontanilla's blood. It was hard to tell where she ended and he started. Her thoughts shifted to her own legs. Were they still there? Would she still be able to ride Chappel? Her legs were intact.

Then she thought about her face: Was it burned? She'd met a young soldier back at Fort Richardson before she deployed. He had taken shrapnel from a rocket-propelled grenade to the face. His lower lip had been burned so badly that it was hanging off. The doctors had to stitch it back together. She touched her face and lips with her fingers to make sure they were still whole. She seemed to be in one piece, yet blood continued to run down her face. Her upper arm burned from where a piece of shrapnel had punctured her bicep.

The explosion occurred to the left of the vehicle, spraying shrapnel on Phelps's side. Robitson, the driver, got a cut on the back of his neck.

Her right arm felt like it was broken. It hurt so badly she wanted to scream. Then she wanted to laugh. Every time Rykowski got into a Humvee, she had to figure out the doors. The handles vary somewhat from Humvee to Humvee. Earlier that day, she checked out the doors on a few different vehicles in case she was trapped or felt trapped and had to get out fast. This vehicle had a different set-up. She threw her whole self at the door to open it and felt a jolt of pain shoot through her arm. Suddenly, Robitson was there. He tried to pull her out, but she still had her seat belt on. She unlatched it and got out. She was told to go behind another vehicle and sit down.

Rykowski was talking but wasn't making much sense. She was going into shock.

"Where's Phelps? What's he doing?"

She repeated those questions over and over again. She had no idea where he was. Then she panicked because she left her M16 in the Humvee. Soldiers are trained never to leave their weapons behind. She still had her pistol but thought she had screwed up. She was told Robitson had it.

Now she was sitting beside someone she didn't know. She asked him his name. It was Specialist Shannon Sanders, who held a bandage on Rykowski's arm. She was definitely feeling loopy. When Sanders shifted, she yelled. He apologized and told her he wasn't a medic. If he hurt her, he was sorry. She asked him what he did, and he said he was an explosive ordnance disposal technician. "Well, that's okay," Rykowski said. "I'm already blown up so you can't hurt me that much." Eventually, Sanders left to assess the damage and analyze the incident.

Rykowski was put on a stretcher and told that a medevac would be there soon. She was a little combative and did not want to leave because she still didn't know where Phelps was.

"Where's Phelps? What's he doing?"

"Turn your head," someone said.

"Why?"

"You don't want to see what's in the other direction."

Rykowski was loaded into a helicopter. As she lay on a litter, she thought about being told to turn her head. Who didn't they want her to see? She was feeling angry. Then someone started cutting off her blouse. She could barely move her arm. She held it over her head in an L shape. Now someone was cutting off her pants. She had a lot of stuff stashed in her cargo pockets—in her left pocket she carried a red leather *Shorter Christian Prayer* book, a journal, an Army Combat Uniform cap, and an extra American flag patch. In her right pocket was an envelope with cash that she planned to distribute to Iraqi nationals for their injury, damage, and death claims. Rykowski was terrified that the money would get lost or stolen.

"There's a lot of money in my pocket," she yelled to the medic over the noise of the aircraft's engines. "Take that money and put it in my right hand. And by the way, that's my hurt arm. If you touch it, I will scream." She was given the envelope, which she clenched in her hand. Rykowski couldn't see Fontanilla, the gunner who had landed in her lap, but she thought he was in the same aircraft.

When the helicopter arrived at the 28th Combat Support Hospital in Baghdad, someone wanted to take the money from Rykowski, and she said no. A colonel who worked at the hospital assured her that he would put the money in the hospital's safe.

The patient was wheeled into the hospital on a stretcher and covered from the neck down with a sheet. She was thankful for the coverage since her uniform had been cut into pieces and she was feeling exposed. At one point, she was taken back outside to go into another part of the hospital for a CAT scan. She remained alert, watching everything, including the overcast sky. As this was happening, she thought about how, that morning, it had never dawned on her that she would end up in a hospital that afternoon.

"Where is Phelps? How is he? How is my specialist?"

She was told that the one who came with her didn't make it. Fontanilla had died.

Someone asked her if she knew what happened to her specialist.

"He looked unconscious to me."

The fact that he wasn't at the hospital could be good or bad.

Later, the same colonel who took her money returned with another colonel.

There's someone here to see you. Rykowski had no idea who he was. He wore an Army patch on one side of his uniform.

"I'm Colonel Martins. How are you?" he asked.

"I'm okay, sir."

Rykowski made a joke, saying that it was okay that she was bleeding red, the bad blood, as long as she didn't lose any of the good blood—blue and maize, the school colors of her alma mater, the University of Michigan.

Sometime later that afternoon, Rykowski felt brave enough to ask about Phelps. "Is he okay? Please say yes."

"I'm sorry," Martins said gravely. "Phelps is deceased."

"No! No!" Rykowski said. She rolled over on her side, facing away from the colonel. She was done talking. She had seen and heard enough for one day.

Rykowski had a nasty hole in the middle of her bicep from shrapnel. It looked like a piece of fruit that had been blown open, and it was her greatest source of discomfort. She was given Fentanyl to quell the pain.

Nothing, however, could soothe the emotional pain that she was experiencing in those minutes and hours. There were five soldiers, including Rykowski, in the Humvee. By now, she had learned that two of the soldiers, Fontanilla and Phelps, had died. She had no idea what was going on with Robitson and Albrecht. Rykowski felt guilty that she had been medevaced for her wounds. Granted, she had burns and shrapnel wounds, but her arm wasn't broken. She had a cut that a medic was going to wrap. She would heal.

She had arrived at the hospital at three o'clock in the afternoon, and at about seven, she was handed a huge pair of pants, a T-shirt that said "The Chicken Got the Best of Me," and flip-flops. She walked down the hall to the bathroom and looked in the mirror for the first time.

Oh my God.

She barely recognized herself. Her face was swollen and peppered with cuts, scratches, and blood. The burn caused by the heat of the explosion turned her face red, except for the white areas protected by her sunglasses and the strap from her Kevlar. Parts of her face were still caked with dirt. Her long brown hair was wild. As she walked back to her gurney, Rykowski got disoriented, sat down, and passed out on the floor. Her head was spinning. She was hungry. Someone took her blood pressure. It was low. She was sure she didn't have internal injuries because she had been wearing her Kevlar and flak jacket at the time of the explosion. She was hungry, dehydrated.

The medical staff gave Rykowski more fluids and sedated her so she could rest. She had to be able to walk on her own before she could leave the hospital. Martins stayed with her for hours. She overheard him say that the general might want to pin a medal on her, and if he was going to do that, Rykowski would want to leave the hospital in uniform, not oversized pants and a T-shirt. Could someone find her a uniform? They did.

After Rykowski was able to stand up and walk around, she was given the okay to leave. She put on a uniform and stopped by the pharmacy on the way out of the hospital for some pain killers, ointment, and extra wraps to change the dressing on her arm twice a day. Then she and Martins walked outside to an airfield and waited for an aircraft.

"Where are we?" Rykowski asked.

"FOB Washington."

"Who are we waiting for?"

"General Petraeus."

Martins and Rykowski were already sitting in the aircraft when General David Petraeus, the commander of the Multi-National Force in Iraq, arrived. He shook their hands. Rykowski flew to Camp Victory in eastern Baghdad with Petraeus and his top legal advisor, Colonel Mark Martins. The colonel was serving as staff judge advocate for Multi-National Force–Iraq. They were all wearing earphones with mouthpieces so they were able to talk while they were flying. Petraeus asked Rykowski questions such as where she was from and what schools she had attended. They spoke for most of the trip. He seemed interested in learning about her and expressed his condolences for the soldiers who had been killed.

When the helicopter Rykowski was flying in landed, Capt. Shanna Conner, now Cronin, was waiting for her at the flight line. Rykowski doesn't have any sisters, so she enjoyed the female camaraderie first at Saint Mary's College and then with the women in the basic course. Cronin was part of both of those bands of sisters. She and Rykowski graduated together from a class of fewer than 400 women at Saint Mary's. They met up again at the Judge Advocate Officer Basic Course, and now they were both in Iraq, though at different bases. Cronin was the trial counsel in charge of the military justice shop for the Multi-National Division–Center (MND-C), 3rd Infantry Division, Fort Stewart, Georgia. She coordinated trials that came through her division and tried courts-martial. She worked on a variety of cases in Iraq, including ones related to drugs, rape, and larceny. Each multi-national division has brigades attached to it, and Rykowski was trial counsel for one of those brigades. She believes that when you find a female friend in the JAG Corps, you just hold on to her. They're few and precious.

Cronin watched as Rykowski walked off the helicopter and, using her bad arm, saluted the colonels nearby. She took one look at her friend before they wrapped their arms around each other and started to cry. Before seeing Rykowski for the first time, Cronin worried because she didn't know the extent of her friend's wounds. The initial injury report had said Rykowski was dead. Then it was updated and listed her as an amputee. Cronin knew Rykowski loved to ride horses. She thought about how different her life would be if she didn't have her legs.

They drove from the flight line to the joint visitor's bureau where they would spend the night. Rykowski would have running water that evening and be able to get cleaned up. On the drive, Cronin shared the tissues that she had brought, and the friends held hands. Cronin was still trying to get a good look at Rykowski's face but didn't want to stare. The right side looked completely normal but when Rykowski turned her face Cronin could see the white areas from where her eye glass protection and chin strap had been, and where she had been burnt from the heat of the explosion. It was like someone had drawn a line down the middle of her face.

The first thing Rykowski wanted to do was shower. She still had dried blood and soot on her from the explosion. She could barely lift her right arm, however. It had been exposed during the explosion as she was retrieving her water bottle from Phelps. She did the best she could, and then Cronin washed Rykowski's hair in the sink and combed it out. After showering, Rykowski took a good look at her face in the bathroom mirror. She wondered if her wounds would ever heal but allowed herself very little time for self-pity. *It could have been worse. People died today.*

Once she realized she was going to be okay, it was time for Rykowski to call her parents. It was just shy of five o'clock in the evening in Michigan. Her hands were shaking. Rykowski didn't want to talk to her mom if she was alone so she called her father thinking she could reach him before he left work for the day. She knew going out on missions in Iraq was the most dangerous part of her job and wouldn't tell her mom when she was traveling. However, she would call he father, an engineer, before she traveled and ask him to pray for her. She hadn't called him that day because it was too hectic, so he wouldn't necessarily have been worrying about her.

After they greeted one another, Rykowski told him that she was okay. Rick immediately wondered why she would say that. She didn't say that the last time she called home.

"Did something happen?"

"I was in a convoy today and got hurt. I'm in Baghdad. I was released from the hospital. I'm fine."

He didn't ask too many questions.

For Rick, the good news was that he talked to Sarah. She sounded fine. And it was his daughter telling him that she was okay, not another soldier. He didn't have to read between the lines. He was getting a firsthand account of how she was doing.

"What do you want to do about mom? Do you want me to call her when you're home?"

There was a family bridal shower that weekend, so they decided to wait until that was over. When he got off the phone, Rick immediately sought out a friend at work whose son had served in Iraq. He needed to talk to someone.

After Rykowski had showered and was ready for bed, she and Cronin sat around and talked about what happened that day. Rykowski was second-guessing where she sat in the vehicle. Each person usually has a specific job that is carried out from a certain seat. But she and Phelps didn't really have roles on this convoy. They were being transported, so they were free to choose their seats in the back of the vehicle.

Cronin and Rykowski also talked about their five-year college reunion that was being held the following weekend. Their classmates would be going out to bars and having teas. As they talked, Rykowski took half an Ambien to help her sleep.

That night, Rykowski's parents' phone rang back in Michigan, but their caller ID indicated it was an unfamiliar number. They let the call go to voicemail. No message. The next morning, the phone rang at six o'clock. Jenny answered. The soldier on the other end of the line was from Fort Wainwright, Alaska. "Is your husband there?" Jenny reached over in the bed for Rick, but he wasn't there. He hadn't slept well the night before and was outside watering the lawn.

Jenny panicked. They don't get many calls at six in the morning, especially from Fort Wainwright. The soldier didn't want to talk to Jenny by herself. She definitely thought something terrible had happened to her daughter. She ran down the stairs yelling for Rick at the top of her lungs.

"Rick, it's the Army on the phone."

She yelled for him to come in, and they both got on the phone. The time between answering the phone and learning what had happened to Sarah was the longest thirty seconds of Jenny's life. The soldier told them what he knew, which was basically what Sarah had already told Rick.

Prior to the call, Jenny had let herself be lulled into a false sense of security about Sarah and her deployment. She knew the dangers involved in just being in Iraq but thought her daughter was safe because she was working in an office on a base. So it came as a shock to her that her daughter had been wounded.

Following the conversation with the soldier on the phone, Jenny, a devout Catholic, prayed. She asked God, "Why didn't You prepare me for this? Why was I so naïve in thinking Sarah would be safe?" It was the same feeling Jenny had the day Sarah was born. Sarah was still in the nursery when the pediatrician called Jenny and said he wanted to talk to her and Rick the next day. Sarah's head was a little big. She might need some surgery. Jenny, who is a nurse, knew what that meant. She had the same reaction back then: "God, why didn't you prepare me for this? Everything seemed fine during the pregnancy . . ."

Jenny thought of the book, *The Hiding Place*, a memoir of Corrie ten Boom, who, along with her Christian family, helped their Jewish friends escape the wrath of the Nazis during World War II. Early in the story, a young Corrie ten Boom learned about death when a neighbor's baby died. She was so traumatized by the experience that she couldn't eat dinner that night. When her father came to her room to tuck her into bed, Corrie burst into tears.

"I need you!" I sobbed. "You can't die. You can't."

Father sat down on the edge of the narrow bed. "Corrie," he began gently, "When you and I go to Amsterdam—when do I give you your ticket?"

I sniffed a few times, considering this.

"Why, just before we get on the train."

"Exactly. And our wise Father in heaven knows when we're going to need things, too. Don't run out ahead of Him, Corrie. When the time comes that some of us will have to die, you will look into your heart and find the strength you need—just in time."

Ten Boom would need great strength over the years to endure the needless and early deaths of so many family members, friends, and strangers who died in concentration camps.

Jenny felt God was telling her that she didn't need to know about Sarah's illness before she was born or her wounds on the battlefield before she was injured. She needed to continue to trust that God would give her the strength she needed when she needed it. Shortly after that phone call, she sent her daughter an e-mail in all caps: I NEED TO HEAR YOUR VOICE.

Rykowski immediately found a phone, called her mom, and reassured her that she was okay. She told her mom that it had been a horrible week for the brigade, but she couldn't reveal how many soldiers they had lost that week and how many more had been wounded.

The morning after the explosion, Cronin struggled to keep up with Rykowski, who was running on adrenaline from the moment she got up. At 8:30 A.M., Rykowski received a Purple Heart. General Petraeus pinned the medal on her uniform. Many soldiers attended the ceremony and went through the receiving line. Lunch was prepared by an Army cook whom Rykowski had met back at Fort Bliss in Texas before she deployed. He came up to her and said, "Ma'am, I told you to come visit me in Baghdad, but you didn't have to get yourself blown up to do that."

It wasn't until after the Purple Heart ceremony that Rykowski learned that Albrecht had died from his wounds. Cronin showed

Rykowski the program for the memorial service. Phelps's picture and bio were on one side, with Albrecht's information on the other side. The explosion had killed three of the five people in the truck. Rykowski and Robitson were the only survivors.

When Major General Scott C. Black, judge advocate general, arrived, Rykowski met with him. He was there to do an Article 6 visit, checking in on the judge advocates and paralegals at various installations. It's a way for the officers and soldiers to get to know their leadership and vice-versa. There was a gathering of JAGs and paralegals, and for the first time all day, Rykowski wasn't the center of attention. She was grateful for that. Black talked to her after his main presentation. He was going to Phelps's funeral in Kingman, Arizona, and wanted to know if he could take anything to the family from Rykowski. She asked him to give them huge hugs from her and let them know that he was on that convoy because he was doing his job.

Later in the day, Rykowski flew back to her unit in Kalsu. She didn't care that her face was bruised, scratched from debris, and burned, but she did mind people staring at her. Normally, she played the piano for the Catholic Mass and Christian service but she wasn't in the mood. She didn't want to have to answer any questions. She just wanted to be alone. If she were home, she would be spending time with Chappel. It was moments like this when he was so comforting.

The brigade held a memorial service for Phelps. Tears streamed down Rykowski's cheeks, and her fellow soldiers tried to comfort her. It was so easy for her to feel guilty for being the one who came back, the one who survived. The soldiers were sensitive to this.

One specialist from Phelps's unit said, "Ma'am, can I tell you something? I hated you when you first came back and Coty didn't."

"I understand."

"But then I thought about it," he said. "I know you, and I know Coty, and he would have hated himself if he came back and you didn't because he was there to take care of you. That was his job. You know that he loved you. He loved working for you."

Rykowski went for a mental-health check-up and was told to visit the chaplain and not to come out until she had talked to him. He gave her constructive ideas for handling her grief, including talking to a psychiatrist, which she did.

The days immediately following the explosion were particularly difficult. Rykowski is more open with her emotions than the average soldier. Sometimes, she couldn't help crying in front of the troops although she preferred to shed her tears behind closed doors. Once she finished crying, she would try to lighten the mood by telling a funny story about Phelps. It helped to remember the happy times.

Going to the office was hard since Phelps's desk was right outside her door. He always greeted her in the morning. When Rykowski first arrived in Iraq, she addressed him by his rank, calling him Specialist Phelps. He preferred to go by Phelps and requested that the captain address him by his last name and not his rank. It took her a while. One morning, a week or two after she got there, Rykowski said, "Good morning, Phelps." He walked around her desk and shook her hand. He was so pleased she hadn't called him specialist.

After Phelps was killed, Sergeant Adam Welch, his close friend and fellow paralegal, took his position. At first, Rykowski felt overprotective of Welch and the other young soldiers. Soldiers expect to lose buddies on the battlefield, but they don't necessarily expect to lose paralegals and attorneys. This war was indiscriminate, killing many soldiers serving in support roles. The JAG Corps has lost numerous soldiers, both officers and enlisted.

Rykowski wanted to grab every other soldier and tell him or her how important they were and not to do anything that could harm them. She wanted to shake Welch before he went on a mission and tell him to be careful. But she knows he's a soldier and has a job to do. When you're at war, that job is often dangerous. You can't lock yourself or your soldiers in a room. Watching Welch go out and come back in one piece was good for her to see.

When something traumatic happens, like the death of a friend, your body and mind need time to grieve. Yet it's hard to work and grieve at the same time. Rykowski sometimes wanted to hide under her desk but knew Welch and the other soldiers were counting on her. She was an attorney handling Iraqi claims and prosecuting American soldiers. She provided legal assistance for soldiers who had problems back home. She helped maintain order and discipline so soldiers could do their jobs. Numerous people were relying on her. She had to do her job.

Adding to her frustration was Rykowski's inability to lift her weapon. She could wear her 9-millimeter in a shoulder holster but couldn't take it out because she'd have to use her sore arm to remove it and hold it up to shoot. She couldn't straighten her arm and keep it steady. Since she couldn't fire her weapon, Rykowski wasn't allowed off base. This was disheartening because if she couldn't go to other forward operating bases, she couldn't do her job. And what she wanted more than anything was to throw herself back into work. Eventually, she did get back to work. She investigated and prosecuted two detainee abuse cases, three murder cases, sexual assault, larceny, fraud, and minor soldier misconduct. Plus, she handled foreign claims in Kalsu and Iskandariyah.

Shortly before leaving Iraq, Rykowski had a long conversation with her Brigade Operational Law Team's noncommissioned officer-in-charge, who told her to just be the best she could be. He pointed out that Rykowski had done the best she could do, and that's all they needed from her. She didn't need to be Wonder Woman. That brought her back to earth.

Rykowski returned to Alaska on November 19, six months after the explosion, and then to Michigan on December 15. She doesn't think she started healing until she saw her parents and knew they weren't going to be okay until they were able to see her with their own eyes. And as her mom needed to see her daughter to know that she was okay, Rykowski needed to see her aging horse to know he was all right. She wasted no time visiting Chappel in his stall.

Since it was December, it was cold when Rykowski saw her horse for the first time. She didn't ride him right away because although she was back in her comfort zone, she wasn't as functional and lively as she normally was given everything that had happened. She was tired. Just seeing Chappel was enough for the time being. She did have the presence of mind to realize that she was with him, and at that moment, she was the most important thing to him and vice-versa. She spent more time than usual grooming Chappel and scratching and rubbing his back.

As Chappel has matured and slowed down, Rykowski has learned to enjoy that time in the barn—so much so that she just goes out to the barn to groom him because it's her way of spending time with him. He puts his head on her shoulder and nudges her head sideways with his nose as he is prone to do just to remind her that he is there. Chappel is a solid horse, so when he stands behind Rykowski and hangs over her shoulder, she feels protected and safe. And he warms her with the hair and skin that covers his muscles. Then Chappel starts sniffing Rykowski for a treat or chews her hair, and he bumps her in the direction of his feed bucket. When she finally did ride again, it was just another ride, like the thousands they had shared over the years.

While the adjustment period between horse and soldier was seamless, the relationship between family, friends, and soldier sometimes required an extra dose of understanding, love, and prayers. Rykowski's parents had to come to terms with their daughter's near-death experience and its affect on all of them. Before Rykowski was wounded, her dad was counting down the days until his daughter's return. After the explosion, he realized the days didn't matter. He could count all he wanted to but, in reality, anything could happen on any given day. It didn't matter if his daughter had months left in Iraq or just one day. Battlefield casualties couldn't be predicted through odds and probability. He just had to pray that she would be safe. He couldn't be consumed with what could happen.

The relationship between father and daughter was good before the explosion, but when Rykowski returned home, it got even better. Rick takes advantage of opportunities to see and call Sarah now that she is back in the U.S. He can't help worrying about how she is dealing with the aftermath of the explosion. He knows the events of May 17, 2007, can consume her thoughts and overwhelm her at times. He wants to help but knows he can't fix it. Instead, he focuses on their relationship, making sure it's solid and continuous so that when she needs to talk, he's available.

Her mother grieved for her daughter and her loss of innocence. As a nurse, Jenny knows what Sarah saw in the truck that day. They are images she will never be able to forget. Jenny wishes Sarah didn't have to see death at such a young age. As a parent, Jenny also has survivor's guilt. She prays for Phelps's mom every day, for her to be comforted and strengthened. Rykowski has reached out to his family, and her kindness has been warmly received.

After spending the holidays with her folks in Michigan, Rykowski moved to Virginia to begin working as an appellate counsel for the Government Appellate Division of the U.S. Army Legal Services Agency in Arlington, Virginia. The spring of 2008 was difficult for Rykowski as she tried to move on with her life while doing justice to Phelps's life. She had days when she didn't want to get out of bed, when she felt crushed under the weight of knowing that Phelps wasn't there, that he was never coming home, that he would never be able to do all the things he should be able to do. On those days, she would close her office door and let her mind wander, send an e-mail to her mom, or phone another relative or friend.

She attended two events commemorating Phelps's service and sacrifice and remembered him on his birthday, when he would have turned twenty-two. On March 27, 2008, the Army JAG School held a dedication for Phelps. When a member of the JAG Corps is killed in action, the school dedicates a stained-glass window in memory of the fallen soldier. The glass includes the soldier's name, rank, unit, date and place of death, and unit insignia.

Rykowski arrived at the JAG School the day before the memorial service. She was extremely anxious. She didn't know if she would be able to get through the next couple of days. She was going to meet Phelps's family for the first time. So many thoughts were going through her mind. Does Phelps's little brother or sister look like him? Did he look like his dad? How would his family greet her, knowing that she had come back and their son hadn't? Would they blame her for his death? Would meeting the family and attending the dedication bring closure for Rykowski, or would it add salt to a fresh wound? Some people feel better after they have attended a funeral, and that may have been the case for Rykowski if she had had the opportunity to go to Phelps's funeral. But she was in Iraq when he was being memorialized in Arizona. Given different circumstances, she would have been there in a heartbeat. She was hoping to get some peace of mind from the dedication, and she did.

When Rykowski met Phelps's parents, they wrapped their arms around her and told her it was good to finally meet her. They knew her name but hadn't been able to put a face to the name. It was helpful for the family to get to know the people who had served with their son, especially during his final days, and it felt good for Rykowski to meet the people who had shaped the young paralegal of whom she had grown so fond.

That first evening, Rykowski went to dinner with the Phelps family. Throughout the night, family and friends grew more comfortable with one another by sharing stories about Phelps. They talked about how he was the life of every party, how much he enjoyed himself and others. Rykowski told the family the story of the missing cake. Her mom would send her cakes from her favorite deli, Zingerman's, in Ann Arbor. Captain Cory Young, who was also an attorney, Rykowski, and Phelps were working in the office late one night. Rykowski and Young were ready to quit for the evening. They'd eaten part of the cake. They left Phelps and a few friends in the office. Young and Rykowski were expecting to eat more of the cake the next morning for breakfast. No such luck. When they went to the office the following day, Phelps and company had licked the plate clean. They yelled for Phelps. He came into Rykowski's office, faced her, and stood straight and tall, except for when he moved his head around to make it disappear between his shoulders, like a turtle does.

"I'm sorry, ma'am, but I was hungry," he said humbly, although he was fighting hard not to smile. Rykowski laughed and told him she wasn't mad, and they got back to work. The cake, after all, was for all the soldiers. One of the things Rykowski always appreciated about Phelps was that if he made a mistake, he would own up to it, but more importantly, he would never make the same mistake twice.

Rykowski also told the family about the time she and Phelps were getting ready to travel to another FOB and both were loaded down with gear. He was carrying some of her gear and got stuck walking through a door. He totally lightened the mood. Rykowski was so happy to be able to tell Phelps's parents how much she loved working with their son and how much she appreciated having that last day with him. She wanted them to know that she would be there for them, no matter what, as their son was there for her.

Two months after the dedication at the JAG School, Rykowski flew to Fort Richardson, Alaska, where the courtroom was dedicated in Phelps's honor. It's now the Corporal Coty J. Phelps Memorial Courtroom. The following day, she attended the dedication of the Spartan Memorial for all soldiers from 4-25, including Phelps, who were killed during their tour.

There are days when Rykowski has flashbacks, when she cries for no apparent reason. Of course, there are reasons. Sometimes, she thinks about going to counseling but tells herself that she's okay. But then she cries and thinks that maybe she isn't all right. Reading a newspaper or magazine article about a soldier killed in Iraq can put her right back in a funk. Seeing a little boy playing and imagining Phelps right there on the floor with him can cause her to pause.

When she returned from the dedication in Alaska, Rykowski decided it was time for counseling. While she felt good about attending the dedications at the Army JAG School and Fort Richardson, they were only two months apart. That meant Phelps had been on her mind frequently. And his birthday was coming up in June.

Rykowski tries to make sense of survivor's guilt, which sometimes falls under the label post-traumatic stress disorder. The symptoms can include depression, anger, irritability, stress, and avoidance. She wants to be the best person she can be. She asks herself, "Am I doing what he [Phelps] would want me to do?" In some ways, things seem pointless. Instead of trying to be the best at something, now she tries to do the best she can and lives with the results. She relies in part on her Catholic faith to move her beyond the explosion and all the pain that's attached to it. She's determined to do more than walk through life like a zombie—if not for herself, then for Phelps. She believes it would be a complete waste to go through the motions. There's a reason why she is alive. She's still trying to figure it out, and that's what keeps her going. She has much more to do in life, like being a better officer, attorney, and Christian.

Jody Suda, a counselor and Global War on Terror specialist, said it's not so much the death that motivates people like Rykowski who have survivor's guilt, but the concept of the sacrifice. She often hears survivors say they want to be better to honor the one who isn't here to live out what they fought for. She cautions survivors not to become over-involved with a person who is no longer here or try to live out another person's life. When Suda hears people say they want to do their best because someone died, she looks to see if that action assimilates into the survivor's life in a clinically healthy or unhealthy way. If it motivates survivors to make the best of their lives and be their best to honor the cause their friend died for, that can be healthy. If it becomes obsessive and they are overwhelmed with guilt when they fail, it's not so healthy.

Processing the grief and the loss are the real clinical concerns. Suda urges survivors to feel the feelings associated with their loss and allow them to take their natural course. "I didn't deserve to live," "Why am I still here and they aren't?," "I deserved it more than they did"—these are all part of the survivor's guilt that stumps some and causes others to get stuck in the healing process.

The best medicine for Rykowski is spending time with Chappel. She tries to get back to Michigan as often as she can to see her family and visit her horse. It means the world to her to walk into Chappel's stall, wrap her arms around his neck, and feel his head on her shoulder.

In the early days of their relationship, when she was ten and he was twelve, the focus was on competing. Chappel also spent that time guiding Rykowski through her adolescent years. As Rykowski entered high school, Chappel wanted her to show him her stuff. He made her work harder to get him to behave. When Rykowski had a bad day at a horse show or lesson, Chappel grounded her. He would bump her face with his nose as if to say, "Hey, I'm still here. It's going to be okay. You're crying now, but I'd like dinner. How about getting me a carrot?"

Once she entered adulthood, Rykowski and Chappel became equals. She had earned his respect. Now it's about them spending time together. He thinks she's the best. Nothing else matters. She still struggles, but Chappel has taught Rykowski that just because she had a bad ride one day didn't mean she wasn't going to have the ride of her life the next day. This lesson has helped her professionally. As a lawyer, she lost some confidence in her ability to argue and speak in public after Phelps died. But toward the end of her deployment, Rykowski bounced back and regained her professional poise.

She still questions whether she did the best she could in Iraq or why her best didn't seem good enough. If she could just make the mental connection and apply the lessons she learned from riding . . . So she didn't come home from Iraq with a blue ribbon. As with riding, being a lawyer is fun, and it is what she loves to do. It's what she believes she was born to do and fought so hard to do. Isn't that enough?

"I'm fighting again, and I really like that," Rykowski said. "If I had been thinking of Chappel more while I was in Iraq, I would have been more grounded. My whole world spun off its axis in

Iraq, and I couldn't call him and have him tell me I was being stupid."

Chappel is twenty-nine years old now. That's old for a quarter horse. Some would say he should be dead by now, but he continues to surprise everyone. When Rykowski talks about Chappel, she could just as well be referring to her own situation. It makes no sense that three soldiers in her vehicle were killed and two survived. But she is dealing with the loss of Phelps as she moves forward with her life, and for that, she deserves a blue ribbon.

Army Specialist Ashley Pullen

ON MARCH 20, 2005, SPECIALIST ASHLEY PULLEN BECAME A HERO to her country. She also became hated by her fellow soldiers. It was the day she would earn her Bronze Star for valor and the day jealousy started to eat away at the other soldiers in her unit—all because she was in the wrong place at the wrong time.

Pullen, who deployed with the 617th Military Police Company out of Richmond, Kentucky, was doing route patrol behind a thirty-vehicle convoy just south of Baghdad. She was driving one of three Humvees when the crackle of gunshots and the boom of rocket-propelled grenades suddenly filled the air. Pullen and the two other security trucks pulled ahead to counterattack, flanking the insurgents so they couldn't escape. Pullen got out of her Humvee and braced herself against the back of it. She and other soldiers unleashed a torrent of gunfire and grenades on forty to fifty insurgents who were attacking from a nearby orchard. She could see the enemy clearly, armed with dozens of AK-47 machine guns and grenades. She blasted away with her M4 rifle, emptied a thrty-round magazine, then reloaded and opened fire again.

Pullen ran 200 or 300 feet to a wounded sergeant who was screaming in agony. She wasn't thinking about the dozens of Iraqi insurgents who had just ambushed the convoy, their piles of guns and grenades, or the bullets ripping through the air around her. Her bloody comrade lay on the road, and she had to help him—fast. So she hustled as quickly as her short legs would carry her, ignoring the heat, the ferocious battle, and her heavy gear.

When she got to the wounded soldier, she realized she left her combat lifesaver bag in the truck. Dodging bullets, she ran back to the truck, grabbed her bag, and returned to the wounded soldier. She dropped to her knees to help her comrade. "It hurts! It hurts!" he yelled. She got him out of his bloody vest, lifted his shirt, and saw a single slug had pierced his stomach through his back, leaving a hole the size of a quarter.

Pullen tried to bandage and calm him. "Think of green grass and trees and home," she said. "Think about your little boy. Think about *anything* but here." Pullen herself was thinking of the first blush of spring at her Kentucky home.

As she was tending to the wounded soldier, a medic from her company fired a shoulder-held rocket launcher at a sniper's nest. "Back blast clear!" he shouted, a warning to stay far away. Pullen blanketed her body—all 5 feet, 2 inches—over the wounded sergeant to protect him. The blast knocked her on her backside.

When the firefight was over, more than twenty-six insurgents had been killed, and another six were wounded. Three civilians in the convoy were killed. The three wounded members of Pullen's company all survived. The insurgents' arsenal, according to a military report, included 35 AK-47s and other machine guns, 16 rocket-propelled grenades, 39 hand grenades, 175 full or empty AK-47 magazines, 2,500 loose rounds, and a video camera with footage of the ambush.

In June 2005, while still on the battlefield and halfway through her deployment, Pullen was awarded a Bronze Star with the V device for valor. Several other soldiers in the unit were honored as well, including Sgt. Leigh Ann Hester, who was given the Silver Star—the first woman to receive that award since World War II—for her bravery.

After the awards ceremony, Pullen felt a dramatic change in the atmosphere of the 617th Military Police Company. The awards had caused a great deal of animosity between her squad and the rest of the company. It was so intense that she wanted to slit her wrists or do whatever it would take to go home. She didn't have a death wish; it was a cry for help.

A couple of days before she left Iraq, she was out-processing, and the soldier handling her paperwork asked her why she got a Bronze Star. "You didn't do anything special," he said.

"I saved someone's life," Pullen said.

Over and over again, she has been forced to defend her Bronze Star.

Her PTSD symptoms started to reveal themselves in Iraq. Even before the ambush, Pullen was having nightmares of zombies coming after her. Once a patient person, Pullen started to have severe mood swings and anger easily. The other soldiers couldn't talk to her at all without her going off on them. Prior to the ambush, she called her family and husband regularly. After the ambush, she'd call back to the States every now and then, but talking to family depressed her. They were living their lives without her. She felt like she was being left behind.

Pullen and her unit returned home on Halloween in 2005. They had been gone for fourteen months, including eleven in Iraq.

The VA rated Pullen 100 percent disabled for severe PTSD. She attributes 95 percent of her PTSD not to the ambushes, firefights, and IEDs, but to the animosity and isolation she faced within her unit in Iraq. She was in a company of 198 soldiers and felt so alone.

Now she doesn't like going out in public by herself. She learned in Iraq that it wasn't safe to be a woman there, and those feelings carried over when she returned home. Post policy mandated that no one could go anywhere alone.

She is paranoid. If she doesn't know her next-door neighbors, she won't bother talking to them. Before, if someone new moved into the neighborhood, she would stop by to introduce herself. She used to bake homemade cookies at Christmas with her mom and sisters and take the cookies to the neighbors. "Now, unless you come and talk to me, I won't talk to you," she said. She doesn't like leaving the house, but her husband tries to get her out.

Her husband quit his job to stay home and help Pullen take care of herself and their son. Pullen has struggled to establish and maintain a bond with her son. People with PTSD detach emotionally from others, she explained. That's how some learn to cope.

"Like most mental illnesses, you learn how to cope with it and live on your terms," she said. "If you don't, you will drown. I'm a survivor. I'm not going to drown."

Pullen was working with the VA on getting an aide to come to her house and help her take care of her son, but it hasn't been easy. "It's difficult when people can't see your wounds," she said. "It's one thing to be housebound due to physical problems; it's another to be housebound because of emotional and mental problems. There are days when I can't take care of my son. I'm trying to have a normal life."

She wants to draw attention to PTSD and let people know that you can have PTSD and still have a life. "It isn't easy," Pullen said. "There are times when I just want to find me a bottle and find me a corner."

But she has discovered that the more she talks about the PTSD, the easier it is to cope.

Elainena Filion with her husband and son

Black Rose

It was June 28, 2005. The tent was empty except for Army Specialist Elainena Filion and her battle buddy, Private First Class Jessi Allen, who was sound asleep in the bunk above her. Everyone else was out on missions.

Filion had just fallen asleep when she felt someone else in her bed. She thought she was dreaming. She heard a voice say, "Em, I'm horny as hell."

"Huh?" said a sleepy Filion.

"Em, I'm horny as hell."

Em? Filion thought, slowly waking up. *That's not my name.* She felt a hand move across her chest and jumped up.

Filion grabbed her knife and turned around, ready to cut someone.

"Oh shit," said a voice in the dark, followed by the fading sound of footsteps running out the back of the tent.

Filion was twenty-five, married, and the mom of a ten-month-old. This was her first brush with sexual assault.

She immediately told her platoon sergeant, first sergeant, team leader, and female staff sergeant what happened. The platoon sergeant asked Filion to describe exactly what had taken place. They knew who Emily was, so they went to her tent and questioned her. Emily denied that the male soldier who climbed into Filion's bed was looking for her. They searched for the soldier in more than twenty tents but never found him.

Filion grew up in Washington, D.C. She went to Largo High School, where she was a competitive swimmer for three years. She swam the butterfly, and her school came in third place in the state finals during her junior year. She loved swimming but wasn't into getting an education at the time, so she dropped out of Largo her junior year. Later, she realized the importance of a high school education and enrolled at Croom Vocational High School. She got her high school diploma at the age of twenty-one.

Between the ages of eighteen and twenty-three, Filion became a volunteer firefighter and a certified nursing assistant working in dialysis. She attended Maryland Fire and Rescue Institute at the University of Maryland for firefighting and emergency medical services training. She has a thick notebook filled with certificates and awards she has received over the past decade from her careers in firefighting, nursing, and the military.

Filion was working as a firefighter and emergency technician when the United States was attacked by terrorists on 9/11. She had already planned to join the Army but hadn't started the process. She went to the site of the World Trade Center for a couple of days but had to leave. She saw too many bodies—or what were once bodies but had decomposed—all over the place. *This is not happening to us.* She was ready to enlist in the Army and get even.

She comes from a long line of family members who have served their country, and she wanted to add to that legacy. Her father was in the Army National Guard and Air Force, and her brother was a first sergeant in the Army. When Filion was growing up, she attended military family functions and got the impression that the Army took care of its people. She'd visit her aunts and uncles at posts and bases and see them in their uniforms, see them filled with pride. She wanted to be a part of that. She joined the Army on July 29, 2003.

She got to her unit, the 69th Transportation Company in Mannheim, Germany, on December 29, 2003. There she would learn how to drive Humvees, five-ton trucks, and twenty-two wheelers, and become a heavy-wheel vehicle operator.

Two weeks after she arrived in Mannheim, she went to the troop medical clinic. She thought she was either sick from the flight to Germany or had the flu. It's mandatory for every female soldier who goes to the clinic to have a urinalysis done to rule out pregnancy.

"You're pregnant," the captain said.

"No, I'm not," Filion said. "I have the flu. You must have me mixed up with another female."

"Want to do it again?"

"Yeah."

"When?"

"Now. You scared the piss out of me. I've gotta go now."

She asked the captain how long it would take to get the results. He said about five minutes. So Filion walked outside the building and smoked about five cigarettes while pacing back and forth. Then she went back in.

"Are the results in?"

"Have you been smoking?"

"Yes, sir, I was smoking."

She had just moved to Germany, alone. Her husband, Brian, wouldn't be joining her for another month. She was scheduled to deploy to Iraq at the end of the year, and now this? Yes, she was smoking.

"You might want to sit down," the captain said.

She said she would stand.

"Okay. Well, you're pregnant," he said.

Her legs went out from beneath her. The nurse and captain had to catch Filion and help her into a chair.

In January 2004, Filion found out she was pregnant. Her husband arrived the next month. She did various administrative tasks over the next nine months. Brian Jr. was born in August. Before deploying, Filion was re-assigned to the Army's 70th Transportation Company, 4th Platoon. From November 15 to December 3, 2004, she trained for 120 hours on a Humvee and a fourteen-ton tractor with a forty-foot trailer to prepare her for her deployment. She shipped out on January 6, 2005.

On the bus drive from Mannheim to Ramstein, Filion cried. Leaving her five-month-old baby made her heart ache. That night, she and the other soldiers stayed overnight in Ramstein. Knowing she was still in Germany and couldn't see her baby made the separation anxiety even worse. On the flight to Kuwait, she did her best to sleep and not think about her baby and husband.

Filion was stationed at Camp Arifjan in Kuwait but didn't spend much time there. She went on more than twenty-seven missions and delivered more than 115 pieces of equipment to coalition forces throughout Iraq. On nearly every mission, an IED exploded and crippled a truck in the convoy she was riding in, and they constantly came under sniper fire or were ambushed.

As a truck driver, Filion had been trained to spot IEDs on convoys, but when one went off nearby, she froze. Her convoy was driving just outside the town of Hilla when it passed its turnoff. More than one hundred U.S. Army and foreign-national trucks in the convoy had to turn around. Filion saw trucks parked along the side of the road that belonged to the Iraqis but no one was in them, and the roadside stands were empty. Then she heard an explosion.

"Oh shit," she said into the radio. "This is Black Rose. An IED just went off."

"Black Rose, say again. What's your location? Where are you in the convoy?"

"Eleventh truck in the convoy. An IED just blew."

"You see anything?"

"There are some Iraqis at my two o'clock." Iraqis who drove the trucks that were parked along the side of the road and who worked in the now-empty markets were just standing around in the dirt a short distance away.

No trucks were damaged by the IED. Filion was a good eighty-five feet away, but the explosion shook her and her truck.

When they reached their destination, Ramadi Forward Operating Base, Filion talked to her team leader, Staff Sergeant Sheldon Edwards, who was like a big brother to her. She told him she didn't feel right. She had been in Iraq for four months and was having nightmares and cold sweats in her sleep. She'd wake up in a puddle. It was as if she had gone to the bathroom in her sleep, but the puddle was around her shoulders and neck. She'd wake up in a panic from her nightmares. In her nightmares, she'd be hugging and kissing Brian Jr. one second, and her truck was being hit by an IED and coming under attack the next. As she fled the firefight, she took out several Iraqi soldiers but was captured and taken hostage. Gunfire in the dream would wake her. She'd touch herself to see if she had been shot in the gun battle and to make sure there was no blood.

"What do you mean you don't feel right?" Edwards asked.

"I don't feel right," she said. "It's hard to explain."

He told Filion to go to the mental-health clinic when she returned from the mission and talk to a doctor. She was already taking an antidepressant and a sleeping pill to help her deal with her separation anxiety. The doctor increased her doses. She was a truck driver in Iraq taking sleeping pills and an antidepressant, which can have many side effects, including increased fatigue and anxiety.

Filion would live to regret the one time she didn't go out on a mission. In June 2005, she was pulled from the mission to go on rest-and-relaxation leave in Qatar. Her friend, Private First Class Doug Kashmer, went on the convoy. He had a tattoo of his three-year-old daughter's face on his leg so that she would always be with him. The wrecker he was driving was going about seventy miles an hour when it hit an IED hole, went off the road, and flipped several times. Kashmer was killed instantly. Filion liked Kashmer because no matter how bad a day he was having, he never showed it. He always had a smile on his face and something positive to say. He didn't complain about every little thing and knew the right thing to say to get her out of her funk.

Filion took Kashmer's death hard because she thought that with her nursing background, she could have done something, anything, to help save his life. Yet if she had been on that mission, she could have been killed.

Another mission hit her hard. Filion was driving along a road when the third-country nationals in the truck in front of her threw food out their window. A child dashed to grab the food. Filion was driving about fifty miles per hour and couldn't stop quickly enough. The corner of her truck hit the kid. She heard a thud and watched in her rearview mirror as the boy's small body was flung backwards. She called it in on the radio. She wanted to stop. She thought she had killed him. The convoy stopped a short distance up the road, and a combat lifesaver in another truck treated the boy. Filion wanted to see him but was told to stay with her truck and pull security.

At first, she didn't see any Iraqis, but suddenly, they started coming out of nowhere. They seemed to be popping out of the sand. They all wanted to see what had happened to the child. He was still alive but had a gash on his head and his collarbone was broken. He was medevaced to a hospital, and Filion wouldn't see him again.

One foggy night, Filion was driving her M915A4 truck in a convoy to Camp Anaconda when her convoy commander came over the radio telling them to keep their night-vision goggles on and stay alert. There was a firefight up ahead. The fog was so dense that Filion couldn't see anything until it was right in her face. As she drove up a hill, the road split. An American M1A1 Abrams tank was patrolling the road to her right. She could go either straight or left. She was supposed to go straight. The third-country nationals driving in front of her sped up, and she couldn't see their tail lights in the fog. The sergeant in the truck told her to go to the left, so she did. All the trucks were heading the opposite way. She called them on the radio but was having a hard time hearing because the line was breaking up. Then the line went dead.

"Oh shit."

She stopped and locked and loaded her M16. She couldn't keep going because if she did, she would end up in the middle of a firefight. She got on the radio to inform them she was separated from her convoy and lost. She gave them her coordinates. It seemed like it was taking them forever to find her. She put on her goggles. In the distance, she saw four Iraqis peeking out the windows of two apartments. Then the rooms went dark. Next thing she knew, there were two men on the roof top. Five patrol Humvees eventually showed up at Filion's location to escort her back to her convoy.

Filion returned to Germany in January 2006. She met her husband and eighteen-month-old son at a gym on base in Mannheim. She and the other soldiers walked in formation and waited to be released. While she was waiting, Filion searched for her husband and son. When she left for Iraq, Brian Jr. had almost no hair. When she found him in the crowd, she saw that his hair had grown in spicy brown and curly. She'd been gone a year and couldn't wait to hold little Brian. She'd thought about this moment every day. When she was released, Filion cried as she ran to her husband and son. She was so happy to see them. She reached out and took little Brian into her arms and pulled him into her bosom. All she wanted to do was to hold him and kiss him.

He pushed her away with his little arms and reached back for his daddy. Filion was crushed. Little Brian knew her voice from phone calls and had seen her face often enough because they used the webcam on their computers to talk, but it didn't replace interacting with his mom in person.

When they got home, Filion sat back and observed her son. Her husband got little Brian a picture of his mom and said, "Who's this?"

"Mommy," little Brian said.

Then big Brian pointed to Filion and said that's mommy.

Little Brian looked at the picture, then Filion, trying to make the connection. It would take a while.

Filion started seeing a counselor right after she returned from Iraq to talk about what she had gone through during her deployment and what she was going through back home with her family. "I knew how to be a soldier," she said. "I didn't know how to be a wife and mom." Her counselor advised her to make one-on-one time for her husband and son and to take baby steps. Daddy had been there for little Brian while she was gone. Mommy would have to rebuild her bond with them, and it wouldn't happen overnight. This wasn't easy to hear. The first two to three months were the most difficult, but it's still hard, two years later, for Filion to see her son go to his daddy for things that a child would typically go to his mom for.

In October 2006, Filion reported to her new duty station, Hunter Army Airfield in Savannah, Georgia. In November and December, a noncommissioned officer to whom she reported, Sergeant Smith, started making sexual advances toward Filion.

It began when Filion went to her sergeant requesting approval to apply for an Army emergency relief loan to help her offset the cost of relocating. As an enlisted soldier, she had to go through her team leader and chain of command before applying for the loan. Sergeant Smith was in the office while Filion completed a budget spreadsheet and made a copy. When she finished, they began to talk. She was still fairly new to her unit, so she was making an effort to be friendly toward everyone. He told her he and his wife had split up, and he had moved into an apartment. She asked him if he had any furniture. He had some but needed a bed, dining room set, and a coffee table. Filion told him about some furniture stores in the area and gave him directions. He didn't know where they were, so she said she would show him. He could follow her to the stores. She took him to a few stores. While they were looking around at the third store, he realized he had to go right away so he wouldn't be late for a meeting.

"Close your eyes," he said.

"No," she said. She looked away. "Here's a nice set at a good price."

When she turned back to look at Sergeant Smith, he tried to kiss her.

"What the fuck are you doing?" she said.

"I was trying to give you an anniversary present," he said. That didn't make sense to Filion.

She walked off. Others shopping for furniture came around them, so Sergeant Smith didn't say anything else. He was going through a tough time, so Filion let his advances slide. She figured it was a one-time incident and wouldn't happen again. They left the store and went their separate ways.

"I never have and never will date a coworker," Filion told Sergeant Smith on another occasion.

"So you're telling me," he said, "that if we were both single, you still wouldn't date me?"

"No," she said. "I like light to white; Mexican's all right." Sergeant Smith was black, dark black.

Filion and Sergeant Smith were both controlling and would often butt heads. She saw how he talked to people. He wouldn't be able to talk to her like that. She would snap at him. She knows how she is. She likes to be in charge. No one was going to control her in a relationship.

A week later, Filion was told to report with Sergeant Smith to the first sergeant's office for news about her loan. When she got there, she was told that it was approved and that Sergeant Smith was going to take her to the AER building to have her paperwork processed. The building wasn't within walking distance, and his truck was low on gas, so he asked Filion to drive. When they got to the building, the computers were down. Filion would have to return the next day.

As she walked back to her truck, Filion started to cry. She had never had to ask for a loan before. She felt overwhelmed and ashamed. Now she was sitting in the driver's seat, and Sergeant Smith was sitting in the passenger's seat. He seemed to be sympathizing with her, but the next thing she knew, he was reaching over and trying to grab her breasts.

"Stop," she said, as she pushed his hand away.

He tried to grab her thigh.

"Stop!"

She drove him to his truck and left.

A couple of weeks later, Filion was in the office with Sergeant Smith and asked to use his computer after he had finished working on it. When he was done, he got up and told her to go ahead. As she walked by him to get to the chair, he stuck the lower half of his body out to try and rub up against her. When she sat down, he leaned over her like he was reaching for some papers and tried to rub against her chest. She turned around and told him that he needed to stop.

Filion was scheduled to have surgery on her knee, so she couldn't do regular physical training. She had to do profile physical training, which meant walking around the airfield every day and doing minimum physical training. Sergeant Smith was also doing profile physical training that required him to walk around the same airfield.

Filion was walking one morning. Sergeant Smith was walking behind her with a female sergeant.

"Come here," he said to Filion.

"I'm not going to walk all the way back," she said, "but I'll stand here until you catch up with me."

He told the female sergeant to go ahead. She kept walking.

"You know we're going to wind up fucking down range," he said. Filion was scheduled to go back to Iraq with her current company, though she didn't know it yet.

"No. Why do you say that?" she said.

"Because we are."

"Well, no, we're not," she said.

They went back to the grassy area by the battalion for formation. Once they were dismissed from training, Filion asked Sergeant Smith for a cigarette. He said they were in his truck.

They walked over to the truck. She was on the passenger side, sitting with the door open and smoking. Sergeant Smith was a

certified nursing assistant and asked her about medical profes-
sions. Then the conversation shifted to comedians. He told an
off-color joke that involved sex. She told him that if he was going
to talk about sex, she didn't want to be a part of that conversation.

"Okay, let's go back to nursing," he said.

They talked about the nursing profession for a while longer.

"Okay, well, if I pull my dick out and beat it, will you watch?"
he asked.

Filion, who had just taken a drag on her cigarette, nearly
choked on the smoke. She coughed.

"If you do that, I'm leaving," she said, looking away.

"Okay, okay," he said. "I'm just joking. I wouldn't do that."

"I'm not playing," she said, looking away. "Don't do that. It's
disrespectful."

"Okay, okay," he said. "You already said you ain't into me like
that. I wouldn't do that."

"I'm not playing," she said. "That's trifling."

"All right, all right, all right." After a moment, he said, "Filion!"

"What?" she said, turning toward him.

He had his penis out.

"That's fucked up," she said, throwing her cigarette and walking off. She got in her truck and drove off. She called her platoon
sergeant and told him that she needed to talk to him as soon as
possible.

She went home, showered, and returned for formation at nine
o'clock. She didn't see the platoon sergeant, so she called him
again and left a message. Later that day, they went to the M16
range. Sergeant Smith ordered Filion to come over to him. She
didn't want to, but when a noncommissioned officer tells you to
do something and you don't, it's a sign of disrespect. She did what

she was told to do, but with an attitude. He ordered her to stand at parade rest so she would have to look directly at him. She told him he could write her up and she walked off with tears in her eyes. When the tears come, that's when Filion knows she's mad and ready to kill someone.

It was her time to qualify on the range. She shot a disappointing marksman, which in her opinion is barely passing. She was used to being a sharpshooter, which is damn good. That's when you're on point and are recognized for it. She was obviously rattled, and her poor score made her even angrier.

She saw her platoon sergeant when she was turning in her weapon and told him that she really needed to talk to him. She explained everything that happened. He said they would sit down and deal with it.

One day went by, and they hadn't sat down.

Meanwhile, every time Sergeant Smith said something to Filion, she snapped at him. If he instructed her to go to the motor pool to do maintenance on a truck, she would say something smart, do an about-face, and walk off. Other soldiers senior to her didn't know what was going on, so it looked like she was being disrespectful for no reason.

Another day went by, and her platoon sergeant still hadn't contacted Filion about the sexual harassment charges. Filion called him and asked when they were all going to sit down because she couldn't remain in Sergeant Smith's chain of command any longer. He told her this was the only truck driver platoon they had. They needed their numbers to be staffed, and they were counting on her to deploy with them after her surgery.

She told her platoon sergeant that she didn't have a problem deploying; she just didn't want to deploy with Sergeant Smith and that company.

"Give me a chance to find out what's going on," he said.

Forty-eight hours had already passed, and he hadn't dealt with these serious charges.

"Whatever," Filion said.

The next day, Filion and Sergeant Smith were called into the platoon sergeant's office to address the sexual harassment charges. After the meeting, the platoon sergeant told Sergeant Smith not to talk to Filion unless another noncommissioned officer was present. Filion still had to work with him but didn't want to, and the platoon sergeant wouldn't move either one of them.

Angry and frustrated, Filion started to act out more and more. It was the second time in two years that a man had touched her without her consent. It was too much.

From then on, whenever Sergeant Smith told her to do something, she said, "Roger" or "Roger that." She said as few words as possible. She worried about having to work for him on their upcoming deployment to Iraq. She wanted to be reassigned to another company. *If I go with him, I will unload my clip—all 210 rounds—on him.*

One Friday, Filion told a female private whom she thought she could trust that she was going to talk to the sergeant major on his open-door policy. The private called the platoon sergeant, who in turn contacted the first sergeant. Filion hadn't told her first sergeant because he had said he'd deal with it and he hadn't. They hadn't removed her from the hostile situation. And he hadn't told the commander.

That evening, she called her brother Ron, an Army first sergeant, and told him what was going on. While she was talking to him, she stepped outside to have a cigarette so that her husband couldn't hear the conversation. Up to this point, Filion hadn't confided in Brian. She knew he had a temper, and if he found out another soldier was sexually harassing her, there's no telling what he would do. A window was cracked, however, and Brian, a former Army Ranger, heard everything. He stormed outside and said, "Get your platoon sergeant on the goddamn phone now!"

She went back inside the house and called her platoon sergeant. Brian told him that he better deal with this shit, or he was going to kill the soldier who was harassing his wife. "No one messes with my wife and violates her like this," he said. "Do something, or I'm going to fucking handle it myself."

The platoon sergeant told him to calm down.

"I don't want to hear that shit," Brian said. "I've been a soldier. I chewed my fucking dirt." They hung up.

Filion and her husband were at home watching a movie and playing with their son when the calls started. It was around nine o'clock. The platoon sergeant wanted to know why Filion had requested to speak to the sergeant major. She didn't have to tell him. Her meeting with the sergeant major was supposed to be confidential. The platoon sergeant called back about five times. He'd talk to the first sergeant, then call Filion, talk to the first sergeant, call Filion. Then she got another call, this time from the female private. She said that the first sergeant and the platoon sergeant were going to burn her if she talked to the sergeant major.

"I'm just warning you," the private said.

The phone calls were driving Brian crazy. He wanted to leave the house and go hurt someone, and Filion was trying to calm him down. She got between him and the door, and he pushed her out of the way. She called her platoon sergeant back. "You're all trying to fucking burn me," she said. "You won't have to deal with me anymore."

Brian took the phone from her and threw it at a family picture, shattering the glass.

He was yelling at her.

"Why won't you fucking let me protect you?" he screamed. "What do you want me to do? Just stand by and let this shit go on? I'm gonna end it right now. What the fuck, Lana? I'm your husband and protector."

Before her husband could leave the house, Filion walked out. "I can't take this shit anymore." She got in her truck and drove off.

She drove past all their houses—the sergeant, the platoon sergeant, the first sergeant. She didn't have a gun with her, but as a firefighter, she knew how to start a fire. She was upset and felt betrayed and wanted to get even.

She drove to a church and tried to open the door, but it was locked. So she went back to her truck, sat there, and did the only thing she knew to do. She had a conversation with God. *Tell me something. Tell me what to do. I can't deal with this. I can't take it.* She was crying, screaming, and shaking. She had Paxil, her anti-anxiety pills, with her. She took one. It wasn't calming her down fast enough so she took two more. Still nothing. She sat there for a good hour. Still nothing. So she took the last fifteen pills in the bottle. *I can't go through this again. I'm not going to go through this again. I did what You wanted me to do. Yes, You brought me back from Iraq safely, but I'm not going through this harassment again. I'm not going to let anyone violate me. This time, I can control someone violating me. I couldn't control it in Iraq because I had taken sleeping medicine and didn't see who violated me. Tell me something because if he says one more word to me, I'm going to kill him.*

As the Paxil kicked in, Filion's body started to calm down. In fact, she was experiencing a big calm. Her stomach started to feel queasy, so she used her cell phone to call 911 dispatch and asked to speak to someone on the medical side. Having worked for the fire department, she knew every dispatch office had a nurse or medic that could advise her.

"If someone takes fifteen Paxil pills, what are the side effects?" Filion asked.

"Why, did someone do that?"

"Yeah," Filion said, crying.

The dispatch traced her call.

"Why would you do that?"

All Filion remembers saying is, "I'm a good soldier. I served my country with honor. I do not deserve to be harassed and assaulted."

The dispatch contacted the military police station at the base. They got Filion's home address and drove there. In the meantime, she drove home, went to her bedroom, and sat on her bed, crying. Next thing she knew, the Savannah police were knocking on her door. One of the policemen was a retired military officer. After hearing her story, he urged her to go to the hospital. He told her she didn't deserve to be treated that way and gave her his business card. If she was ever harassed outside the post, she was to call him, and he would arrest the offender. She went to St. Joseph's Candler Hospital to make sure the pills hadn't done any serious damage. The doctors did blood work and gave her an IV to hydrate her and flush out the Paxil, and charcoal to absorb the medication. She also took something to quell the queasiness. The lab work showed that it wasn't an overdose.

By trying to calm herself, Filion realizes she had made a huge lapse in judgment. The doctor recommended she be taken off Paxil and put on something stronger to control her mood swings. He switched her to Celexa, which worked much better.

Filion's commander showed up in the emergency room and wanted her senior noncommissioned officer to take her to the base hospital, but she didn't go that night. She was released from St. Joseph's later the next morning and admitted to the mental-health unit at Winn Army Hospital at Fort Stewart. She stayed for more than a week but didn't feel like she fit in. She wasn't trying to kill herself. By trying to calm herself, she nearly overdosed on pills whereas the other patients had tried to shoot themselves, slit their wrists with razors, drove their vehicles off the road, and took a bunch of speed pills.

She was admitted under an adjustment disorder. Her doctor determined she hadn't fully adjusted from what she had been through in combat and in transitioning home. Shortly before being discharged, the doctor added to his report that she had a borderline personality disorder.

"Hell, I ain't got no issues," Filion said.

When she left the hospital, she began outpatient treatment. The outpatient doctor, Major Jones, told her she didn't have a personality disorder. She had an adjustment disorder. He told her she had post-traumatic stress disorder symptoms, but that wasn't his call, and he didn't change anything in her medical paperwork. That was the VA's call, and they have strict guidelines. If Filion were diagnosed with post-traumatic stress disorder, the Army would have to pay her disability. Major Jones explained that with continued treatment, she would be able to fulfill her career obligations in the military.

In May 2007, Filion was honorably discharged from the Army. Personality disorder, not post-traumatic stress disorder, was listed as the reason for her early departure. "It wasn't my personality that made me break down," she said. "It was the shit they were putting me through and the cover up."

In September 2008, the VA diagnosed her with post-traumatic stress disorder as well as combat and sexual trauma. Filion is taking Depakote for her mood swings and anger, Celexa for anxiety and depression, Topamax for severe migraines, and Trazodone to help her sleep.

Filion never got to speak to her sergeant major. If the sexual harassment charges against Sergeant Smith had been treated more seriously by her chain of command, she and Sergeant Smith could have gotten professional help. Sergeant Smith never got into trouble. It came down to he said/she said, and an E-5's word over an E-4's word. He denied sexually harassing Filion. Case closed.

A Pentagon survey on sexual harassment and assault in the military showed that a third of women and 6 percent of men reported being sexually harassed in 2006. Filion believes the number of women sexually assaulted and harassed is much higher. The reason why the reported number is so low is that women don't report the abuse because they're afraid they'll receive the same treatment as Filion.

As far as Filion knows, Sergeant Smith is still in the Army, possibly harassing other female soldiers, and Filion, who wanted to be a career soldier, is struggling to make it through each hour of each day. If she wanted to go back into the Army, she would have to wait two years and then be re-evaluated.

Filion didn't want to get out of the Army. She wanted to get treatment for her adjustment disorder and move to another company. She joined after 9/11. She knew she would have to go to Iraq and was willing to go back. In fact, she wanted to go back because she knew the roads she had traveled in Kuwait and Iraq like the back of her hand. She knew them better than stateside roads. She misses being around her battle buddies. Friends call her, crying, from Iraq to say they wish she was there to watch their backs. Then she cries because she wishes she was there, too. Sometimes she wakes up and thinks, *Why am I here? I should be on the front lines with my battle buddies.*

Now she lives in Mitchellville, Maryland, and works as an assistant property manager for a storage company. She thought about going back to school for nursing but couldn't do that with the medical issues she faces on a daily basis. She wouldn't be able to lift and move the patients, and she couldn't handle more death. She's considering earning a bachelor's and master's degree in sociology so she can help returning soldiers, especially those who have been sexually assaulted. "I want to help my brothers and sisters," she said. "This country doesn't have the manpower to help the returning soldiers."

Filion blames the Army for a good portion of what she has gone through. She is reminded of the recruiting slogan, "Army Strong." She believes the slogan implies that the Army and its soldiers look after one another. How else could they be Army strong? Yet that wasn't her experience. No one looked after her. If her Army had been strong, it would have taken her sexual harassment charges seriously and corrected the situation. Instead, soldiers were trying to get one up on each other and the system. The Army causes its soldiers to break down when it doesn't deal with the small issues because, eventually, the little things add up to big things. Filion said "Army of One" was a more fitting slogan because of the way soldiers stabbed each other in the back to make rank.

To release some of her anger and frustration, Filion likes to open up her motorcycle to more than 100 miles per hour on the road. When she's driving that fast, she can scream, and no one will hear her. And the stress blows off her like the wind. Sometimes, she'll go swimming; her favorite spot is at the bottom of the pool, where it's quiet, and she can just sit and think. Church helps. So does going to the small-arms gun range.

She'll feel fine one second, and the next, she cries uncontrollably. Two years after returning, she still doesn't feel as though she has reconnected fully with her husband and son. She still feels like she's all alone. She doesn't like taking Depakote or Celexa because when she wants to get mad, the pills prevent her from reacting the way she normally would. She'd prefer a shot of Grey Goose or tequila.

She won't see male doctors; she has a difficult time trusting men since she was sexually assaulted. She often questions why a man is looking at her. Sometimes, she cringes when Brian touches her in her sleep. She jumps if he tries to put his arms around her and hold her at night or tries to become intimate with her. More than anything, she wants to get back to being normal and having fun with her husband and son. She feels like her body came home but her mind didn't.

She tries to remember to tell herself: Just press through your struggles. They won't last forever. God knows your trials. Through him, we shall prevail. Stand still. Stay in the word. Pray through your pain. And smile through the tears.

Necia Williams with her husband

Full Circle

THE FIRST TIME NAVY COMMANDER NECIA WILLIAMS DEPLOYED TO Iraq was with Bravo Surgical Company at the beginning of the war. She worked out of a tent as the company followed Marines from Kuwait to several different camps in Iraq. During her second deployment, from February to September 2005, Williams was stationed at Al Asad Airfield. At the time, violence dominated the far western part of Iraq near the Syrian border. The casualties— wounded Marines, Iraqi police, international forces, and insurgents—were transported to Al Asad. The surgical team—which included Williams, a general surgeon, an orthopedic surgeon, a certified registered nurse anesthetist, OR nurses, and surgical technicians—treated whoever was brought to them.

Williams saw it all—patients wounded from firefights, mortars, rocket-propelled grenades, and IEDs. She saw burns, head wounds, and amputees. Some patients didn't make it out of Iraq alive, like the Navy corpsman who was serving with a Marine unit. He stands out in her mind because the Marines were protective, and when they brought in one of their own, they would share particulars with the medical staff. This corpsman had a wife and children waiting for him back home.

The surgical team worked together for several hours as the surgeons struggled to get control of the corpsman's traumatic bleeding, and the anesthesia team provided continuous resuscitation with fluids and blood while administering medications to stop pain and keep the patient unconscious. It was a true team effort, requiring the full focus of everyone involved. The young corpsman was still alive when he was moved from the operating room table to a litter and loaded in a helicopter for transport to a larger U.S. military field hospital in Iraq. Williams later learned from one of the Marines in the corpsman's unit that the patient died several days after leaving her surgical company. Although he had been critically wounded and was in serious condition when he was flown out after surgery, Williams had maintained hope that he would survive and make it home to his wife and young children. It was hard for the medical team that took care of him. There was the frustration of knowing that sometimes their best efforts weren't good enough, the deep sadness that they had lost one of their own, and the understanding that a family back home was receiving heartbreaking news. To this day, Williams keeps the families of those who lost loved ones in her prayers.

The corpsman didn't make it, but most do survive their battlefield wounds. More than 4,000 American troops have been killed in Iraq, whereas it's estimated that more than 55,000 have been wounded. And with so many warriors coming home wounded, helping them deal with their pain has become a critical part of the recovery process. Troops are surviving with wounds that would have killed them during the war in Vietnam. The protection that the troops now have—up-armored vehicles, flak, Kevlar—and emergency medical services so close to the battlefront, have dramatically increased the survival rate on the battlefield. If someone made it to one of the surgical companies like the one Williams was working in, they stood about a 90 percent chance of survival. Back in the rear, it was the duty of the military hospitals and the VA system to take care of them.

For the most part, Williams didn't know how her patients did once they left her surgical company, and that could be frustrating. The surgical team would spend hours treating a patient, who would then be sent back to Germany and the U.S. for additional care. Once the patient left the surgical unit, all Williams could do was hope and pray. Sometimes, they'd hear how a patient was doing through word of mouth, but that was the exception to the rule. When she returned home, Williams wouldn't have to wonder any longer. She chose to continue to take care of the wounded troops and in doing so learned firsthand how they were coping.

As is the case in one's life journey, people change, and so do their passions. Williams started college at the age of sixteen and graduated from Virginia Tech with a degree in industrial engineering and operations research. She worked for IBM for seven years as a system engineer. It was rewarding, but after a while, boredom set in. She had traveled, was married, had children, and was ready for a career change. She considered teaching high-school math and science but then became interested in medicine. So she took some pre-med courses, applied to medical school, and was accepted. Now she needed a way to pay for her medical degree.

She was attending the University of North Carolina at Charlotte when she heard an Army recruiter talking about the Health Profession Scholarship Program. She was more familiar with the Navy because her father had been a sailor, so she called a recruiter to see if they had a similar program. Before she knew it, she had received a scholarship with the Navy and was on her way to the University of North Carolina Chapel Hill School of Medicine. On her thirtieth birthday, she was sitting in Berryhill Hall at Chapel Hill, filling out the registration forms for medical school. She's probably one of the best investments the Navy ever made.

Williams finished medical school and did her internship at the Naval Hospital in Portsmouth, Virginia, after which she was assigned to Cherry Point Air Station in North Carolina, where she was the general medical officer at the hospital. There, she worked with emergency medical services, disaster preparedness, the Substance Abuse Counseling Center, and Military Sick Call. She had decided at that point that she wanted to work in emergency medicine or anesthesiology.

She chose anesthesiology because she liked the intense relationship between the anesthesiologist and her patient while taking care of the patient in the operating room. She interviews patients before their operations and gets to know them. Then she tries to optimize the situation for the patient so that he has a successful anesthetic and is stable with good pain control when he wakes up and heads to the recovery room.

She applied to the anesthesiology residency at the National Naval Medical Center in Bethesda and got in. Within the residency, residents rotate among different specialties. She requested additional rotations in cardiac anesthesia and in the pain clinic. She graduated in July 2002 and in August started working at the Naval Hospital at Marine Corps Base Camp Lejeune in Jacksonville, North Carolina. Six months later, she deployed to Kuwait and was with Bravo Surgical Company when the unit went into Iraq to provide support for the Marines of Task Force Tarawa. She served with the Marines twice more in the following two years providing anesthesia services in Haiti in 2004 and returning to the Anbar Province of Iraq in 2005.

One of Williams's most vivid memories from Iraq struck a nerve more with the mom than with the anesthesiologist. The last time Williams was in Iraq, she had a patient on the operating table who was just two weeks older than her youngest son, who was in college at the time. They had both recently turned nineteen. She felt a connection to an unknown mother somewhere whose son she was treating in a field hospital thousands of miles from home.

"It was like I was on an amusement park ride, and my stomach was up in my throat," Williams recalled. "It was hard to breathe. It was fleeting, but at that moment, when I was looking at the patient's paperwork, I realized how close the patient's birth date was to my own son's. It was pretty powerful. These things affect you." It was a startling and very personal reminder of the impact of war. That Marine made it; although his wounds were severe, they were not immediately life-threatening.

Williams is smart, attentive, and reserved. She cares deeply but doesn't necessarily share that side of herself. What is apparent is her dedication to family and country. As a mom who deployed with the Marines three times in three years, she missed some family milestones back home—like her youngest daughter's sixteenth birthday, her oldest daughter's high-school graduation, and her oldest son's college graduation. She can't get those back. But she's patriotic and does her job and understands that you can't be in two places at once. When she has personal time, she likes to sail, walk, and bike ride with her husband, Tommy, a retired Marine master sergeant.

When she returned to Camp Lejeune after her second deployment to Iraq, Williams worked with the Marines assigned to the just-opened Wounded Warrior barracks. The barracks are operated by the Wounded Warriors Battalion–East, which maintains a comprehensive program to track and support wounded Marines and sailors who are residents east of the Mississippi River. The program also provides assistance to the wounded and their families until they return to duty or have been medically discharged or successfully reestablished in civilian life.

The Marines with whom Williams interacted at the Wounded Warriors barracks weren't necessarily the worst off. They were at Walter Reed and Bethesda. Some of the Marines at the Wounded Warrior barracks had chronic pain as a result of their injuries. Through her work with them, Williams was inspired to apply for pain fellowship training, a subspecialty within anesthesiology. She was approved for a one-year fellowship and had the option of doing her Navy-funded fellowship in a civilian or military hospital.

She wanted to get some training in advanced regional anesthesia techniques along with her pain medicine fellowship. Some of the Marines she was treating in Camp Lejeune could benefit from these types of pain interventions. Advanced regional anesthesia can help a patient who, for example, had severe upper limb pain following a traumatic injury. A catheter can be placed in the shoulder area or below the clavicle and an infusion of medicine given to completely block pain in the arm or hand.

Williams looked around at some civilian pain fellowships but didn't find one that would allow her the flexibility to choose electives that would optimize her skills in taking care of the troops who had developed pain from wounds sustained while serving their country. She wanted to work directly with the troops, so she contacted the person in charge of the pain fellowship at Walter Reed. The pain fellowship was full, but they created a spot for Williams, and the Navy approved.

During the acute-pain months in her fellowship training at Walter Reed, Williams worked with Marines, soldiers, sailors, and airmen. It was an intensely challenging time. The rapid military transport system resulted in severely wounded troops reaching Walter Reed within days of their wounds in Iraq and Afghanistan, some with sand still on their skin and in their hair. This reminded

Williams of being in Iraq, where virtually all patients arrived at the field surgical company covered in sand.

Finally, some of the questions that had lingered in Williams's mind about how her patients in Iraq had fared were now being answered—and perhaps more importantly, she was able to complete the cycle of treatment she had started in the field surgical company and eventually achieve some closure. Sleep did not come easily during this time.

Williams has chronic insomnia. Being on call 24/7 for months on end in Iraq can affect someone's sleeping pattern. She goes through periods that she calls "Every Other Night Sleeping." Especially during the months of regional anesthesia, she'd have nights where she'd get maybe three to four hours of sleep. The next night, she'd sleep well because she was so tired, and then the following night, she wouldn't sleep well. It was a tough but rewarding time.

When she couldn't sleep, Williams would try to figure out how she was going to help a patient with his or her pain. Or she'd reflect on the fact that the war was still going on and that she had been in Iraq and asked herself whether she could have done anything differently when she was there. It was during this period that she processed many of her experiences from Iraq. "When I was in Iraq, I didn't know how the troops did when they left," she said. Sometimes, when she was treating patients, she would think, "We did everything we could, but there's just no way they can survive," or, "They'll never be the same."

Sometimes, she doubted whether a patient would make it simply because he didn't have the level of specialty care or supplies in his surgical unit to meet the needs of all the wounded. A surgical company on the front lines has a general surgeon and often an orthopedic surgeon who focus on immediate life- and limb-saving procedures, followed by evacuation of the patient to a higher level of care. Once the wounded got to one of the large combat surgical hospitals in Baghdad or Balad, they could receive more services from neurosurgeons and cardiothoracic surgeons, intensive-care units, full laboratory services, and a CT scanner.

Having now served on both sides, the battlefield and Walter Reed, Williams realizes that many of the wounded make it home. It was worth going the extra distance on every Marine and soldier they treated. It was worth every sleepless night.

At Walter Reed, she discovered, "Yes, many of them survived and many of them are incredibly resilient. Now I feel very strongly that we take care of them through the continuum, and that allowed me to achieve a lot of closure. I have no regrets from Iraq. We went all-out on everybody, keeping in mind there are just so many things you can do in the field. Working in a surgical unit in Iraq isn't the same as having Walter Reed in the middle of the desert."

Once she finished her fellowship, Williams went to work six miles away at National Naval Medical Center in Bethesda, Maryland. She divided her time between providing anesthesia services in the operating room and working in the pain clinic. When patients are being evaluated in the pain clinic, the goal is to identify what is causing the pain and develop a treatment plan to try to minimize the pain and increase the patient's ability to function in his or her daily life. Williams would sit down with a patient who was having chronic pain, such as phantom limb pain or complex regional pain syndrome, and get his full history. That might include problems with sleep because of traumatic brain injury (TBI), post-traumatic stress disorder (PTSD), or the pain itself. The patient could have had an amputation, but that might not be the source of his pain.

"When you first see someone that's had an amputation, you almost think the amputated leg is going to be the problem because phantom limb pain can be so common," Williams said. But the blast that caused the patient to lose the limb may have also led to back pain, and that could be the greatest source of what's bothering the individual a year after the wound. If he was recovering well from the amputation, the pain clinic would focus on his back, neck, or hip pain.

Success means getting a patient's pain under control. In the past, there were few options other than narcotics like morphine for treating pain. Now, if somebody comes in and is in a great deal of pain and isn't doing his physical therapy, one of the ways the medical staff can get the pain under control is through regional pain blocks used with catheters for local anesthetic infusions. The patients are alert, can interact with their families, and are able to participate in their rehab.

One young enlisted soldier was using a Dilaudid PCA (patient-controlled analgesia, a method to deliver IV anesthetic through his veins), in which he could press a button to deliver a bolus of the medication. He had an amputation to one of his legs and severe wounds to the other. Williams and her staff talked to him about having regional catheters placed in his lower extremities. He had pain in both of his legs but refused to allow them to use the regional catheters. He opted for IV narcotics instead and was sleeping most of the time. When he woke up and moved, he would cry out in pain. The acute-pain clinic service always made sure he had pain treatment available. They won't use regional catheters without the patient's approval.

When the patient was having his dressings changed, he was in so much pain that the staff had to take him back to the operating room and provide anesthesia for dressing changes. Once his legs had healed to the point that he didn't need to go under anesthesia for daily dressing changes, the dressing changes were done in his hospital room. The discomfort he felt with these daily changes

302 _____ *The Girls Come Marching Home*

led to his decision to try the regional anesthesia catheters. These catheters are placed near the nerves that supply sensation to the area of the wound.

With the regional catheters in, the patient's pain was controlled to the point that he no longer had to use his PCA for pain relief. Because he had been using the narcotics for so many weeks, his body had developed a dependency on the medicine, and he experienced some physical withdrawal symptoms as a result of suddenly stopping the medication. This is a physiologic reaction, not an addiction, and can be very uncomfortable for the patient. Anyone who uses pain medicine over a long period of time will develop a physiologic dependency. His withdrawal symptoms were treated by the pain service team because they did not want him to experience the discomfort of withdrawal.

With the catheters in place, the patient was much more alert in the day and would ride around the ward in his wheelchair and tell the new patients, "You've gotta get these catheters. They're a lifesaver." It was the best advertisement.

The patients aren't the only ones who benefit from the regional catheters. When the patients are in less pain and feeling better, the same can be said for the spouses, parents, and children who spend time on the ward.

The regional catheter is just one of many techniques that were not available twenty years ago. The anesthesiologists could do some regional blocks, but they weren't using the catheters. This war has inspired medical progress. Catheters have been used in the civilian world for a while, but in a wartime setting, it really only started in 2003. An anesthesiologist from Walter Reed, Colonel Trip Buckenmaier, pioneered the use of advanced regional anesthesia using catheters placed at the combat-support hospitals in Baghdad and Balad and continuing that use throughout the medical evacuation process, all the way back to the U.S.

This meant that the patients didn't have to become dependent on morphine and could be transported on planes back to the U.S. with less worry about respiratory depression and nausea that are associated with narcotics like morphine.

Williams had one patient at Walter Reed who was involved in a motor-vehicle accident in Iraq and ended up with a herniated disc that was pressing on his nerves. He was in a great deal of pain. The patient can have the disc surgically removed, but there are newer techniques in the pain clinic. They placed a needle through the skin and into the disc. Then they used a device to remove some disc material. That allowed the disc to shrink back down and resulted in substantial pain relief. He was able to avoid surgery and return to full duty within a few weeks.

Another patient in excruciating pain went to the clinic because he wanted to avoid surgery and its lengthy rehabilitation. He had been promoted, and his unit was going on a training exercise in California; he wanted to go along. If he had the surgery, the rehabilitation would make him miss the training. He had worked so hard to get where he was and wanted to be with his unit. The clinic was able to treat the pain. A week later, the Marine flew out to join his unit, and Williams hasn't heard back from him. She hopes no news is good news because he was doing well when he left.

Because there is about a 60 percent symptom overlap with PTSD, TBI, and chronic pain, Williams sees each patient who walks into the pain clinic as a "human puzzle." The challenge is to figure out the symptoms and address them. Since sleeplessness and depression are among the overlapping symptoms, the pain clinic staff have to be very careful. Just like a patient can have high blood pressure and diabetes, a wounded soldier can have PTSD, TBI, and chronic pain at the same time. If the medical staff focuses only on the PTSD, the patient may get somewhat but not entirely better. The combination of TBI, PTSD, and chronic pain is likely to result in disability unless each condition is addressed appropriately. The pain clinic staff works closely with other medical specialties to make sure the troops receive the comprehensive care they need.

"The patient care has to be individualized," Williams said. "That's the real art of medicine. There's no cookie-cutter way to treating the patients. We have to figure it out. If somebody has PTSD and chronic pain and I just address their pain, their improvement will not be nearly as good as if I identify the PTSD, and make sure they're seen and treated for that."

While many wounded soldiers start out in the pain clinic, it's not unusual for some to begin treatment in behavioral health for PTSD and end up in the pain clinic. As the patient starts to heal emotionally, he may begin sleeping and interacting better and feel less anxious, but then his pain starts waking him up, so he's referred to the pain clinic. The pain clinic works closely with its mental-health colleagues. It has even started an initiative to send a pain physician to the warrior clinic, which is a primary-care clinic that Walter Reed has developed to care for wounded warriors. There, the pain physician evaluates patients to optimize their treatment and to schedule them if they need to have a procedure done.

Within the military, there are specialty leaders for each field, and in 2008, the specialty leader for anesthesiology was Captain Ivan Lesnik. During a phone conversation, Lesnik asked Williams where she saw her career going. She told him she saw herself continuing to take care of the troops, either by going back to a Marine Corps base or deploying again. He told her that she had done her share of deployments and went on to compare the anesthesiology community with aviation. Everybody wants to fly, but sometimes, people have to stay back so others can fly. He needed her to stay back and train the people who will be going to the field and taking care of the wounded soldiers.

Walter Reed and Bethesda are academic institutions and teach anesthesia residents. Williams was one of those teachers, leading by example, conscious of how she is perceived, and taking her teaching role very seriously. She develops close professional relationships with her residents so that they take care of the patients with her and assume increasing responsibility throughout their residency. When they finish their training, they will be prepared to provide care where needed. This might be in a stateside military hospital, an overseas base hospital, or a tent close to the battlefields.

If a twenty-year-old Marine or soldier is lying on a litter in Iraq or Afghanistan two years from now, he may be cared for by an anesthesiology resident that Williams and her team is training today. She feels compelled to do everything she can to make sure those future troops are being cared for by anesthesiologists who have had the training they need to face the challenges of providing care on the front lines.

As a result of the 2005 Base Realignment and Closure Commission, in 2011 Walter Reed Army Medical Center and the National Naval Medical Center will come together to form one hospital called the Walter Reed National Military Medical Center. Williams was appointed the Integrated Chief of Anesthesia for both Walter Reed Army Medical Center in Washington, D.C., and the National Naval Medical Center in Bethesda, Maryland.

In her role as Chief of Anesthesia, Williams's primary job is to bring the two institutions together to provide anesthesia services to all patients. This includes comprehensive pain care for the wounded troops. In that role, she and her staff follow their patients from the time they arrive at Walter Reed or Bethesda to the time they leave and go through outpatient rehabilitation in the area and then the VA center they may be going to. Or if they're going back to their commands, she and her staff ensure that follow-up care has been arranged so that they don't feel abandoned along the way. Patients will sometimes return to Walter Reed or Bethesda if they develop a problem or need additional care.

Being able to continue to serve the wounded warriors has been personally and professionally satisfying for Williams. "The opportunity to take care of these troops and to complete the loop is the reason why I stay in the military," she said. "To see the wounded warriors go through rehabilitation and do well is a beautiful thing. That's why I want to devote my life—at least the rest of my career—to this."

When Williams reflects on her deployments, she thinks about how rewarding they were and how she would go back to Iraq in a heartbeat if she were asked to go. She and her husband have an agreement, however: She won't volunteer to go, but if asked, she'll go. Williams said that if she wasn't willing to deploy at a moment's notice to help the troops, then why bother being in the Navy. She might as well be a civilian anesthesiologist.

Once she retires from the Navy, Williams plans to go to work for the VA. "I can't imagine not following these patients through their lifetime," she said. "The troops are my heroes, and it is an honor for me to work with them."

"Everything happens in God's world for a reason," Williams said. "There's a reason why I went to Iraq, and there's a reason why I'm taking care of the troops. I just do the best I can every day."

Marine Sergeant Major Irene O'Neal

IN THE FIRST GULF WAR, SERGEANT IRENE O'NEAL WORKED AS AN imagery interpreter in intelligence. In 2003, now a first sergeant, she kept track of about 300 Marines from the 7th Engineer Support Battalion, Force Service Support Group, from Marine Corps Base Camp Pendleton, as they provided support for different units in the outskirts of Baghdad.

Two years later, O'Neal deployed to Camp Fallujah in Iraq, but this time, she was filling a sergeant major's billet for a combat-service battalion made up of more than 1,000 Marines. O'Neal's job was to be there for her Marines from the beginning to the end. That was especially tough when they lost a Marine. One sailor and six Marines were killed during this deployment.

The first time Marines were killed from the battalion, four were lost in one day. "It's hard to lose any Marines, never mind four," O'Neal said. Their mission was to bring everyone back, and now that wasn't going to happen. "People think Marines and soldiers in combat support are not on the front lines, but they are."

One death that hit O'Neal hard was that of a twenty-year-old lance corporal who was a combat engineer and part of a small detachment assigned to reconnaissance. His job was to use mine-detecting equipment to locate caches. While on a mission, the lance corporal saw an Iraqi running. He realized something was wrong with the scene and tried to warn the others to stay away. It was too late. A cell phone had already triggered the IED. The young Marine was killed instantly, and others were wounded. The Marines were devastated. Anytime a Marine is killed or wounded, the commanding officer and sergeant major are notified immediately.

O'Neal and her commanding officer went to Charlie Surgical Company. O'Neal stood outside the surgical shock-and-trauma platoon to see what other Marines were coming in and who was affected by the death of this lance corporal. A gunnery sergeant, also a combat engineer, came by to check on his Marine. O'Neal shook her head to indicate that he hadn't made it. The Marine started crying. O'Neal put her arm around him and walked him over to the side. She gave him a hug and told him there was nothing they could do about it now. She needed the gunny to be strong for his Marines. So O'Neal had to be strong for the gunny and the gunny for his Marines.

By now, she had already seen two of her Marines in body bags. "It's tough," O'Neal said. "You think about it when you are there and it happens, but you don't dwell on it. You think, 'What do I have to do now?' You keep pressing on. Then you come home, and that's when it all starts."

In Iraq, everything was so fast-paced. O'Neal would go to work at six in the morning and leave at ten, midnight, or two in the morning. When she came back to the States and had time to think about her deployment, she would cry in private. She didn't disclose her combat stress right away, not even to her Marine husband. She talked to medical, and they confirmed that she had combat stress and that what she was experiencing was "normal." She was always there for someone else but who was there for her? Counseling opened the flood gates.

In 2008, O'Neal was one of twenty-one female sergeant majors in the Marine Corps.

Postscript

I DIDN'T SEE IT COMING.

In fall 2007, I unknowingly embarked on an intense emotional journey. That's when I started interviewing women warriors returning from the battlefield in Iraq, delving into their hearts, and capturing their voices for *The Girls Come Marching Home.*

That same fall, I told my mentor about the subject of this book. He predicted that I would need counseling somewhere along the way to get through this venture. I stored that comment and started traveling the country to interview female Marines, soldiers, sailors, airmen, and their family members. I first realized this book was going to hit me hard when I interviewed the mother of a female Marine who was burned over nearly 20 percent of her body. About ten minutes into the phone interview, the mom said she was nervous about talking to me. It had been more than two years since her daughter was wounded in Iraq, and she hadn't talked about it at any great length in a long time and was concerned she would break down. I told her not to worry. I began crying as soon as she started retelling her and her daughter's story.

About nine months later, after having interviewed all of the women for this book at least once, I spoke to Vet Center counselors in New England about *Band of Sisters* and this book. By that time, I had become so immersed in *The Girls Come Marching Home* that it was impossible for me not to talk about it. It was the first time I had spoken about the struggles of our female veterans, and apparently, I was getting emotional. In the question-and-answer period that followed my talk, the first question turned out to be a statement: "I hope you're getting help." I mumbled something about walking on the beach and going to church. But in all seriousness, I wasn't getting help, and I needed it.

I had spent the past year listening to and then writing stories about trauma. Like a counselor, I wanted to know what the women were feeling. Unlike a counselor, I believed that to be true to the women and their stories, I had to actually feel what they were feeling. I blindly jumped onto their emotional roller coasters. I had no idea that their pain would become my pain. Some of the women told me personal and painful stories they hadn't yet shared with their counselors. I was humbled by their candor but also felt helpless at the end of the interview when I put away my pen, pad, and tape recorder. I knew I had helped them by listening, but I didn't have any tools to make them better. I wasn't a therapist. I was a writer who had entered their world.

Emotions poured out as I sat at the computer and wrote and rewrote each word, sentence, and paragraph that describes how it felt when a female soldier survived but the soldier beside her in the Humvee died or why a female soldier to try to overdose when she returned home.

The deeper I got into their worlds, the more I grew depressed. I went out less. I detached from family and friends. I wasn't sleeping or eating well. I spent way too much time in bed. I'd go to sleep tired and wake up tired. Small errands like going to the grocery store, post office, and bank felt like cross-country excursions. I put them off as long as I could.

Trauma changes people. It changed 1st Sgt. CJ Robison and everyone who knew and loved her, including me. I was two-thirds of the way through writing the book when I sat down at my computer one day. I looked at a picture on the screen of Robison in her Army uniform, flanked by her daughter on one side and son on the other. I read the first two paragraphs of her story. I couldn't write. There was no way I could do her story justice. No way. Not after what she had been through. Did I seriously think I could capture her experiences in Iraq and then after coming home—the IED explosions, the falls from a truck and helicopter, hearing loss, back and leg pain, and traumatic brain injury? Could I really show what it felt like to be a single mom who returned from war only to want to go right back not out of love for war but to protect her soldiers and maybe even save some lives? Who did I think I was?

I felt so inadequate, but also intensely sad for what she had gone through. I was grieving what Robison and other women had left behind on the battlefield, and I was angry about what they had gone through when they returned home. Their bodies came back jostled, burned, broken, shattered, and ripped apart. They had post-traumatic stress disorder, traumatic brain injury, and military sexual trauma. Those who were fortunate enough to make it home alive and in one piece weren't off the hook. They still had to wait for their emotions to catch up. At some point, they would begin thinking about a fellow soldier who had been blown up on the battlefield or an Iraqi they had a hand in killing. These women were fragile beyond belief. They couldn't sleep. They couldn't eat. They smoked too much, drank too much, slept too little. How to go on? I asked this of them, and I posed the question to myself. How do they go on after what they'd been through? How would I go on after hearing and internalizing what they had experienced?

I had made many friends with female service members during the writing and publication of *Band of Sisters*. They had already experienced firsthand—to a much greater degree—what I was going through. They recognized what was happening and encouraged me to find a counselor—*now*. I knew they were right but figured I'd keep working as long as I could . . . until secondary trauma caught up with me.

Secondary trauma affects people who experience trauma secondhand. Sometimes called vicarious trauma, it can seriously affect mental-health counselors, first responders, critical-care nurses, and other health-care professionals involved in treating those exposed to traumatic events. It can resemble post-traumatic stress, which includes having nightmares or flashbacks, being easily startled, and avoiding situations that remind one of the trauma. A Geisinger-led study suggests that hearing repeated stories of suffering from trauma victims causes serious psychological stress in clinical social workers. In writing the stories of our women warriors, I had exposed myself to their trauma over and over again. Like many of the women who return from the battlefield not realizing they are beset with post-traumatic stress, I was being traumatized and didn't even know it.

In addition to being traumatized by their stories, I could also relate to some of their challenges. For instance, service members struggle tremendously with a sense of belonging when they come home, especially if they were part of a reserve or National Guard unit that dispersed when they returned from the battlefield. For some, the desire to be around other soldiers is so intense they would go back to the battlefield if it meant that they could continue to be a part of that community. During the writing of this book, I moved from Jacksonville to Wilmington, North Carolina. Between the move and my traveling and writing schedule, I lost any connection I once had to other communities. I understood our female service members when they said they felt alone or lonely. It was during the writing of this book that I learned just how universal our feelings, such as loneliness and abandonment, are.

In the same way women came home from the battlefield and kept themselves busy so that they wouldn't have to think about their wartime experiences, I also stayed active in researching, writing, and speaking so that I wouldn't have to think about how the women's experiences were affecting me. As one therapist put it, I kept pedaling and pedaling until one day I stopped. And as soon as I stepped on the brakes, I also hit an emotional wall.

This was when my fingers froze at the computer keyboard and I cried. Tears replaced words; emotions took the place of my intellect. I had lost my voice to tell these stories. It had hardened like ice, and I was becoming numb. My deadline came and went. Winter would turn to spring. I had to thaw so I could feel again. It would happen, but not without a great deal of help.

I had to do something different because what I was doing wasn't working. Most of the women I was writing about had faced loneliness, fear, and abuse on the battlefield and hopelessness, isolation, and depression at home. In researching and writing their stories, I was overcome with feelings of unworthiness, helplessness, and despair. I would have to face those emotions if I was going to be their voice to the world at large, if I was going to ensure their stories were not only told but that they were heard. How could I finish what I had started?

Fortunately, while working on this book, I met some counselors who are experts in dealing with trauma. A counselor at Pope Air Force Base, whom I had interviewed for a couple of stories, suggested I get professional help. I knew whom to contact. Months earlier, a female Marine had given me the name and number of her counselor. Of course, I didn't act on it right away. I was too busy pedaling. Time passed. I attended the friend's mili-

314 _____ *The Girls Come Marching Home*

tary retirement and met her counselor there. In late 2008, when I seemed to have lost my ability to write about our women warriors, I called her. In the months ahead, my counselor would gently guide me while my female military friends told me to "suck it up."

Therapy is hard. I initially went to my counselor to talk about the stories in the book, process them, and start writing again. It wasn't long before I became the focus of these sessions. Having gone through months of counseling now, I understand why so many people don't follow through with it. But I also see why it's so important. Sometimes, people quit counseling because they are afraid of their own vulnerability and the depth of their emotions. Yet when someone ends their counseling prematurely, they are postponing healing. Emotions must be felt in order to heal.

My counselor, who has worked with many service members, describes therapy as boot camp magnified 100 times. Like boot camp, counseling can feel awful—that is, until it feels better. I realize that being vulnerable is seen by many as a weakness that goes against military training. However, I have learned that it takes courage to be vulnerable. Counseling isn't for the weak; it's for the strong. I'm not saying this just because I've been through it; after all I question how strong I am every day. I'm saying it because I've experienced it firsthand and know how hard it is to look inside and fix what is broken. A weak person can't do that. You have to be strong to release the emotional toxins in your system. It's hard.

If you want or need help and haven't sought it, I encourage you to do so. Please see the resources on the following page or on my website, *www.girlscomemarchinghome.com*, for more information.

Vet Centers
www.vetcenter.va.gov
Vet Center staff are available toll free during normal business
hours at 1-800-905-4675 (Eastern) and 1-866-496-8838 (Pacific)

Women Veteran's health care in the VA
www.publichealth.va.gov/womenshealth/index.asp
1-877-222-8387

VA Center for Women Veterans
www1.va.gov/womenvet
1-800-827-1000

VA National Suicide Prevention Hotline
1-800-273-TALK

United States Department of Defense
Sexual Assault Prevention and Response
www.sapr.mil
1-800-342-9647

National Center for PTSD
www.ncptsd.va.gov/ncmain/veterans
1-802- 296-6300

Band of Sisters:
Where Are They Now?

VERNICE ARMOUR, FORMER MARINE CAPTAIN, REALIZED ANOTHER dream and passion in June 2007. She is the founder/CEO of VAI Consulting and Training, LLC (www.vernicearmour.com). Armour is working with companies, organizations, and associations as the *Zero to Breakthrough*™ Expert. Focusing on leadership, teamwork, and accountability, her *Zero to Breakthrough*™ Success Model is based on the process she used to EXCELerate from beat cop to combat pilot in three years. Outside of work, Armour loves mentoring youth as they go for and achieve their dreams. *Zero to Breakthrough* and *Bringing Your Dreams to Life* are two of Armour's upcoming books.

Robin Brown, former Army captain, and her husband, Jason, got out of the Army and moved to Corvallis, Oregon, where Jason taught Army ROTC at Oregon State University (Go Beavs!) and Robin ran unsuccessfully for state representative. They have a son, Hank, who is now two. Robin opened her own linen shop, Brown House. She worked on the board of a veterans' organization for three years to help pass legislation for Oregon veterans. In early 2009, Robin sold her business and moved with her husband and son to Lafayette, Louisiana, where Jason began work with a natural gas drilling company. Robin gave birth to a baby girl, Merli Alysse Brown, on April 8, 2009.

Marine Sergeant Chrissy DeCaprio re-enlisted and is stationed at the 1st Marine Corps District in Garden City, New York. She received numerous acknowledgments and awards for her actions in combat, including the Sergeant Major Bertha L. Peters Award for sustained exceptional performance of duty while serving with a Fleet Marine Force Unit. She was meritoriously promoted to sergeant and was awarded the Combat Action Ribbon, an award few female Marines wear. A dinner was held in her honor, and she received the Hometown Hero award in New York. DeCaprio speaks about her experiences to various groups, such as high school ROTC programs and veterans. She uses her experiences to motivate people to appreciate what they have and to improve themselves. She loves speaking to women of all ages and encouraging them to be as successful as they can be. She is a certified fitness instructor and is taking many different health and nutrition classes. She is also attending the Academy of Art University, where she is working on a degree in interior architecture and design.

Angela Jarboe, former Army sergeant, and her family are doing well. Angela is currently working on her associate's degree, which she will finish in the summer of 2009, and plans to transfer to Austin Peay University, where she will pursue her bachelor's degree in social work and eventually a master's degree in social work and rehabilitation counseling. She plans to use her degrees and experience to help disabled veterans. She is currently substitute teaching when she's not in classes.

Marine Sergeant Priscilla Kispetick was chosen to participate in a Joint Task Force exercise, Austere Challenge, in Grafenwöhr, Germany. She received a letter of appreciation from the Army and two coins, one from Gen. Kenneth Hunzegar, the commanding general of the V Corps, and the other from Richard Cody, the vice chief of staff for the Army. She has a son, Aidan Michael, who is one. Kispetick has transferred to MASS-1, MACG-28 at MCAS Cherry Point. She plans to re-enlist and deploy with MASS-1 or re-enlist and become a Marine combat training instructor at Camp Geiger. She still loves the Marine Corps and hopes to stay in for a long time.

Navy ABH3 Marcia Lillie's last active-duty tour was on the USS *Eisenhower* during the first half of 2009. She planned to get out of the Navy in July and enroll in college in the fall of 2009 to study atmospheric science and astronomy. She will be attending under the NASA student program at Langley Air Force Base. Upon graduating from college, she hopes to work either for NASA or with the Department of Homeland Security as an Immigration and Customs Enforcement (ICE) agent in the Human Trafficking Division. She will also join the Active Navy Reserve, where she will cross-rate from Aviation Boatswain's Mate–Aircraft Handler (ABH) to Master at Arms (MA).

Marine First Sergeant Yolanda Mayo was assigned to Charlie Company, 4th Landing Support Battalion. After completing a successful tour as the company first sergeant, she was transferred to II Marine Expeditionary Force (MEF) to be the reserve first sergeant for the Individual Mobilization Augmentation Detachment. In spring 2009, she was selected for sergeant major. In her civilian life, she continues to serve as the protocol coordinator for II MEF. She signed on to assist the Marine Corps in its campaign to protect the fleet at home. She has completed three safety videos for the Marine Corps: *I'm in Charge*, which tells Marines to take charge of their lives and not drink and drive; a motorcycle safety video; and one on binge drinking. She also stays in touch with many of the Marines and soldiers whom she supervised in Baghdad in 2003 and 2004. In 2009, Mayo and her husband, Greg, were proud to have their daughter, Sydney, receive an invitation and attend the presidential inauguration. They are also looking forward to their son Tony's graduation from high school in 2010. Tony's high school essay: "My Mom—My Hero."

Marine Major Amy McGrath is engaged to be married in December 2009 in her hometown in Kentucky. She was promoted to the rank of major in 2007. She most recently completed a tour to Japan with her old squadron of VMFA (AW)-121, this time as a pilot.

Gunnery Sergeant Rosie Noel retired from the Marine Corps after more than twenty years of faithful service to God, country, and Corps. Her retirement ceremony was held on October 29, 2008, the third anniversary of her Purple Heart ceremony. When she grows up, she plans to finish her degree in education and teach special-needs children. Her primary job for now is being mom to her two teenage boys—a fulltime job! When time permits, she has fun traveling with her very good friend, Kirsten Holmstedt, to help promote *Band of Sisters.*

Air Force Colonel Polly Padden (formerly Montgomery) joined the Special Operations Command at Fort Bragg, North Carolina, where she deployed for six months to Afghanistan and ran the air support in manhunting operations. In Afghanistan, she earned the Bronze Star and Defense Meritorious Service Medal. She attended the Army War College in Carlisle, Pennsylvania, for one year after Fort Bragg. She then moved to Maxwell Air Force Base in Alabama. She's now a full colonel and was named chairman of the Air War College's Department of Leadership and Strategy. Her three children are attending the same elementary school she attended thirty-five years ago.

Rachelle Spors, former Army sergeant, is teaching Spanish in Omaha, Nebraska, and bought a house. She is no longer dating Aswald Hooker, but they do talk on occasion. She feels good and started doing yoga, which has helped immensely with the tightness in her chest and muscles around her scars.

Acknowledgments

THANK YOU TO MY EDITOR, CHRIS EVANS, AND ASSISTANT EDITOR Dave Reisch of Stackpole Books, and my agent, Robert Guinsler of Sterling Lord Literistic. From the beginning, they appreciated the importance of a book that would capture the emotions and voices of women returning from war. I am eternally grateful for the support of my parents, Anne and Herb Holmstedt; my siblings, Herb, Mary, Eric, and Heidi; their spouses and children; and my special friend David Weber. Your encouragement and enthusiasm mean the world to me. Betsy and Jim Chaffin—your friendship and kindness afforded me the opportunity to complete *Band of Sisters* and *The Girls Come Marching Home* in a serene and peaceful setting. Thank you!

I can't put into words how much I admire our female service members. Your courage and resilience motivate me every single day. In addition, I would like to offer my deepest appreciation to a group of women whom I leaned on during this project and who, in my opinion, embody the best qualities of a band of sisters. Every woman needs her own band of sisters. Each of these women helped me work through the pain I was experiencing and the tears I was shedding while completing this book. For that, I will be forever grateful. Thanks to your encouragement—sometimes on a daily basis—I was able to write a book that I hope will validate what our female service members are going through and persuade those who need help to get it.

Micaila Britto inspires me daily.

Leanne Lyon Burns is a kindred spirit who never ceases to amaze me.

Emily Delp believed in me when I kept questioning myself.

Dru Elliott was on call 24/7 and always answered the phone.

Jeri Fountain, a faithful friend, edited portions of this book between visits to a cabin that she and her husband built in western North Carolina.

Robyn Morgan, a poet and world-class wrestler (on the Internet), generously edited portions of this book.

Rosie Noel has been my traveling companion and friend since I interviewed her for *Band of Sisters.* A retired Marine gunnery sergeant with a Purple Heart, Rosie has had my back since day one.

Lauren Korn gave me hope not only in myself, but also in the counseling profession. I can honestly say there are people who care out there.

Jody-Lynn Suda taught me that like a rainbow, our emotions are made up of a spectrum of colors, all of which are beautiful.

Doris Weber is a dear friend and cheerleader.

Thank you to Ken Marts, World War II naval aviator, and Ed Russell, an Army Ranger during Vietnam, for their steadfast friendship and encouragement, and to Lt. Col. Kathy Platoni, clinical psychologist, for her expertise.

Index